GATSBY

The Cultural History of the Great American Novel

Bob Batchelor

Contemporary American Literature

ROWMAN & LITTLEFIELD
Lanham • Boulder • New York • Toronto • Plymouth, UK

Published by Rowman & Littlefield
4501 Forbes Boulevard, Suite 200, Lanham, Maryland 20706
www.rowman.com

10 Thornbury Road, Plymouth PL6 7PP, United Kingdom

British Library Cataloguing in Publication Information Available

Library of Congress Cataloging-in-Publication Data

Batchelor, Bob.
Gatsby : the cultural history of the great American novel / Bob Batchelor.
p. cm. — (Contemporary American Literature)
Includes bibliographical references and index.
ISBN 978-0-8108-9195-1 (cloth : alk. paper) — ISBN 978-0-8108-9196-8 (ebook) 1. Fitzgerald, F.
Scott (Francis Scott), 1896–1940. Great Gatsby. I. Title.
PS3511.I9G8228 2014
813'.52—dc23
2013024293

♾ The paper used in this publication meets the minimum requirements of
American National Standard for Information Sciences Permanence of Paper for
Printed Library Materials, ANSI/NISO Z39.48-1992.

Printed in the United States of America

To Lawrence S. Kaplan,
for teaching me how to think like a historian,
and to
Kathy and Kassandra Dylan,
as always, the sunshine in my life!

CONTENTS

PREFACE

I'm awfully tired of being Scott Fitzgerald anyhow as there doesn't seem to be so much money in it and I'd like to find out if people read me just because I am Scott Fitzgerald or, what is more likely, don't read me for the same reason.—F. Scott Fitzgerald, 1939

For one afternoon in January 2013, students at Berea High School, in Cleveland's western suburbs, went back in time to experience the 1920s complete with sultry black dresses, tuxedos, jazz music, and even a make-believe speakeasy. Only knowing the secret password garnered admission. The riotous celebration marked the culmination of a cross-disciplinary study of *The Great Gatsby* between the school's sophomores and juniors, the media center, the Cuyahoga County library, and Baldwin Wallace University.

While some students banged away on the piano, many others learned the Charleston and other period-specific dances, bringing smiles to everyone involved. More importantly, though, for teacher Bill Boone, the gala helped the young people understand the Jazz Age better: "They can get personally involved with this. If we can get them a little more enthusiastic for American Literature and American History with this type of presentation, our goal has been met." The outcome is palpable, according to high school junior Natori Santiago, who confessed, "I don't really like to read, but I loved *The Great Gatsby*. I would have loved if I lived during that time." Thus, another generation influenced by Fitzgerald's masterpiece is established.[1]

Given the global excitement regarding the new *Gatsby* adaptation directed by Australian Baz Luhrmann and featuring Hollywood star Leonardo DiCaprio in the title role, 2013 is a special year for Fitzgerald's masterpiece. Not only are there 1920s-themed parties and celebrations taking place around the world, but the elation surrounding the film has influenced popular culture across the globe. Nations one would imagine are far removed from the novel's themes or the movie's fashions are caught up in the wave of *Gatsby* mania.

The Internet and the constant churn of content, such as film trailers, clips, music, and other visual and filmic elements, drive the craze for Fitzgerald's book. However, a pleasant corollary is that the novel itself, including a film-related release with DiCaprio and others on the cover, climbed back to the top of the best-seller lists. So, whether the film sparked new audiences to buy the book or vice versa, the resulting sales demonstrated yet again the ubiquity of *Gatsby* within American popular culture.

DiCaprio's intense, slightly sinister interpretation of Gatsby is attracting praise and a large following. The legend of a drunken, defeated Fitzgerald intertwines with the murdered Jay Gatsby to spin into a tale of woe. Yet what the reader should also pull from *Gatsby*'s pages is the sheer joy in the poetic writing, vivid descriptions of life, and the intellectual heft of the slim volume.

META-*GATSBY*

One of the central ideas in *Gatsby: The Cultural History of the Great American Novel* is that Fitzgerald's masterpiece has transcended its place as a Jazz Age novel to become a touchstone across American culture. I label this overarching idea "meta-*Gatsby*," which symbolizes the way the novel is employed across mass media and in the collective public consciousness. For example, if one were to walk up to any stranger and say the word "Gatsby," the receiver would immediately conjure up some image that related to the book or one of the film adaptations. It might not be a specific example, but instead a general impression, like a mental picture of a decadent party or a remembered photograph of a Jazz Age flapper. One's idea could also bounce to something concrete, like a picture of Fitzgerald or Robert Redford from the 1974 film adaptation. The ubiquity of the novel and its tangents created meta-*Gatsby*.

An interesting aspect of meta-*Gatsby* is that while using "Gatsby" as a sign symbol is universal, not everyone who uses it actually employs it properly. From examining the tens of thousands of pages of uses across the global mass media from the 1940s to 2010s, one sees that a kind of misdirection is common. Unfortunately, what it also reveals is that either people using "Gatsby" in this manner do not understand the novel and its characters well or that it is just an easy example to pull out of one's writing bag of tricks, regardless of its meaning.

In other words, "Gatsby" is reduced to a generic group of synonyms, such as "wealthy," "lavish," or "rags to riches." In many respects, this taxonomy is the dominant one employed when journalists and other writers refer to the novel or film. The important question here is what it means for a novel to enter the cultural mind-set of a nation, particularly if that appearance opens the book up to wild, speculative, or even incorrect uses. Over and over again, "Gatsby" is used in ways that reduce the novel to some basic idea that usually oversimplifies what Fitzgerald actually wrote to the point of trivializing his ideas.

Moreover, not only does "Gatsby" mean something across mass media and popular culture, but often "Gatsby" also is employed as a stand-in for the word "novel." Similarly, "Fitzgerald" has become almost the generic image of "writer."

The idea of meta-*Gatsby* is important when one connects the use of the novel in countless high school and college classrooms with the wider goal of public education. What this book advocates even beyond the study of *Gatsby* and meta-*Gatsby* is that books, literature, and the humanities greatly matter in contemporary society. That I even have to make this statement demonstrates how far such a reasonable suggestion has fallen. We find many ways to marginalize intelligence in the United States, particularly given the link between hard work and the American Dream.

Based on our agrarian past, the notion that working with one's hands is a higher calling came to dominate a nostalgic view of the nation, yet today fewer and fewer people hold these kinds of jobs. This position enables some opponents of literature and the humanities to stress that practicality and job training should be elevated at the cost of "soft" disciplines. While I will not cast aspersions on those who emphasize science,

math, and technology training since these are important parts of an educated society, I will battle for the humanities as equally important.

There are simply concepts and beliefs that must be developed through
deep reading and engagement with great written work. I agree with the
link that eminent scholar Louise M. Rosenblatt makes between literature
and metalearning. She explains that "active participation with literature"
leads to the kind of thinking we should aspire to attain:

> Development of the imagination: the ability to escape from the limita-
> tions of time and place and environment, the capacity to envisage
> alternatives in ways of life and in moral and social choices, the sensi-
> tivity to thought and feeling and needs of other personalities . . .
> partnership in the wisdom of the past and the aspirations for the future,
> of our culture and society. The great abstractions—love, honor, integ-
> rity, compassion, individuality, democracy—will take on for him hu-
> man meaning.[2]

This call to arms is not an intellectual pipe dream. It is a plea that avails
us to a better future.

Books open minds to different eventualities. According to scholar
Mark William Roche, "Morality is not one subsystem among the others,
such that there is art, science, religion, business, politics, and so forth,
alongside morality. Instead, morality is the guiding principle for all human endeavors."[3] The outcomes furnished via stronger critical and contextual thinking can change worlds. We may not need *Gatsby* to operate
computers better or solve mysteries about the physical body, but I contend that we need the novel and other great works of art to help people
develop more compassionate, ethical, and humane worldviews.

WHO IS F. SCOTT FITZGERALD?

Some readers might pick up this cultural history of *The Great Gatsby*
with little previous knowledge of Fitzgerald (1896–1940), so let us briefly put the great writer in context. The public image of Fitzgerald is from
the go-go 1920s, a dashing young man with movie star looks and Zelda, a
beautiful, spirited wife on his arm. His celebrity status reached iconic
proportions, the kind reserved today for those at the pinnacle of Hollywood, TV, and music's A-list. During their Jazz Age heyday, one ima-

gines that Scott and Zelda were the Brad Pitt and Angelina Jolie of their era.

In what seemed like the blink of an eye, though, Fitzgerald plummeted just as hard. Even *Gatsby* (1925) could not generate the kind of sales that would help him back up. The novel met with decent sales and lukewarm critical reception. An excruciating nine years later, Fitzgerald published *Tender Is the Night*, full of hope that it would be his ticket, but the novel wilted under the same fate as *Gatsby*.

Two years after *Tender*, with continued health, alcoholism, and writing challenges, with his wife ensconced in a sanitarium, where she would basically spend the rest of her short, tragic life, Fitzgerald attempted to outline his worldview for his fifteen-year-old daughter Scottie, explaining, "A whole lot of people have found life a whole lot of fun. I have not found it so. But, I had a hell of a lot of fun when I was in my twenties and thirties; and I feel that it is your duty to accept the sadness, the tragedy of the world we live in, with a certain esprit."[4] Shortly after, Fitzgerald left for Hollywood, his last chance at reviving himself physically, emotionally, and (most importantly) financially.

When he arrived in Hollywood in the summer of 1937, Fitzgerald lived on a $1,000 a week salary from Metro-Goldwyn-Mayer (MGM). The studio later extended his contract for a year at $1,250 weekly. A princely sum in the late 1930s, the money enabled the writer to pay back his considerable debts, but he made little headway on his fiction. When his contract expired at the end of 1938, Fitzgerald scrambled as a free lance scriptwriter and putting out stories for *Esquire*. His creditors, including the Internal Revenue Service and Zelda's North Carolina sanitarium, continued to demand payment.

Without studio backing, Fitzgerald spent the last eighteen months of his life in chaos and near collapse. The most pressing day-to-day concern was money. Overnight, Fitzgerald's income plummeted to virtually nothing. He searched for bit studio writing gigs and resorted to begging friends and acquaintances for money, which he had done prior to the Hollywood work.

At one point in September 1939, Fitzgerald pleaded with Zelda's doctor because he could not pay her bills. Describing his own dire situation, including a recent recovery from tuberculosis, he claimed, "It is simply impossible to pay anything . . . when one drives in a mortgaged Ford and tries to get over the habit of looking into a handkerchief for blood when talking to a producer."[5] Showing his deep concern for his wife, but realistically examining the situation, Fitzgerald hoped "that this does not mean Zelda will be deprived of the ordinary necessities . . . [but] if things go as bad as they have for another month, the hospital can reimburse itself out of life insurance. This is a promise."[6] Not long after, he died.

The Fitzgerald at the end of his life looked back on the boy genius he had been with scorn and more than a healthy dose of envy. The older man, physically broken by booze, debt, and failing health, however, did not allow his spirit to be destroyed. At the end of his life, in the Pat Hobby short stories and unfinished novel *The Love of the Last Tycoon*, he produced a new vision of Hollywood, completely different than one would have assumed from his early work. Subsequently, Fitzgerald's Hollywood at the end of the 1930s is a bitter, lonely place, even though the stories themselves are filled with real-life figures, such as Orson Welles and Ronald Colman, and culled from Fitzgerald's work as a scriptwriter for MGM and other prominent film companies.

What one cannot overlook, however, in assessing Fitzgerald is the power of his work as a novelist, particularly in *Gatsby* and *Tender*, or the ten to twelve short stories he authored that are considered in the upper echelon of those ever written. According to critic Charles Poore:

> Buffon said that the style is the man. In Fitzgerald's case the unity is more expansive: the style, the man, the stories, the novels, the legends, the influences, the friendships, the loves, the disasters make one great mass of infinitely exploitable material.[7]

In the end, it is the writer that stands above the playboy, party character, and the craft that should outlive the legend. We cannot completely untangle these dual personas in the public's mind, but we can assess the work and its meaning to demonstrate how pervasive meta-*Gatsby* has been in contemporary America.

***

What does it mean for someone or something to be called "Gatsby-like" or compared to the fictional character? If you called an acquaintance one of these terms, how would he or she react? What if an employee said that the boss's house or a company celebration were "Gatsby-esque"? I can imagine that such declarations might lead to a wry smile or a punch in the nose. Does it mean something different, though, when we label Donald Trump "Gatsby-esque" or some local real estate mogul? Regardless, a person making these kinds of claims would get a reaction, which exemplifies meta-*Gatsby* at work.

While the 2013 film adaptation is arguably the best movie version of *Gatsby*, part of the challenge in putting the novel to film is meta-*Gatsby*. People hold ideas, visions, and impressions of the book and its characters, which influence their subsequent feelings about an adaptation.

Another challenge is that *Gatsby* is a novel of ideas, rather than a novel of action. This distinction makes Fitzgerald's masterpiece elusive and difficult to film. For some readers, too, this dichotomy either results in one loving or hating the book. Many simply do not realize that *Gatsby* is a novel of ideas masked within a novel of action. The cloaking that occurs is the result of Fitzgerald's ability at managing the intricacies and his beautiful writing style.

Using Nick as a narrator enables Fitzgerald to emphasize the storytelling aspects, while concurrently casting the unreliability in that recounting. According to literary critic Arthur Mizener, "Nick is in the middle, torn between the superficial social grace and the unimaginative brutality of the wealthy and the imaginative intensity and moral idealism of the socially absurd and legally culpable self-made man."[8] Because Nick is all over the place in retelling the story and weaving it with his own judgments of the action, the reader finds room for interpretation that other novels attempt to force. Thus, *Gatsby* lives on into the twenty-first century in a way that other books of that era have not.

ACKNOWLEDGMENTS

I have read or listened to *The Great Gatsby* hundreds of times and spent my career as a cultural historian, but the idea for this book took root in early 2007 in a seminar on Ernest Hemingway and F. Scott Fitzgerald directed by Phillip Sipiora. *Gatsby: The Cultural History of the Great American Novel* has been percolating in my mind ever since and the hoopla surrounding the new film adaptation for the last several years made it time for the book to be written. It might seem odd to thank Fitzgerald for writing this book, but to me it would be strange not to, since the creation of this book marked a turning point in his life and, we would later surmise, for the nation, too.

Researching *Gatsby*, I have incurred many debts. Many educators spoke with me about the novel and film and their joy in teaching it to high school and college students. I would like to thank Quincey Upshaw, who provided wonderful insight from a high school teacher's perspective, and graciously allowed me to read several papers and assignments of her former students. I would also like to thank Denise Douglas of Greenfield High School (Tennessee). Denise not only gave me her thoughts on *Gatsby*, but her students participated in my research, answering questions about the novel and 2013 film. Thanks to the young people who took part: Taylor Alderson, Colten McAlister, Logan Galey, Jeremy Lannom, Jessica Witherington, Savannah Ricketts, Lauren Rush, Austin Pence, McCall Scates, Brody Stanford, Kayla Totty, Kalee Kesterson, Tiffani-Amber Whitworth, Kendal Cook, Ashton Pence, Leasha Allen, Alison Williams, Brittany Ricketts, Ashley Cooper, Bethany Cole, Holley Carpenter, Brittany Roney, Matthew Sawyers, Jeffrey Johnson, Jason Fortner, Russell Williams, Jessica Boettner, and several others who chose to remain anonymous. Their insights were invaluable in representing how high school students interpret the novel and film.

I feel fortunate to have a fantastic group of mentors and friends who I can turn to when writing a book takes on the guise of an emotional roller coaster. Thanking them here is a drop in the bucket compared to what they provide. Phillip Sipiora, Don Greiner, Gary Hoppenstand, Lawrence Mazzeno, and Keith Booker are wonderful scholarly role models and guides. Thanks to Jim West, Don Greiner, Phil Sipiora, and Morris Dickstein for early words of encouragement on this project. Other friends offered cheer along the way, including Chris Burtch, Larry Leslie, Kelli Burns, Thomas Heinrich, Gene Sasso, Bill Sledzik, George Cheney, Josef Benson, Ashley Donnelly, and Tom and Kristine Brown. I have been lucky to have many fantastic mentors, whom I would like to thank: Lawrence S. Kaplan, James A. Kehl, Sydney Snyder, Richard Immerman, Peter Magnani, and Anne Beirne. Thanks to my popular culture scholarly teammates: Brendan Riley, Brian Cogan, and Leigh Edwards! I would like to thank my new Thiel College friends, particularly Troy VanAken and Lynn Franken, as well as my colleagues in the Department of Communication and other members of the Thiel family.

From the moment Stephen Ryan and I talked about creating the "Contemporary American Literature" series for Scarecrow Press, I knew we were onto something extraordinary. As the first book in the new series, I hope that *Gatsby: The Cultural History of the Great American Novel* demonstrates the kind of interdisciplinary, exciting work that we want to publish. Thanks to Stephen and everyone at Scarecrow/Rowman & Littlefield for their work on this book, especially the design team that created the outstanding cover.

My family is incredibly supportive and kind, considering that writing books necessitates long hours of writing and thinking time. Thanks to my parents, Jon and Linda Bowen, for everything they do to make our lives infinitely better. My daughter Kassie thinks I should have written "The Great Catsby," based on her love of cats and other animals. Her smile and bright eyes bring love and laughter into every moment. My wife Kathy is my pillar of strength and soul mate.

INTRODUCTION: WHY *GATSBY* MATTERS

Would the 25 cent press keep Gatsby in the public eye—or is the book
unpopular. Has it had its chance? Would a popular reissue in that
series with a preface not by me but by one of its admirers . . . make it a
favorite with class rooms, profs, lovers of English prose—anybody.
But to die, so completely and unjustly after having given so much.
Even now there is little published in American fiction that doesn't
slightly bare [sic] my stamp—in a small way I was an original.
—F. Scott Fitzgerald, in a letter to Maxwell Perkins, May 20, 1940

More than any other American novel, *The Great Gatsby* has transcended
its era to become a touchstone within the broader culture, essentially
establishing itself as one of the most important books ever written. As
such, I contend that *Gatsby* is the fabled "Great American Novel," that
vaunted title that so many writers have spent their lives attempting to
produce. Concurrently, as the novel has developed into a cultural lynchpin, I maintain that there its employment has taken on a broader meaning—a "meta-*Gatsby*"—or overarching idea of what the taxonomy encompassing *Gatsby* connotes.

However, since Fitzgerald's masterpiece centers on ambiguity, commentators, analysts, journalists, writers, and others have employed its
themes and imagery in their own work, which is sometimes congruent
with what Fitzgerald might have had in mind and other times, completely
off kilter. Therefore, as the ideas at the heart of *Gatsby* have spread
throughout our common cultural discourse for more than eighty-five
years, its importance grew, too, thus enabling it to ascend to folklore or

Americana prominence to sit at the very heart of what it means to concep-
tualize the nation. Whether it is interpreted correctly, incorrectly, vague-
ly, or in some other manner, meta-*Gatsby* possesses meaning for audiences.

The rest of *Gatsby: The Cultural History of the Great American Novel*
lays out my argument in greater detail, but I will briefly outline my
rationale here so that the reader may wrangle with my position as it
unfolds. Boiled down to three essential points, I claim that *Gatsby* is the
Great American Novel because of its sales and readership over the past
nearly ninety years, its ubiquity in high school and college classes, and its
use as a cultural touchstone within the wider mass media as a fill-in for
certain terms, themes, and ideas. These items combine to earn Fitzgerald's book this title.

Examining each part of this equation on its own merit, the evidence
becomes more overwhelming. First, I estimate that *Gatsby* has sold about
350,000 copies per year averaged out for the last fifty years, which totals
17.5 million books. Moreover, this figure increases geometrically when
one considers the used-book industry on one hand and the library/class-
room pass-along market on the other. Certainly, countless sales are driven
by the widespread use of the novel in high school and college classrooms.

Readership also grows by multitudes if one adds in the countless
students who attempt to shortcut the process by reading any number of
cribbed versions, such as CliffsNotes or SparkNotes. Others attempt to
circumvent reading by watching one of the several film adaptations. Woe
among these who are students when their teachers or professors find out!
From the readership viewpoint, an attempt at quantifying this total might
be a fun exercise, but one that could never be definitely proven and
ultimately might drive the researcher insane.

The third leg in the equation is one that database research helps us
uncover, though the results are not comprehensive because the extant
databases cannot search across all publications. Regardless, the returns
are staggering. Searching "Gatsby" via Factiva yields 11,813 uses from
1971 to 2013, though Factiva's figures prior to the late 1990s are sketchy.
In contrast, a Newsbank's North American source search yields a remarkable 38,612 results from January 1980 to February 2013. Drilling down
even further, LexisNexis finds 6,928 hits in the 2000–2010 period alone.
Similarly, a *New York Times* historical search for "Gatsby" generates
362,000 results.

When one attempts to be more inclusive, the results multiply geometrically. A search for *"The Great Gatsby"* via Google in mid-May 2013, for example, yielded some 110 million hits. Obviously such a broad search on Google does not provide much context, but it does speak to the pervasiveness of "meta-*Gatsby*." Furthermore, an examination of these results taken together reveals the depth of the novel's grip on American popular culture and its place within our national folklore.

* * *

The Great Gatsby matters because its inherent ambiguity enables readers to use the novel as a barometer for measuring their own lives and the culture they inhabit. Therefore, the central themes and ideas emerging from the book, ranging from the fulfillment of the American Dream to the role of wealth in society, resonate with contemporary readers who struggle with similar uncertainties today. As a matter of fact, the ambiguity at the heart of *Gatsby* is its lifeblood and embraced by audiences, particularly American readers who hope and anticipate that its contents will help them comprehend their lives and the larger world a little better.

Simultaneously, however, we cannot ignore the ongoing anti-intellectual and antihumanities era now under way. This breakdown, represented by the combination of the web and high-definition television, actively undercuts deep thinking, reflection, and reading with technological beeps and whirling imagery. "Literature and literary criticism have never been doubted by the general public as much as they are today and so the question of legitimacy is central to the future health of the discipline," concludes literary scholar Mark William Roche.[1]

One needs to simply look at online video figures to see the change the web has facilitated. For example, according to marketing firm comScore, Google/YouTube videos reached 150.7 million unique viewers in February 2013 who watched an astounding 11.3 billion videos of a total of thirty-three billion that month alone.[2] I think it is safe to estimate that in one single month, more minutes were spent watching online videos than all the time people dedicated to reading books in a decade. The commitment to reading remains important, though, particularly when examining the methods used to teach in the K–12 and higher education systems. So, while the balance has tipped mightily toward technology in people's personal lives, education is still reading based.

This tech/nontech paradox is one of many puzzles in contemporary life, so it is no wonder readers find the pulse of *Gatsby* oddly comforting, while concurrently confounding. "Ephemeral" is the word scholar Jonathan P. Fegley uses to describe the way Fitzgerald represents Gatsby. "Fitzgerald has rendered Gatsby through the only means possible," he says, ". . . in the process of becoming, not in a state of being, and thus exists in an ephemeral state."[3]

Gatsby, therefore, is almost ghostlike in his physical manifestation, always somewhat illusory as he floats above the novel's other players, cast upward by the power of his dream. Nick sees this in the way that he watches the man and experienced it after first meeting him, not even recognizing or realizing that he was talking to his host at the first party he attended. A resolute midwesterner who made it through Yale and survived the Great War (if we can believe he actually went to war), Nick watches Gatsby soar above the crowds and wants a piece of that action, even though he does not really know what to make of the man.

This section searches for clues in answering its title, which I contend is a key question that has entertained scholars, readers, and others for many, many decades. There are numerous reasons why *Gatsby* matters, ranging from its foundational place as part of the literary canon to its ubiquity in popular culture. The most obvious tie is to the American Dream, that broad notion about the United States that each of its people keeps at the center of his or her belief system or worldview.

Jay Gatsby and Tom Buchanan seem to be the keys to this equation. It is Jay, the hero/antihero who is so caught up in his love for Daisy that he makes her the center of his fictional world, risking everything and eventually losing his life as a result. Tom, on the other hand, symbolizes the corruption of American capitalism and represents the idea that if one has enough money, he can stand above the law. Furthermore, in Tom's heart of hearts, we find that he is a racist, philanderer, and snob. Juxtaposing the two characters provides the good versus evil narrative that drives so much of our popular culture, even though the great magic of Fitzgerald's novel is that we forgive Jay for his crimes because his romanticism and the purity of his dreams elevate him to a higher plane.

The ambiguity and mystery surrounding Gatsby is attractive for many readers. In several instances, Fitzgerald claimed that the character's murkiness stood as one of the novel's weaknesses. Yet in modern America the secretiveness of Gatsby's rise to power enables the reader to use the character as a prism reflecting the ideas he or she wants to accentuate. Furthermore, Gatsby's many masks enable the reader to reassess and rethink him on subsequent examinations. Each new reading opens up the novel and its titular lead to further inspection and analysis.

An answer to this section's primary question is that *Gatsby* is so important to our conception of ourselves that meta-*Gatsby* developed as a result of the novel's ubiquity. "It is reasonable to assert that Jay Gatsby was the major literary character of the United States in the twentieth century," says scholar Harold Bloom. "No single figure . . . was as central a presence in our national mythology as Gatsby."[4] This is uncommon ground for a novel. While the nation has many ideas and iconic figures that are part of our national mythology, few are based on novels and even fewer have exhibited the staying power of meta-*Gatsby*.

LITERATURE MATTERS

The crux of the argument for literature holding meaning, thus for why *Gatsby* matters, is also contingent on believing that the humanities are worthwhile. While this statement is pretty straightforward, countless gallons of real and virtual ink have been spilled on the question of the role of the humanities in an educated society. Reading and the kinds of books and novels that should be read are part of this debate.

Perhaps an even larger issue is whether one can learn or gain wisdom or perspective from literature. We have already seen how technology is reorienting the way people spend their leisure time, so it seems only a matter of time before technology moves from its tangential place in the education system to front and center. The humanities and technology do not have to be at odds, though, if the goal is toward building, developing, and strengthening critical and contextual thinking skills. As Roche states, "Literature enriches us partly through its intrinsic value, partly as a result of its ability to address neglected values, partly through its simple vitality."[5]

It is this idea of combining the hard work of deep reading with the simplicity of opening a book or e-book that keeps literature prized. Literature scholar Frank B. Farrell explains:

> Referring to literature as truth-revealing includes those moments when we do not simply gather information but have some fundamental character of being human, and especially of human relationships, brought intensely into view . . . some truth about human interaction emerge[s] from shadows into light, so that we seem to understand it clearly for the first time . . . one can feel moved by having a vista seem to open up suddenly on the world in its character as such, or on the patterns of the psyche's investments in the world, its attachments and losses.[6]

Thus, literature highlights and accentuates what it is to be human, to perceive and contemplate emotion, and to feel alive in the moment that the staleness of the technology world cannot.

Roche believes that critics should elevate texts that speak to virtues, such as courage and humility. In this respect, *Gatsby* becomes a way of addressing those ideas by presenting us with characters who are less courageous and lack humility. Demonstrating these virtues via literature enables critics to demonstrate the "existential worth of literature . . . as an end in itself and recognition of those virtues elicited in aesthetic experience but neglected in modernity."[7]

Of course, to grasp the existential, one must be open to the idea that one can learn from literature and that it has something to pass along in the act of reading and assessment. Once could argue that the current K–16 education system is set up in absolutely the wrong way—burying, rather than exulting the existential spirit. One needs to look no further than the way children read and choose books, comics, and other materials when provided choice, versus the way they are *assigned* readings in elementary school.

READING MATTERS

Literary scholars and literature departments have come under increasing fire over the last fifty years to prove their relevancy in a changing world, but no one doubts the primacy of reading as a cornerstone of the American education system. Somehow a disconnect formed in many people's minds between what literature scholars do and how that reflects in classrooms, not only in teaching young people deep reading skills, but also in training future generations of teachers. One could certainly argue that scholars brought this challenge on themselves by focusing on politicized or postmodern readings to interpret texts, rather than preparing students for comprehending and evaluating materials. As a result, students who were unsure about how to actually read deeply and bring new ideas from their efforts into their lives were instead bombarded with interpretations and politicized ideas.

One of the easiest and most persistent criticisms of *Gatsby* that took hold in the late twentieth and early twenty-first centuries is that a narrative focused on wealthy, white elites no longer held lessons for a multicultural readership, particularly immigrant populations and others that scholars should champion. Opponents of the canonization of the novel argued that readers would find deeper meaning in works by writers they could identify with based on gender, ethnicity, or race.

While the movement toward inclusion seemed logical and many writers certainly benefited from the political correctness movement in higher education that brought more diversity to the high school and college classroom reading lists, writer Lawrence Samuel found that the young people he taught in and around Boston realized that *Gatsby*'s themes of "possibility and aspiration" had meaning for them as individuals, in spite of their ethnicity and backgrounds. [8]

A fourteen-year-old female Chinese immigrant who had only been in the United States for a couple of years, for example, spoke eloquently about her *Gatsby*-esque aspiration, saying, "My green light is Harvard." As Samuel points out, this kind of thinking is important as the idea of the American Dream continues to evolve. *The Great Gatsby*'s role is also critical, given that the novel is required reading, Samuel reports, "at half the high schools in the country." Despite its 1920s setting, teachers find that it resonates with teens, many either new to the country or only a generation or two removed from the immigrant experience. [9] As it has for decades, Fitzgerald's creation continues to inspire readers who see something of themselves in Jay Gatsby's self-creation and desire for a new start.

In examining contemporary literary theory, scholar Frank B. Farrell makes a case for the power of reading and its potentially transformative consequences. One of the terms he uses in defining literary space is that it is *ritualized*, which means that the act of reading itself commands change in a safe environment, and produces "ultimately, a more satisfying sense of one's relationship to the forces of the cosmos and to one's community." [10]

This idea may seem lofty to someone who is not a self-described book lover, but it is a common enough concept, usually described as getting *lost* in a book. Farrell explains, "By giving oneself over to these ceremonial patterns, the reader enters slightly hypnotic states determined by the rhythms and sounds as well as by the scenes and images of the text."[11] What Farrell has outlined is the beauty in the way young children read—developing an awe and sense of wonder at the way words are shaped and the meanings they produce. What is critical in this idea of reading is that the person is altered in the process and that some fundamental shift has occurred in the way that the reader views the world. Roche, in turn, argues, "Literature teaches us the nuances of intersubjective relationships, the strategies, the limits, the possibilities of human interaction."[12]

It is telling that we usually only discuss these kinds of transformative moments after someone has read a gripping or powerful text. If one were to chart a second-place finisher in this regard, it would be film. Ironically, given our technology enslavement, one never finds a web user touting this kind of overwhelming joy. The Internet simply does not train people to be contextual or critical thinkers; rather, it merely throws facts and imagery at the person, akin to a tidal wave or avalanche.

British critic and novelist David Lodge views reading as a kind of physical activity that mixes in deep probing, which he describes as "a very delicate and complicated activity . . . both involved and detached" that forces the reader to accept and reject ideas simultaneously while also searching for ideas and significance. He explains:

> The novel unfolds in our memories like a piece of cloth woven upon a loom, and the more complicated the pattern the more difficult and protracted will be the process of perceiving it. But that is what we seek, the pattern: some significantly recurring thread which, however deeply hidden in the dense texture and brilliance of local coloring, accounts for our impression of a unique identity in the whole.[13]

While the reader makes mental notes of the aspects of the novel that work and do not, Lodge says, he or she is piecing together the whole, constantly (perhaps consciously and subconsciously) making decisions about how all these strands will flow into one united narrative. When the reader then senses that he or she has deduced the meaning, the realization "sends a shock like an electric charge through all the discrete observations." Make no doubt about it, though, the reader is engaged in the process.[14]

Readers are so engaged in holding the actual book that the simple idea of doing so has become important. According to writers Jane Mount and Thessaly La Force, "Perhaps we're guilty of sentimentalizing the book as an object. But in an era when digital technology (of which we are nevertheless fans) threatens irreversibly to change our reading experience, there is nothing that parallels the physical book. There is nothing like its weight and smell and the crackle of its spine."[15]

HISTORY MATTERS

Fitzgerald understood the role history, heritage, and nostalgia played in people's thinking about themselves and the world around them. As a result, his novel works on two levels: a specific portrait of life in and around New York City in summer 1922 and an examination of how history's broad sweep influenced the nation from the Civil War through the Jazz Age. According to literary theorist Mark William Roche, "Studying the past as a genuine partner in conversation gives us alternatives to the passing modes of the present. What becomes valuable is not the newest but the greatest that has ever been thought." This kind of interaction is transformative and powerful, he explains: "To have such an encounter with the past is humbling for the present."[16]

Undoubtedly, given the terror of World War I ("the Great War"), Gatsby's reach back into a nostalgic vision of the past makes the novel more interesting, nuanced, and open for interpretation. Scholars Jason P. Leboe and Tamara L. Ansons discuss the role of nostalgia in fueling the kinds of reactions that readers get when reading *Gatsby*, explaining, "Nostalgic experiences represent a distortion of both the past and the present. The 'good old days' may not have been as good as they seem in retrospect. In turn, the present is only as bad as it seems when compared against an unrealistic ideal."[17] In this regard, the reader confronts nostalgia from multiple perspectives, including Jay's and Nick's yearning for a romantic West and one's own assessment of life in the Jazz Age as typified by the novel's plot.

One interpretation of Jay Gatsby would be to anoint him a Horatio Alger–type example of the success one can have in achieving the American Dream. Yet, Gatsby is also a con man. He fakes his way into a life that he does not deserve by letting Daisy assume that he is wealthy, then steals and cheats his way to wealth later without regard for the consequences. This conflicting image heightens the mystery, because the reader knows so much more about Gatsby than the other characters do. We see him through multiple lenses hinging on his secret identity, a narrative trope that fills popular culture from the time of Homer's *Odyssey* to the comic book pages of Superman, Batman, and Spider-Man.

World War I is never far from the action in *Gatsby*, even though the events in the novel take place as it creeps into the past. Or, perhaps the war is still on people's minds. In response, they are just attempting to throw mud in its face by partying as hard as possible in the aftermath— dancing in the streets to avoid facing the devastation nations unleashed on one another. Early in the novel, Nick irreverently calls the war "that delayed Teutonic migration" and claims that he "enjoyed the counter-raid so thoroughly that I came back restless."[18] This feeling of unease led him east to New York City to set up a career selling bonds and sets off the action that summer. Yet, the reader can only imagine what horrors Nick witnessed or the consequences because he never partakes in that kind of self-analysis. He narrates, but his grasp of his own history is not what he wants to serve up.

As it seems is inevitable in talking about *Gatsby*, Fitzgerald plays a role here too when looking at history. According to famed literary critic Alfred Kazin, Fitzgerald's status as the voice of his generation helped establish the Jazz Age and the way people interpreted it. He says, "Mothers swooned and legislators orated; Fitzgerald continued to report the existence of such depravity and cynicism as they had never dreamed of. The shock was delivered; Fitzgerald became part of the postwar atmosphere of shock."[19] *Gatsby*, a rather immoral novel for its times, becomes part of the history of the era, as its author assumed celebrity status that afforded him a platform for making various prognostications. According to Kazin, "In 1920 he was not so much a novelist as a new generation speaking; but it did not matter. He sounded all the fashionable new lamentations; he gave the inchoate protests of his generation a slogan, a character, a definitive tone."[20]

STYLE MATTERS

The popular image of Fitzgerald with a martini glass in one hand and Zelda in the other while preparing to jump on the go-go 1920s dance floor mocks the solitude, hard work, and dedication the author devoted to the writing craft. The painstaking craftsmanship, however, only emerged long after his death. By that time, his legend had been established.

Much of what scholars have learned about Fitzgerald's style is based on the pioneering bibliographic work of Matthew J. Bruccoli, who not only helped propel the Fitzgerald renaissance, but also devoted great amounts of energy to collecting the manuscripts and galleys that Fitzgerald corrected, amended, and edited by hand. Ironically, Fitzgerald's work became "more collectible" based on his writing style: each new work necessitated extensive revision and editing, which means more items exist written in his hand. Thus, these works become valuable for scholars in understanding Fitzgerald's style, while simultaneously establishing a market for the documents.[21]

"Fitzgerald generated a rich archive by rewriting and revising," Bruccoli and Judith S. Baughman explain.[22] Examining the work in draft stage, which included every ribbon copy and the publisher's proofs, demonstrates that Fitzgerald was an incessant editor and reviser. While the edits do cover simple word replacements, what is most astonishing in looking at *Gatsby* across drafts is the substantial thematic revision the author carried out. One could reasonably argue that the novel takes on its stylistic aura in the final revisions Fitzgerald made in the proofs he received from Scribner's.

What Fitzgerald accomplished with *Gatsby* is never taken for granted by contemporary readers, but to merely acknowledge his style and poetics is not enough to explain what he achieved. According to scholar Morris Dickstein, "Its story trickles out in bits and pieces and its style, fresh and full of surprises, is as sinuous and unpredictable as the narrative . . . [it] achieves resonance as myth and metaphor rather than as a densely populated fictional world."[23] Novelist Thomas Berger notes, *"The Great Gatsby* is as nearly perfect as a novel can be, with not a word, not an emotion, not an idea in excess or lacking or misplaced or corrupted."[24] Scholar and poet George Garrett views the novel as revolutionary. He explains, "Fitzgerald advanced the form of the American novel for the benefit of all American novelists who have followed after him, whether they know it or not. They seem to sense this, to bear witness to it, in their continuing admiration for *Gatsby*."[25]

The singular beauty of *Gatsby* is so complete that people who should possess the words for explaining it often fall back on otherworldly phrasing. "There is something magical about Fitzgerald," says publisher Charles Scribner III, "the real magic lies embedded in his prose and reveals itself in his amazing range and versatility . . . his dramatic vision, his painstaking craftsmanship."[26] Scribner lists the types of prose that teachers hope their students will either enjoy and/or emulate by reading *Gatsby*. While literary criticism is not built on speculation, it is not too much of a stretch to imagine that the novel would be widely read just for the writing style and lyricism if it had not reached meta-*Gatsby* proportions.

Kazin concludes that Fitzgerald the writer seemed to be at war with Fitzgerald the personality, which created a "persistent tension . . . between what his mind knew and what his spirit adhered to; between his disillusionment and his irrevocable respect for the power and the glory of the world he described."[27] As a result of this battle, "He was innocent without living in innocence and delighted in the external forms and colors without being taken in by them; but he was preeminently a part of the world his mind was always disowning."[28]

The tactical aspects of Fitzgerald's writing impresses scholars, particularly as Bruccoli and others uncovered the intricate patterning and revision he conducted after the book was already in page proofs. The outcome, according to Farrell, is that "the stable and well-proportioned architecture of the language allows us to get closer to threatening experiences and insights without fear of being overwhelmed by them, since the architecture of the prose that we identify with seems able to internalize such material without losing its self-sustaining form and momentum."[29]

CULTURE MATTERS

Popular culture provides the central narratives that comprise life in contemporary America. In a sense, therefore, our very existence as language-making creatures centers on our ability to interact with one another as storytellers. These narratives created in society by individuals, groups, and organizations establish, shape, and reflect all that we are and someday hope to be. Popular culture's centrality is self-evident to scholar Ray B. Browne, who views it "as the everyday world around us: the mass media, entertainment, diversions, our heroes, icons, rituals—our total life picture." Importantly, when placing *Gatsby* within this culture, Browne explains, "Popular culture of a country is the voice of the people—their likes and dislikes, the lifeblood of daily existence, the way of life . . . the voice of democracy."[30] Over time, Jay Gatsby has transformed from literary character in a 1925 novel to meta-*Gatsby*, a tool employed to understand that era and all those that have followed.

Audiences like Gatsby the same way they like other seemingly normal underdogs who have extraordinary (but somewhat believable) powers, ranging from the undersized action heroes played by Bruce Willis, Kevin Costner, and Patrick Swayze to the up-by-their-bootstraps figures represented by Barack Obama and Bill Clinton. The notion that a form of congruence exists between Gatsby as a fictional character and various other real and imaginary figures from contemporary mass media demonstrates how ubiquitous Fitzgerald's creation remains.

Like the best individual pieces of popular culture, for example, a film or television series, *Gatsby* provides both a mirror and projection. According to writer Philip Hensher:

> When we are confident, and booming, and full of trust in our own splendor, *The Great Gatsby* seems like a curiosity, an anecdote as it did to its first readers. But when things are going wrong all round, and we are trying to remember what it was like to live within a magnificent dream—to be deceived by what we want—then it speaks to us. It buttonholes us, saying, not quite attractively or in a way that we can trust, "Old sport."[31]

Many commentators contend that popular culture is about individuals from across the celebrity spectrum, perhaps mainly because people interact with mass media from the standpoint of their favorite actor, band, films, or television shows. Others counter with the notion that culture is actually about the larger influences that drive society, such as technology, government, economic structures, and national ethos.

Regardless of the particular perspective one holds regarding the definition of culture, the dominant notion centers on the essential position of popular culture in contemporary society, as well as its role as a teaching tool. As discussed earlier regarding the state of the humanities, literature, and reading, the idea of reading education leading to a more nuanced and deep relation to one's world is critical. According to eminent scholar Maxine Greene, "We need to hold in mind the fact that the arts are almost always inexhaustible. There is no using up of a painting or a concerto or a poem. If they have any richness, say destiny at all, they are inexhaustible; there is always more."[32] As a matter of fact, the scope of arts education is endless and holds countless consequences for people now and in the future.

GATSBY: A GUIDE

The outline of *The Great Gatsby* is relatively simple. A writer is telling the story of a year he spent among friends, relatives, and assorted famous and infamous characters at a watershed moment in American history. What the reader immediately learns, however, is that the writer (Nick Carraway)—because he is a writer—is a kind of professional liar, and boy does he lie, mislead, and generally impose on the story. After all, Nick is in the process of creating the story, which is what writers do.

As readers, we experience the first lie on the front cover, since the title character is neither "Great" nor "Gatsby." Or, at least we are supposed to consider these options as we "listen" to Nick summarize and analyze the tale. As convoluted as it may seem, what Nick does in creating a readable, sellable, and ultimately fictitious Gatsby from the pieces of his own life is exactly what Fitzgerald and all writers have done since storytelling began.

What makes Gatsby great, for Nick, is that the story he represents is about belief in the American Dream, even though the term did not even exist at the time. Nick is a dreamer and believer. In Gatsby, he finds a fellow traveler who ultimately gives his life in an attempt to achieve his aspirations. The title character's commitment to the dream earns him greatness in Nick's mind, since the narrator's own life contrasts rather negatively in comparison. The reader cannot imagine that anyone would consider Nick anything other than average.

Ironically, what makes Gatsby appear "great" is that Fitzgerald/Nick is so reserved in making him real. As a result, the reader is more or less invited to make his or her own determination. Do we emulate the heroic rise of young Jimmy Gatz to opulent Gatsby, or do we condemn the war hero who turns criminal all in the fruitless pursuit of a married woman?

When readers turn to Nick for clues, instead one finds his narrative fraught with inconsistencies and doubt. Interestingly, it is only the "great" Gatsby that Nick holds in awe while writing his book. All the other characters are revealed for their foibles and shortcomings: Tom Buchanan is a racist and snob, Daisy is weak, and Jordan is frigid and a cheat. Of the dozens of characters, only Gatsby is portrayed as meaningful, even if his guiding light is a confused quest for an unreachable aim. Yet, despite all this, readers may freely lionize the title character. As writer Bruce Bahrenburg claims, in each reading and rereading, "It is Gatsby who gains stature. He is heroic in resisting failure, and in defeat his grace is almost majestic."[33]

***

The Great Gatsby matters, if for no other reason, in its exploration of the American Dream and its consequences. Although one might find fault in this book, arguing that its premises are forced or too much of a reach to justify, there is no questioning *Gatsby*'s use as a tool in teaching, assessing, evaluating, criticizing, or reinforcing this essential American notion. As a result, with each new high school or college student exposed to the book or individual who picks it up (or revisits it) based on the film release, the world gains another person with the tools to weigh how he or she fits into the American Dream.

In other words, *Gatsby* provides readers and viewers with a kind of blank slate that can be employed to create and recreate one's personal worldview. And, since the novel carries so many ambiguities, it makes good fodder for doing so. According to literary critic Harold Bloom, this universality is an appealing trait across the lines that usually divide people. He explains, "There are few living Americans, of whatever gender, race, ethnic origin, or social class, who do not have at least a little touch of Gatsby in them."[34] We are all at some point and time dreamers, obsessive, status conscious, lovesick, friends, enemies, voyeurs, among the multitude of ideas and moments that make up a life.

What all this adds up to is a situation in which a novel (of all things) has laid the groundwork for addressing many quintessentially American qualities. I label this broad and far-reaching ideology meta-*Gatsby*, which means that this slim book has become pivotal in our lives as a cultural touchstone that carries value that transcends itself. As a result, *Gatsby* defines what we suggest when we say that a thing is iconic, Americana, or folklore.

We all really do have a bit of *Gatsby* in us, because we certainly do have *Gatsby* all around us. Fitzgerald's masterpiece is essential in our cultural world and foundational in understanding what it means to be American.

Part I

The Faustian Bargain: Creating
The Great Gatsby

I

A LITERARY STAR ROARING THROUGH
THE TWENTIES

Often I think writing is a sheer paring away of oneself, leaving always something thinner, barer, more meager.—F. Scott Fitzgerald, in a letter to his daughter, April 27, 1940

April 3, 1920. Biting winds whipped through the streets and neighborhoods of New York City making last-minute preparations difficult for those celebrating Easter the following day. As they made plans and bought food for the celebration, shoppers on West Forty-Second Street between Seventh and Eighth avenues passed by the remains of a large industrial building that had been literally ripped apart by a booming explosion the evening before. The force of the charge, set off by a storehouse of flash powder at a commercial photography studio, basically split the structure down the middle, like tearing apart a squat telephone book. The resulting fire caused even more damage as the winds pushed the flames toward other buildings in the vicinity not built to withstand fire like contemporary structures.

Witnesses to the blast and other onlookers met a rain of shattered glass and debris. In an adjoining five-story apartment building, the force of the explosion blew one unlucky tenant—Emma Corrigan—from her chair by the window and onto the floor. Others faced life-threatening circumstances as the fire spread. At least five engine companies, several fire trucks, and dozens of police officers responded to the devastation in an attempt to control the chaos. Although fire inspectors immediately real-

ized that flash powder caused the fire, they were puzzled about the exact
reason the magnesium exploded, since it did not spontaneously combust.
Eventually the explosion, fire, and containment efforts landed nine men
in the Bellevue Hospital emergency room.

Despite the pandemonium, several heroes emerged from the wreckage. A reporter from the *New York Times* learned that Robert White, a
street cleaner, and bystander Emil Moller ran into the burning building
and dragged out three injured men, ensuring that no one would die at the
scene. Later, two police officers—simply identified as Nevin and Raddo
in newspaper reports—risked their lives by alerting nearby residents of a
fire in their building. When they got to the top floor, they found a mother
and her three children overcome by smoke. Using blankets, the two men
carried the family to safety, which set off a large cheer from the neighbor-
ing crowds. [1]

Not far away from the remains of that odd chemical explosion, a
young couple in some respects almost as fiery and volatile stood before
Father William B. Martin in the vestry of St. Patrick's Cathedral and
became husband and wife. For twenty-three-year-old Scott Fitzgerald and
nineteen-year-old Zelda Sayre the day marked a tumultuous on-again,
off-again courtship that ended when Scott beat the odds and seemed
destined for literary fame on the sales of his first novel, *This Side of
Paradise*. Leaving the church directly after the ceremony, which neither
bride's nor groom's parents attended, and without holding a traditional
postwedding party, the young couple honeymooned at the Biltmore Hotel
on Forty-Third Street. [2]

Finally, after what seemed an eternity and through agonizing bouts of
self-doubt and pain, Fitzgerald got the rich girl he pined over. Like the
flash powder that lit up the night sky, their lives would explode across
American popular culture as they became the "it" couple of the 1920s and
global celebrities. Young, wealthy, always at the ready for a photo or a
quote, the Fitzgeralds rode stardom across the 1920s. Their union—and
the endless rounds of negotiations and scheming that led to it—set in
motion a whirlwind gallop around the globe.

On the day of their wedding, though, the young couple probably did
not have thoughts of explosions, or fires, or storybook endings of everyday people turned into heroes on their minds. In her last letter to the
future groom, less than a week before the event, Zelda talked about "living happily every afterward" and called Scott "a necessity and a luxury

and a darling, precious lover."[3] There is innocence in these phrases that validated both her love for him and her youthful exuberance. From today's more pessimistic perspective it is easy to overlook their youth and decided lack of wisdom. In 1920, neither Scott nor his teenage bride could be easily labeled "worldwise."

While the news of the day may have passed them by, given the prominence of the occasion, Scott and Zelda did have stardom firmly set in front of them. Caught up in the final capture of his girl and the spectacular sales numbers he received from Scribner's for *This Side of Paradise*, Scott wired her just several days before the wedding: "We will be awfully nervous until it is over and would get no rest by waiting until Monday[.] First edition of the book is sold out."[4] The two events publication and the wedding—were intimately intertwined, just as the compressed sentences in the wire message accidently revealed. Unlike his future character Jay Gatsby, Fitzgerald used his newfound wealth to get his lost love before one of her many Southern suitors beat him to the punch. Luckily for him, no Tom Buchanan—masculine, athletic, and ultrarich—stood in the way.

***

The reader cannot fully understand the birth of *The Great Gatsby* without grasping Fitzgerald's pre-*Gatsby* life and circumstances. In hindsight, perhaps too much is made of Scott and Zelda's celebrity status and its negative consequences. However, we also do not want to play down this standing, either. As scholar Kirk Curnutt explains, Fitzgerald is one of a small handful of "American writers whose life stories threaten to overshadow their art." According to Curnutt, most people do not know anything about him outside of *Gatsby* or *Tender Is the Night* (1934), but they can describe chunks of his life, intertwining it with the highlights and lowlights of the chaotic 1920s.[5]

Yet there is another perspective here, too: How many writers are well known enough that not one, but two novels are still remembered at all these many decades later? So, we cannot completely divorce Fitzgerald from the episodes in his life or his era, even though the thesis at the heart of this book is that *Gatsby* has transcended its time to become a cultural touchstone.

From any vantage point, Fitzgerald became a famous writer after the publication of *This Side of Paradise* and he enhanced this reputation by publishing widely in slick national magazines like the *Saturday Evening Post*, then at or near the top of the magazine circulation figures. His success and broad acclaim increased his fame and wealth, which in turn accentuated the positive and negative aspects of his life, whether circulating among the rich to gain background knowledge for what would become *Gatsby* or, alternatively, engaging in drunken hijinks with Zelda in hotels around the world.

This chapter sets the stage for the publication of *Gatsby* and its consequences by examining Fitzgerald as he roared across the early 1920s, living out his Jazz Age dreams with Zelda and a growing circle of famous friends and acquaintances both in the United States and Europe. During this period, Fitzgerald not only juggled his family life and celebrity, but dealt with the fulfilling of his own aspirations of becoming a literary great, not just a writer who sold a lot of books. What we will also see in this early stage in the young author's career are the internal and external struggles he confronted as he searched for solid footing as a husband and father, as well as an international celebrity and ambitious artist.

While there is a great deal of truth to the conventional image of the Fitzgeralds as dapper young sophisticate and beautiful flapper queen, it is important to remember that few prototypes existed for those newly wealthy or famous to follow. The fame business was young when they struck it big. As such, the couple really flew solo—too young, rich, and outrageous to see the bigger picture or understand the long-term consequences of their actions.

Fitzgerald himself longed for fame and celebrity and achieved it, not realizing the costs the victory would claim or the concomitant hit his literary reputation would take as a result. In retrospect, the greatest challenge the young couple faced was a lack of wisdom. Without positive role models for handling the intense scrutiny, their own personal demons were let loose, which resulted in a meteoric rise and spectacular fall.

As representatives of the Jazz Age and participants in the era's decadence, Scott and Zelda held court in a game that was rigged. What they could not have foreseen is that the spectacular times would end almost as quickly as they began, which initiated a long spiral downward as the world faced economic devastation and world war. In a mere fifteen years from the publication of *Gatsby*, Fitzgerald would be dead and Zelda the victim of incurable mental illness. If one simply looks at the photographs taken of the couple at each end of this spectrum, the images are shocking. From young and beautiful, Scott and Zelda aged far beyond their years, their physical brokenness seemingly matching their mental exhaustion.

"MAKE A NOTE OF THE NAME, F. SCOTT FITZGERALD"

Looking back on Fitzgerald's experience as a struggling writer, one is struck by his dedication to succeeding as a means of winning young Zelda Sayre's hand. After his discharge at the end of the Great War, he went to New York City, taking a job in an advertising agency for ninety dollars a month and writing stories, essays, and poetry at night in an attempt to gain a foothold in the literary world. In the approximately four months in New York, he accumulated some 122 rejections from a variety of magazines, which speaks to his determination. However, Fitzgerald also understood that the ad business would not be a road to quick wealth, either. Zelda was not going to marry someone making so little. [6]

The amazing aspect during this period is that the guy who basically flunked out of Princeton and barely survived the rigors of military life suddenly found a sense of purpose that enabled his talent to shine through via the spotlight of a newfound work ethic. Though he left the agency after Zelda broke off the engagement and went home to St. Paul, Minnesota, to live with his parents, Fitzgerald continued to rewrite his novel, then titled *The Romantic Egotist*. He did not let the stacks of rejections or the fact that the novel failed to sell in its initial form stop him from his quest.

In the army, Fitzgerald had written the first draft furiously, convinced that he would be killed in World War I having "left no mark on the world," so he pushed forth, propelled by "consuming ambition," explaining, "My whole heart was concentrated upon my book." [7] In another burst, this time fueled by his desire to win Zelda before a wealthier suitor swooped in to claim her heart, Fitzgerald rewrote the novel in about eight weeks. By mid-September, he got word that Scribner's editor Maxwell Perkins accepted the revised, retitled *This Side of Paradise*. The energy of the approval enabled the young man to concentrate his efforts on short stories, selling nine quickly, including his first to the *Saturday Evening*

Post in November 1919. By February the following year, he had six more accepted by the high-paying glossy. [8]

Scribner's published Fitzgerald's first novel on March 26, 1920, which it sold for $1.75. The publisher soon realized that it had a hit book on its hands. The three-thousand-copy first printing sold out in three days and the novel would eventually sell more than fifty thousand by the end of the following year. [9] Although not universally praised, *Paradise* served as a launchpad for Fitzgerald. *Chicago Tribune* reviewer Burton Rascoe, for example, exclaimed that the young author wrote "literature . . . [that] bears the impress, it seems to me, of genius." Realizing Fitzgerald's role in the wider culture, Rascoe explains, "It is the only adequate study that we have had of the contemporary American in adolescence and young manhood." [10]

According to scholar Morris Dickstein, "Like Lord Byron in 1812, he awoke and found himself famous. His commercial and literary careers were launched." [11] In short order, Fitzgerald followed up his literary success with marrying Zelda as discussed earlier. Given the then-shocking content of *This Side of Paradise*, combined with the youthful beauty and vitality of the couple, and the emerging youth-focused market, Scott found himself in demand as a spokesman for the new generation. Although he admits to being baffled by this role, he relished it and pursued it with vigor. As his fame skyrocketed, Fitzgerald transformed from "a" hot writer to "the" representative writer of his age. [12]

BOTH BEAUTIFUL AND DAMNED

The dashing young novelist and real-life beautiful flapper seemed typecast for stardom in the early 1920s. In the tradition of many celebrities both then and now, Scott and Zelda realized that they could get as much, if not more, attention for acting silly and juvenile. According to Matthew J. Bruccoli, from their initial stay in New York City, "they were interviewed; they rode on the roofs of taxis; they jumped into fountains; there was always a party to go to." [13] After bouncing around the city, generally wearing out their welcome at whatever hotel they holed up in, the Fitzgeralds rented a house in Westport, Connecticut, so Scott could get back to the business of writing. Given the phenomenal sales of *Paradise*, Scribner's published Fitzgerald's first short story collection in September

1920 with the hip title *Flappers and Philosophers*. Although critics were mixed in the reviews, it sold well and solidified Fitzgerald's standing at the time with the general reading public. The young couple seemed on top of the world.

Despite the public displays of giddiness and devil-may-care attitude, however, Fitzgerald's insecurities got him into trouble—from drinking too much and making a spectacle of himself to worrying about what shenanigans Zelda instigated when she left him alone to write and went off searching for amusement. Throughout their courtship, she held the power. After the wedding, however, Scott's budding fame pushed him to the forefront. The situation grew increasingly volatile. Zelda could not play second fiddle and may have used her more dominant personality to keep Scott in check. Making him jealous and using his friends as pawns offset his blossoming celebrity. The cracks that would eventually expand into full-sized chasms started appearing in their marriage, from wandering or being forced from one hotel or rental to the next to the ever-present money issues.

Neither the birth of their daughter Frances Scott "Scottie" Fitzgerald on October 26, 1921, nor the publication of Fitzgerald's second novel, *The Beautiful and Damned*, in early 1922 seemed to get the couple back on track. Over time, even the most fun-loving antics run their course, and the Fitzgeralds grew more and more desperate in their pranks and hijinks. Eventually, they started to alienate their friends and acquaintances, starting a cycle of alcohol-fueled fighting that led to later apologies and reversals. Their manic energy pushed the envelope; each crazy lark had to be outdone by one or the other on the next binge or drunken outing.

Fitzgerald, already experiencing the money problems that would plague him for the rest of his life, thought that *Beautiful* would sell well enough to alleviate his economic woes and provide more time for writing novels. He had taken an advance of $5,643, which meant that much of his royalties from book sales would go toward repaying the debt before he reaped any additional gain. Eventually *Beautiful* would sell in the forty- to fifty-thousand-copy range, a figure that would have delighted most authors, but not one with expectations (and debts) as high as Fitzgerald's.[14] Caught up in the competing maelstroms of being a famous writer, a new father, young husband, and celebrity, Fitzgerald probably did not realize the different trajectories these moves necessitated. There were too many dichotomies, whether the major conflict between the time required to write and the urge to drink and party or more minute challenges, like balancing the household economy.

Literary admirers, detractors, and those who fell somewhere in the middle all judged each new Fitzgerald novel or story with the voracity of a lion pride on raw meat. Given Fitzgerald's internal demons and sensitivity, this reaction had consequences on his psyche and output. Even his friends, like H. L. Mencken, eagerly pointed to his development and areas where they felt the young author remained stunted. Shockingly, it may have been Fitzgerald's Princeton classmate Edmund Wilson (who the novelist once called his "intellectual compass") who served up the harshest criticism, while also using his insider status against the writer.

Wilson, for example, in an unsigned overview of Fitzgerald's career for *Bookman* magazine, prattled on about Fitzgerald not understanding or being capable of using his talents. The review originally indicted the young writer for his difficulties with alcohol, but Wilson cut those sections after showing a draft to Fitzgerald who pleaded with him to take it out. Wilson's abrasive critique of Fitzgerald's intellect, rather than merely his writing, set the tone for much critical abuse he would face. Bruccoli concludes:

> The effects not only damaged Fitzgerald's contemporary reputation but perhaps also impeded the fulfillment of his genius by depriving him of the critical respect he sought. The popular or mythic view of Fitzgerald still retains the idea that he threw away his genius in orgiastic revelry.[15]

When one considers the kind of critical bashing that Wilson and others served up, combined with the picture painted by the burgeoning tabloid culture, it is no wonder that Fitzgerald's image in many respects outweighs his standing in literary history. Scholar Ruth Prigozy explains, "A public greedy for stories about celebrity hijinks relished the dramatic antics of the Fitzgeralds which gossip columnists painted in expectedly sensational colors."[16] The eventual fall, then, in terms of Fitzgerald's deteriorating health and addictions and Zelda's insanity and continual hospitalization served to cement the two as fallen stars of the Roaring Twenties, a physical manifestation of the wasteland left in the wake of the indulgence of the era, soon swept away by the Great Depression and Second World War.

Yet one also cannot oversell the hype that both Fitzgeralds relished or that they worked diligently to attract more. Bruccoli wisely concludes: "They were collaborators in extravagance and dissipation."[17] It seems clear, in retrospect, that the young couple desperately needed parental guidance or mentorship that may have left them better able to traverse the uncharted rapids they entered. But these kinds of relationships did not exist for them, nor is it clear that they wanted to change their ways. Most of Fitzgerald's male friends were individuals he looked up to or admired, while Zelda found most women boring. In the mostly carefree flirting of the day, it is no stretch either to say that many of Fitzgerald's friends were smitten with Zelda's dashing looks and carefree persona. Before the contemporary days of *Oprah Winfrey Show* celebrity confessionals and the modern-day rehab culture, the Fitzgeralds bopped along, letting alcohol and the next party guide them.

WRITING *GATSBY*

On paper in the early 1920s, Fitzgerald's ambition to become one of the world's greats outpaced what he had yet accomplished. His books sold well and the instant fame that came via *Paradise* and the slick magazines pushed him into a place on the nation's consciousness. Many reviewers had even anointed Fitzgerald as one to watch or a potential superstar. It would have been a stretch, however, to chart his path to that point and say confidently that here stood a candidate that might just write the greatest novel of all time. If the public and others knew the extent of his drunken binges at the time, they may have more seriously wondered if he would outlive the 1920s.

Despite the production of "popular" work (rather than novels considered "literary"), Fitzgerald sensed something in himself that would lead to literary fame. According to Matthew J. Bruccoli, the young author felt he could achieve both: "to make a great deal of money while bringing him artistic satisfaction and acclaim."[18] In mid-1922, while living in White Bear Lake, Minnesota, Fitzgerald wrote to his Scribner's editor Max Perkins that he had begun conceptualizing a new novel. His initial thoughts centered on a story set in New York City and the Midwest in the late 1800s. A month later, in July, he told Perkins, "I want to write something *new*—something extraordinary and beautiful and simple + intricately patterned." From this bold declaration, one clearly sees the high-lights of *Gatsby*'s style and potency, although it would be a torturous several years before the young writer could complete his masterwork. [19]

In fall 1922, Fitzgerald returned to a central theme in his fiction in the short story "Winter Dreams," which explored the love between a poor young man and a rich girl he desired. Combined with another move, this time to Great Neck, New York, which placed him near and among great wealth on Long Island, the novel in progress that would become *Gatsby* began to take a different shape. Although Fitzgerald considered himself a novelist, the manuscript took a backseat to more pressing concerns, which meant that the young writer had to churn out short story after short story to pay for the family's lavish lifestyle in the last months of 1923 and early 1924. *The Vegetable*, a play he had written and expended a great deal of energy creating, turned out to be a flop, which also diverted his attention from the novel and left him $5,000 in debt. [20]

When Fitzgerald emerged from the financial difficulties in early 1924, he and Zelda decided to leave Long Island for the less costly France, where they hoped they could stretch their money. The nonstop parties and extravagant lifestyle of Great Neck left them burned out physically and emotionally and without much money to their names, despite all Scott's hard work. Other crises and tragedies were on the horizon, despite the couple's optimism about the kind of lives they would live in Europe, but they left the United States full of hope.

Far from American shores, Fitzgerald nonetheless labored over the complexity of his new novel. This book would stand apart from his earlier novels and stamp him as one of the world's great literary stars, not just another "popular" author who rode on the back of sales and publicity successes. Every decision about scene, place, and character seemed to hang the entire novel in the balance, yet he carried forth, throwing himself completely into its creation. Reality also pounded its way into Fitzgerald's work life when Zelda began an affair with a suave French aviator named Edouard Jozan. The relationship scarred Scott forever, changing the way he felt about his wife and the way she lived. [21]

Despite the intrusion of Zelda's affair, Fitzgerald reported to Perkins that progress continued on the new novel, which meant that he was not drinking and instead settling into a lifestyle based on hard work. Clearly, as he drafted and redrafted the story, Fitzgerald must have felt delighted in working on the manuscript. He realized he was onto something big.

Later, after the first working draft emerged, the young writer spent about two months in September and October 1924 reworking the typed version, essentially rewriting much of the book. Even long after most writers stop fiddling with the text and the publishers demand as much, Fitzgerald continued to revise. At the galley stage, in early 1925, he still worked on the structure of *Gatsby* and worried about the title right up to publication on April 10, 1925. In some ways, the constant revision and uncertainty regarding the title foreshadowed the general public's reaction to the novel.[22]

What the work of textual analysts and bibliographers reveals, however, is the level of determination and dedication Fitzgerald put in the revision process. Bruccoli states, "The duplicate set of reworked galleys retained by Fitzgerald reveals that *The Great Gatsby* achieved greatness through extensive proof revisions."[23]

Although he faced intense pressures resulting from keeping the family afloat financially, the fallout of Zelda's affairs, and his dissatisfaction with expatriate life, Fitzgerald found the strength to bring *Gatsby* to life in spite of this bedlam. The portrait of Fitzgerald as a hardworking young writer stands at odds with the popular culture picture of him swinging from the ceiling on gold-gilded chandeliers. Thankfully, the work of scholars like Bruccoli provides a truer appraisal of the writer's process and its eventual outcome.

CRITICAL SUCCESS . . . COMMERCIAL FLOP

Fitzgerald understood the potential negative consequences of writing a novel that skirted potentially controversial topics, including illicit sex, multiple adulteries, and murder/suicide. These challenges kept magazine editors who feared public backlash from serializing the book. Fitzgerald thought sales would offset the lack of an additional revenue stream from a monthly, but serialization would have at least alleviated some of his financial burden.

Despite this misstep, the author possessed a keen understanding of the general reading public, as evidenced by his phenomenal success as a short story writer for some of the nation's most popular magazines and early literary success with his first two novels. Fitzgerald's knowledge may have in part led to the bold (often-quoted and basically accurate) declaration: "An author ought to write for the youth of his own generation, the critics of the next, and the school masters of ever afterward."[24] Although there were challenges, Fitzgerald believed the book would sell, raising his boat financially and as a literary star.

Yet, ten days after publication, Perkins cabled his young star with the cold, hard truth: "Sales situation doubtful excellent reviews."[25] The first printing of 20,870 copies did not sell quickly and the second printing some four months later totaled an additional 3,000 copies. Bruccoli's research indicates the vast gap between *Gatsby* and 1925's best-sellers, which sold in the hundred-thousand-copy range. A mere two weeks after *Gatsby* appeared, Fitzgerald penned Perkins a note blaming the commercial doldrums on the poor title and the fact that female readers were not interested in a novel without positive female characters.[26]

Given his hard work crafting the novel, past successes, and the overwhelmingly positive response by Perkins, Fitzgerald's dreams of financial and critical success were smashed upon the rocks when the novel did not fly off the bookshelves. After expending so much, the mediocre sales figures struck a horrible blow to Fitzgerald's ego and financial status. Almost any freelance writer would have felt the liability of a novel that did not sell, particularly when the time spent on it meant diverting one's efforts from more lucrative work. With Fitzgerald dancing gingerly on and around the financial break-even point, never really getting himself righted, it became clear that he would not get the kind of boost from *Gatsby* that would enable him to concentrate on writing novels full-time, particularly given his and Zelda's lifestyle.

Though the novel did not sell the way Fitzgerald wanted, he did receive ringing endorsements from some of the era's greatest literary lights, including T. S. Eliot, Edith Wharton, and Gertrude Stein. Some of his other friends, such as Ernest Hemingway and H. L. Mencken, were less enthusiastic about specific aspects of the work but still found the novel fresh, innovative, and a positive step for Fitzgerald.

***

The enduring portrait of Fitzgerald as sage of the Roaring Twenties and flapper king grew out of a combination of astounding early success and both self-sustained and external marketing campaigns that kept the young star in the spotlight with his beautiful, offbeat wife Zelda. Fitzgerald represented the bawdiness of the 1920s and the growing press corps eagerly anointed him its shining star. He welcomed the crown and gave the press sound bites and content that filled newspapers and magazines with insight into the young generation fueling the Jazz Age.

However, the image of Scott and Zelda as obnoxious, drunken clowns who were more annoying than charming does not hold up to the sentiments of those who knew the young couple. Edmund Wilson, Fitzgerald's longtime friend (and otherwise famous curmudgeon), for example, wrote about their mutual appeal. Scott and Zelda were able to walk the fine line between drunken revelry and playfulness in the early 1920s, he believed. Wilson highlighted the couple's "spontaneity, charm, and good looks."[27] Like most stars, the Fitzgeralds delighted in the attention, which took on a life of its own.

In retrospect, some of the stories and legends enlarged as time passed. Yet it is certain from the reminisces of people who were around them then that the young couple often put on a show, thus earning an inordinate amount of press interest. Some of these hijinks were alcohol fueled and spontaneous, but no small amount took place to entertain those around them and to give the press its nourishment.

The failure of *Gatsby*, though, was serious business and sent Fitzgerald into a tailspin. When the novel did not live up to the sales figures he imagined, the resulting depression and sadness depleted the young man of both the energy and confidence necessary to sustain the heights he now haunted as one of the very best writers of his age. The personal letters about the book's success buoyed him for some time and served to validate his notions of the novel's literary value, but doubts crept in as the reality of low sales figures forced him back to pumping out short stories to stay afloat financially. All Fitzgerald's hopes were in one basket, so much so that to conceive of a different life left him deflated.

The difficulty with Fitzgerald is in attempting to distinguish between the writer as product and the works he produced. Once the publicity machine grabbed hold of Scott and Zelda it kept them in its firm grasp until the times changed and they were no longer useful, just like the fame business has gobbled up and eventually discarded celebrities for centuries. From all the information available to the researcher, it seems as if there is simply no way to extricate these sides of Fitzgerald.

Writing just two years after Fitzgerald's death, the great American literary critic Alfred Kazin realized that the author's legend and his storytelling went hand in hand, saying, "The legend actually was his life, as he was its most native voice and signal victim; and his own career was one of its great stories, perhaps its central story."[28] Similarly, as writer Scott Donaldson explains, both were extremely young and immature: "Like an insecure child he needed approval. Like a willful one she demanded attention. Both sought to occupy the center of the stage, sometimes in collaboration but often in competition."[29] Fitzgerald as husband, writer, celebrity, drunk, friend, and foe are contained within this human vessel, each facet essential in his complete essence.

We all know (at least roughly) the trajectory of the Fitzgeralds' lives, so it is impossible to approach them completely objectively. However, this chapter asks that the reader try to imagine both the Roaring Twenties and the Fitzgeralds as they intersected, which resulted in an explosion of wealth, fame, and notoriety that would fuel the Fitzgerald legend to the present day. They are more than flapper queen and dandy king of the age. Their lives are a case study in numerous traits that demonstrate the importance of culture in American life.

Scott's experiences in total invigorated the world he recreated and reported on in *Gatsby*. That novel's greatness germinated in his own life preceding it, as well as his deep commitment to what this crazy world of the 1920s might mean for his own generation and those in the future.

2

BREAKING BAD: FITZGERALD'S DEMISE, 1925–1940

*Now once more the belt is tight and we summon the proper expression
of horror as we look back at our wasted youth . . . it seemed only a
question of a few years before the older people would step aside and
let the world be run by those who saw things as they were—and it all
seems rosy and romantic to us who were young then, because we will
never feel quite so intensely about our surroundings any more.*
—F. Scott Fitzgerald, "Echoes of the Jazz Age," 1931

In an ironic, cruel twist of fate for a writer foisted into superstardom on
the back of the growing media fascination with celebrity, a tabloid reporter named Michel Mok wrote a hatchet job article on Fitzgerald in September 1936 for the *New York Post*. The piece accentuated Fitzgerald's
drunkenness, loss of faith, and that he existed in "broken health."[1] Mok
put Fitzgerald back in the public spotlight, but as a pathetic, washed-up
version of the 1920s golden boy. Adding to the insult, *Time* used the
story, too, which gave it national circulation.

Fitzgerald, in despair over the long-term consequences of the articles
on what was left of his literary reputation, reportedly attempted suicide by
taking an overdose of morphine, but he threw it up.[2] The incident, on one
hand, took place at Fitzgerald's own doing. His past reputation as the
main party animal of the Jazz Age and ongoing alcoholism combined to
lead to the ghost of a man that Mok profiled.

Yet the writer also took advantage of Fitzgerald, emphasizing the
sensational aspects by playing up to the writer's vanities and woes to

create a kind of confessional situation. This is the kind of celebrity gossip that passed for news in the 1930s and would continue to grow into a mega-industry as the century progressed. So typical of Fitzgerald's later life, the incident with the Mok profile symbolized the mix of his own ills, the reputation that hung like an anchor around his neck, and an outside force that blindsided him. What we certainly know at this point in his life, whatever he had been when he wrote *Gatsby* or what he dreamed he would become after its publication was long gone.

The hard-charging, frenetic lifestyle of the 1920s and 1930s turned Fitzgerald old beyond his years. Although still a young man, Fitzgerald's poor health from 1935 to 1937—when only thirty-nine to forty-one years old—had dire consequences. He could not physically write much of the time, which compounded his writer's block and put him further behind financially. Nearly destitute and living under the umbrella of constant pain, Fitzgerald basically snapped, declaring in early 1937 to his agent Harold Ober, "My biggest loss is confidence."[3] The numerous letters to Ober from this period are filled with Fitzgerald's anxiety, pleas for loans to keep the writer afloat, and a swelling angst that seems to consume his every moment.

The simple fact, if there could be such a thing when applied to Fitzgerald, is that he faced immense stress for this entire fifteen-year time frame. The clues that divulge the high levels of strain are apparent across his extant letters, in the nonfiction essays he penned, and at the core of *Tender Is the Night*, the novel from this period that many scholars and experts consider his best work. That book's main character, Dr. Dick Diver, experiences a catastrophic rise and fall, with Fitzgerald drawing quite a bit of this material from his own life.

What the popular culture caricatures of Fitzgerald as a scion of the Roaring Twenties or washed-out bum of the 1930s often forget, however, is that the responsibility for Zelda and Scottie remained, regardless of his mental state or ability to work. He realized as much, writing his friend Ceci Taylor in early 1937 about quitting drinking and refocusing on work, which he found "more appalling than ever," but "Scottie must be educated + Zelda can't starve."[4] Yes, it is true that if he could have actually gotten off the booze, he may have alleviated much of his personal misery, but he did not leave them or disband the family completely by abandoning Zelda to a state-run sanitarium or forcing Scottie to go to a public school.

Perhaps the best words to describe the final phase of Fitzgerald's life are unsettled and anxious. In retrospect, it seems that he traipsed from one locale to the next, either searching for a better treatment facility for Zelda or in an attempt to focus on his work from a place that would be more affordable. Even when he went west to Hollywood and had a high-paying screenwriting job that would enable him to erase his debts, Fitzgerald's letters and notes are filled with angst. He complained about the energy it took to work for the studio, which then left him too drained to work on his long fiction. Also, always lurking in the background was the threat of alcoholism and the next binge that might put him out of commission.

Ultimately, when examining the last decade and a half of Fitzgerald's life, the amount of tragedy and sadness he encountered is nearly overwhelming for the contemporary researcher. Here stood a great writer, one of the best America ever produced, reduced to groveling to Hollywood studio hacks and megalomaniacs for his meal ticket because he could not make ends meet otherwise. At the same time, he exuded a certain type of nobility that few could comprehend—the utter mental collapse of his true love and soul mate—compounded by their daughter Scottie's racing through adolescence and young adulthood. Fitzgerald had to be a single parent in an era that did not openly acknowledge that status, especially if the father were the remaining parent. Furthermore, the responsibility for supporting the entire rickety structure financially never abated. To do so, Fitzgerald often turned to "loans" from his close business associates and friends, which embarrassed him and broke his spirit a little on each subsequent request.

Perhaps America's version of Mozart, but for the literary world, Fitzgerald burned brightly, creating some of the great masterpieces in history. Yet one cannot wonder if the price he paid would have satisfied him in the end. The wonderful writing abides, but he traded it for his life. Unfortunately, what the contemporary cultural scholar also notes is that if Fitzgerald would have come of age later in American history and had a similar career, he would have been celebrated for many of the chances he took, such as penning the memoir-ish pieces for *Esquire*. It is hard to imagine Fitzgerald making more money since he made so much as a short story writer and selling his work to Hollywood and Broadway, but there would have been other help to get him righted emotionally, physically, and in supporting Zelda.

Yes, I believe that Fitzgerald would have been okay, if he could have just lived through the excesses of the Jazz Age. His bill came due, however, and at his death, his friend Dorothy Parker echoed the owl-eyed man at Gatsby's funeral, muttering, "The poor son of a bitch."[5]

***

From the outside, Fitzgerald's decline seemed somewhat quick, though over the ensuing decades, as the details leaked into the mainstream, observers understood the numerous challenges he faced. Yet, despite the memoirs of those close to him and indications that the writer had turned a corner prior to his death, the national mind-set continued to hold on to the 1920s Fitzgerald—young, handsome, and swinging from chandeliers without letting a drop of bootleg champagne spill. The impression of Scott the life of the party took hold and grew into legend; according to literary critic Clive James, "He became the focal point of numberless journalistic stories about the waste of a literary talent."[6]

This chapter observes Fitzgerald's decline after the commercial failure of *Gatsby*, the agonizing publication of *Tender* in 1934, and carries through to his death in late 1940. The emphasis here is that Fitzgerald, like much of the nation, experienced a roller coaster of highs and lows in this era, compounded at times by national and international forces he could not control, like the onset of the Great Depression. Other calamities centered on his own family and intimate circumstances. Sometimes the demons at his doorstep appeared out of the blue, while at times he stood welcoming them, fanning the chaos with drink and delirium.

It is hard not to conclude that the failure of *Gatsby*, a work Fitzgerald knew in his soul to be a masterpiece, served up a knockout blow that the young man never overcame. The commercial failure, after he had pinned his family's hopes and dreams on its success, ignited a fifteen-year slide that ultimately led to his early demise.

THE GREAT CRASH

In March 1930 a bone-chilling wind assaulted two thousand men standing outside an Episcopal church on Twenty-Ninth Street in Manhattan. The long line twisted its way up Fifth Avenue, filled with people who had heard that the church dispensed food to the poor. A quarter of them were turned away when the rations ran out.

The sight of these needy New Yorkers unnerved the city's residents. Many of those waiting for food were clearly in anguish over accepting charity to survive. Those filling bread lines and taking handouts carried a deep psychological burden as unwilling participants in the economic breakdown. They did not want to take charity, wanted to work, and believed they would be rewarded for this attitude. Most who received welfare aid, from clothing to food and medical supplies, did so reluctantly.

The idea that the national economy could collapse at the hands of Wall Street corruption left the country mentally whipped. Money stood at the center of American culture in the 1920s, and the era's brokers and investment bankers reigned as society's new heroes—the kind of man that Nick Carraway might have become if he had stayed in New York. Wall Street fluctuations, hot stocks, and trading exploits served as juicy gossip.

The growing consumer culture required massive infusions of money. The impulse to live it up necessitated an ever-growing cash flow. Thus, many in the newly moneyed class relied on stocks and a line of credit to finance their lifestyles. The banking industry held a great deal of power determining the economic fortunes of the nation. The "get rich quick" mentality—similar to the go-go days of the Internet bubble in the late 1990s—lured people into the market who hoped for the big score that would take them away from everyday toil. World War 1 bond drives demonstrated the power of investment and the idea of a quick hit that would put an investor on easy street. Large commercial banks willingly facilitated the transactions. Win or lose, big banks and brokerages received their cut.

The national media also followed Wall Street closely, trumpeting its successes. The *New York Times* and the *Wall Street Journal* kept tabs on the stock market's movers and shakers. Despite the widespread panic gripping the nation after the collapse, newspapers across the region brimmed with reassuring stories about the long-term viability of the market system.

Wall Street represented a new religion in the United States. Its priests were the men who ran Wall Street's successful brokerages and investment banks. They formed a sort of exclusive gentleman's club, each belonging to the same clubs, vacationing together, and mainly living on the Upper East Side of Manhattan. These are the men one can imagine

attending Gatsby's galas, chugging out to Long Island in fancy new automobiles with beautiful women in tow. The ultimate club was the New
York Stock Exchange, with a mere 1,100 seats. The only way in was to
purchase an existing seat from one of the members or investment banks
that owned the seat. The men who controlled Wall Street had deep ties to
the Northeast. Most had attended the private schools and elite colleges
dotting the region.

While Wall Street's leaders breezed through an insulated world high
above the trading floor, an entirely different kind of trader fueled the
stock overspeculation that would lead to the crash. Many traders only
cared about stock fluctuation, borrowing enough money to buy and sell,
then quickly moving the stock to make money on the difference. Timing,
not knowledge, mattered most. By the summer of 1929, stock market
value hit $67 billion, up from $27 billion two years earlier.

The economic free fall that took place in and after October 1929
decimated the American economy. Within three years, 75 percent of the
value of all securities—a whopping $90 billion—disappeared. The year
after the crash, more than twenty-six thousand businesses went bankrupt,
surpassed in 1931 by more than twenty-eight thousand failures. In December 1930, the Bank of the United States went bankrupt, wiping out
the funds of about four hundred thousand depositors.

As debilitating as the stock market crash was to the nation's economy,
the crushing blow came from the way it demoralized the American people. The collapse shocked everyone and shook people's faith in the national economic system. Businessmen and corporations, many headquar-
tered in New York, reacted by making drastic cuts, while anxious consumers virtually stopped spending on anything beyond bare necessities.
Millions of workers lost their jobs as businesses desperately cut their
operations to the bare essentials. Construction in New York City, for
example, came to a near halt as 64 percent of construction workers were
laid off soon after the stock market collapsed. Unemployment in 1929
was slightly over 3 percent, but by 1932 the figure had reached 24 percent. Millions more involuntarily worked in part-time roles.

Two years after the crash, some two hundred thousand New Yorkers
faced eviction for failure to pay rent. Many who were not evicted sold off
their valuables so they could raise the money. Others trekked from apartment to apartment. If their furniture had been purchased on credit, many
owners left it behind when they could no longer make payments. In

Philadelphia some 1,300 evictions occurred per month in the year following the crash.

The psychological toll unemployment took on the American people caused high levels of stress and anxiety. While some took to the streets to sell whatever they could gather, others turned to crime in an effort to find food. In Pittsburgh, a man stole a loaf of bread to feed his children, and then later hanged himself in shame. In New York City, hundreds of thousands of unemployed or underemployed workers turned to soup kitchens. By October 1933, New York City counted 1.25 million people on relief. Even more telling is that another one million were eligible for relief but did not accept it. Some six thousand New Yorkers attempted to make ends meet by selling apples on the streets. But by the end of 1931, most street vendors were gone. Grocery store sales dropped by 50 percent during the Depression. Many urban dwellers scoured garbage cans and dumps looking for food. Studies estimated that 65 percent of the African American children in Harlem were plagued by malnutrition during the era.

Tens of thousands of people in New York City were forced to live on the streets or in shantytowns located along the banks of the East River and the Hudson River. These clusters of makeshift abodes were dubbed "Hoovervilles"—a backhanded tribute to the president. The city's largest camp was in Central Park. Ironically, the Central Park shantytown became a tourist attraction and featured daily performances by an unemployed tightrope walker and other out-of-work artists.

Even the rich were not immune to the harsh realities of the Great Depression. From his Manhattan palace, steel king Charles M. Schwab openly admitted his fear. By the early 1930s, the situation was so glum that it became fashionable among the wealthy to brag about how much they had lost in the crash. Even professions one would think were insulated from economic hardship were affected during the Depression. In Brooklyn, one-third of all doctors were forced out of business.

When people learned of the role business leaders had played in the stock market crash, they quickly changed their formerly favorable opinions to outright scorn. The Wall Street collapse proved that these exalted financial leaders did not know what they were talking about in the years leading up to that fateful October as they continually hyped the market. Remarkably, in the days immediately after the collapse, the nation's business leaders (Sears, AT&T, and General Motors, among others) issued cheery reports about swelling sales and stability in an attempt to bolster public confidence.

There is no way to divorce Fitzgerald's fate from the Wall Street crash and ensuing Depression. As the veritable poster boy for the glamour of the Roaring Twenties, the inevitable end of those glory days meant that Fitzgerald would suffer, just as countless millions of Americans were forced to do more with less just to survive. What we can see now, looking back on his life and era, is that Fitzgerald could not have anticipated how the ground beneath his family's feet would shift as a result of the economic collapse.

At first, the chilling retribution would not come professionally, since Fitzgerald continued to make an inordinate amount of money via short fiction sales (some $31,500 in 1931 from stories, out of a total of $37,599).[7] However, Zelda experienced her first breakdown in April 1930 while the family resided in Paris. For almost a year and a half she remained in treatment facilities in Switzerland. She recovered enough to sail to America in September 1931, but the cost of getting her first-rate help put an indelible strain on their financial status.

Punctuating the impact of the Depression, Fitzgerald's main outlet, the *Saturday Evening Post*, dropped his payment in 1932, with its editors complaining that his work was not his best. In retrospect, it seems clear that the preoccupation with Zelda's mental health and becoming a single parent to Scottie weighed on him, which reflected in his writing. His earnings that year dropped to $15,832 and precipitated additional rough financial times ahead.[8]

FAMILY TIES: ZELDA, CRISIS, AND THE TIMES

Fitzgerald continued to struggle with the relentless bills and costs associated with his new lifestyle alone and supporting Zelda from afar. He would not recover until Hollywood threw him a lifeline in mid-1937. Yet, in this strange way of life, Fitzgerald faced the kinds of twists and unyielding challenges that gripped families across the nation. The economic crisis caused the idea of what a family could or should be to change. Ironically, it took World War II to get the nation back on track financially and the postwar period to get people interested in recreating the notion of family life, though that era faced unprecedented changes as well.

Family roles were muddled when the traditional male role of bread-winner disappeared. Merely keeping families together during economic duress became difficult as people lost their jobs and homes. Some couples delayed weddings due to the uncertainty, while others put off divorce because they could not afford to separate. For many children, the Depression altered their role in maintaining family order. Children had to grow up faster during the crisis; many were forced to forgo formal schooling and get a job at an early age while also often taking on parental roles to provide solace to those within their own families.

Domestic violence and child abuse increased during the Depression. Family disputes over finances, food, and other basic necessities caused tensions to increase. Men and boys often simply fled the home out of embarrassment, frustration, or the inability to cope with the new economic reality. Thousands of people, young and old, became traveling hobos, riding the rails in search of work or some form of relief.

The economic pressure on male breadwinners intensified. Men's self-image, which had been strengthened by the nation's victory in World War I and the subsequent prosperity of the 1920s, took a beating during the Great Depression. In many cases, men arrived at work to find the doors locked, with little or no explanation. Some families were able to make ends meet by having the wife and children work, a situation that could be humiliating for the husband and father. Studies, such those undertaken by sociologist Mirra Komarovsky for her book *The Unemployed Man and His Family* (1940), revealed that many unemployed or underemployed men suffered from impotence. The birthrate also slipped as unemployment grew.

During the 1920s, many Americans had begun to equate self-worth with material possessions. Therefore, when times turned bad, people felt worthless. The nation's traditional optimistic outlook was replaced by the reality of economic chaos and confusion. Even among those fortunate or wealthy enough to avoid economic disruption, the Great Depression took a psychological toll. Psychiatrists' offices were packed in the early 1930s with those from the upper classes attempting to cope with the economic mayhem. The confidence the average American held up as tenet of the nation's greatness in the Roaring 1920s fell to a general malaise and inertia as unemployment grew and depression set in. People waited for something to happen, spinning in circles as they fought to survive.

Suicide became a part of everyday conversation, particularly as the stories of bankrupt Wall Street traders jumping from tall office buildings entered the public mind-set. Urban legend regarding mass suicides during the Great Depression far outstripped reality. However, the national suicide rate did increase in late 1929 and continued to increase until 1933— from 13.9 per 100,000 to an all-time high of 17.4 per 100,000.

In one widely publicized example, James J. Riordan, president of the New York County Trust Company, killed himself in November 1929 because of the deep shame he felt over losing other people's money, as well as his own loss of funds. Fearing that news of his suicide would cause a run on the bank's deposits, the board of directors did not release a public statement until after the bank closed on Saturday afternoon.

Franklin D. Roosevelt's New Deal began to reverse some of the psychological damage inflicted by the Great Depression. The New Deal relief programs helped people to realize that the collapse was societal, and not the result of individual failure. The New Deal enabled many Americans to deflect some of the guilt they felt for their personal economic failure.

The entertainment industry helped divert people's attention during the Great Depression. Hollywood actually entered a boom period, with about eighty million people going to the movies each week. Popular radio entertainers, including Bing Crosby, George Burns, and Gracie Allen, also helped distract Americans from their difficulties. Fitzgerald, who always loved the movies, would eventually end his personal financial challenges by going west to Hollywood on a $1,250-a-week contract with MGM. As scholar Scott Donaldson notes, "In 1938 MGM paid him a total of $58,750. Fitzgerald made a fortune from writing. He also spent it all."[9] Yet one must consider that a significant amount of money went for Zelda's care. Her sanitarium expenses were not cheap, and Fitzgerald attempted to find her good care, not run-of-the-mill facilities.

TENDER IS THE NIGHT

In the long nine-year span between *Gatsby* and *Tender Is the Night*, Fitzgerald's life bobbed and bounded around the globe and across the United States, while he and Zelda experienced the travails of stars whose celebrity sputtered. During the long lull he struggled with a number of physical and professional ills, from intensifications of his alcoholism and other acute ailments to his freelance rate dropping and markets going out of business as the Depression churned.

Even though *Tender* is now considered either Fitzgerald's best or second-best work, its publication did not spark huge sales or even provide the author with enough money to support himself or his family. Records obtained from Scribner's by Elaine P. Maimon reveal that in 1936, just two years after *Tender*, the publisher only sold 210 books from the Fitzgerald catalog.[10] The forces conspiring against Fitzgerald included the deepening economic depression that made buying books a frivolous endeavor for many Americans. In addition, Fitzgerald's poster-boy standing as a symbol of the Roaring Twenties worked against him and made *Tender* seem antiquated.

Tender is a novel quite unlike *Gatsby*, and is an even darker examination of the lead character's (Dr. Dick Diver) deterioration based on his own shortcomings and the forces around him that are beyond his control, including the manipulations of the wealthy Warren family he marries into. For the purposes of this book, perhaps the most critical aspect of *Tender* in relation to *Gatsby* is that in his post-*Gatsby* state, Fitzgerald became in many respects more autobiographical, which provides readers a way to think about and consider his spiraling state in the late 1920s and early 1930s.

There are two overt assumptions related to *Tender*'s autobiographical impulses, first that Diver is basically a stand-in for Fitzgerald, but drawing on himself even more than in earlier work. Second, a common scholarly belief is that Fitzgerald's portrayal of the Diver marriage is wholly autobiographical. On the former, Scott Donaldson claims, "This close identification of author and character accounts for a critical shortcoming in this brilliant novel . . . reviewers thought Diver's decline and his rapid acceptance of it unconvincing."[11] In other words, Fitzgerald played with his self-image on the page but could not accept that Diver could be disliked, just as he could not stand when people did not like him. The gap is reflected in the novel. In terms of the marriage, scholar Matthew J. Bruccoli claims, "Zelda Fitzgerald's illness supplied more than factual background for *Tender*: it provided the emotional focus of the novel. Diver's response to Nicole's illness derives from Fitzgerald's feelings about his wife's collapse and relapses."[12]

Like *Gatsby*, money plays a central role in *Tender* and is at the core of the Diver marriage. The Warren riches are an international calling card, giving Nicole Diver's sister Baby Warren tremendous power for a woman in the 1920s. The Warren name alone "caused a psychological metamorphosis in people."[13] However, Nicole's illness inhibits Baby, so she tells Dick about her plan to marry her younger sister off to a doctor in Chicago, essentially buying him as a husband and caretaker. The arrangement will enable Baby to play out her role as a proper aristocrat without constantly worrying about Nicole's whereabouts or state of mind.

Dick is disgusted by the notion of a husband "purchased in the intellectual stockyards of the South Side of Chicago."[14] Since Baby outlines the idea to him, Dick incorrectly believes she is targeting him and using the Chicago example to goad him into action. Later, Baby's request for Dick to escort Nicole back to the clinic is seen as another attempt to "throw us together."[15] Interestingly, one of the major tenets of the book is the Warren family's "ownership" of Dick and how that manifests itself throughout their marriage. However, that entire notion is built on deception and misinterpretation. The all-knowing narrator fills the reader in, saying, "He was wrong; Baby Warren had no such intentions. . . . Doctor Diver was not the sort of medical man she could envisage in the family. She only wanted to use him innocently as a convenience."[16]

Fitzgerald is virtually setting up the characters (and the reader) for a fall. The entire marriage is predicated on this notion of ownership, but Fitzgerald reveals that it was the wrong assumption for Dick to make. The misdirection also enables Baby to maintain a powerful role within the Diver marriage by controlling the money flow. Whenever Dick or Nicole wants cash, they must ask Baby, all based on his perception that he is the husband/caretaker Baby implied she would find for Nicole. For her part, Nicole remains passive when it comes to money. She knows that the Warrens are wealthy, but she grants Baby control in this area.

In Dick's mind, Nicole used the money against him, not only using it to "own him," but also to draw him away from his work.[17] Dick sees it as a plot wearing him down to the point where he feels that he can do nothing but sit and watch time pass. He would not accept the notion of being owned, but his thin mental defense could not overcome the onslaught of Warren wealth and the tag team of Nicole and Baby always tacitly insisting as much.

If one believes Ernest Hemingway's recollection of Fitzgerald's real-life marriage in *A Moveable Feast*, then it would be difficult to argue that the way Nicole tried to keep Dick from working was not inspired by Zelda's attempts to keep Scott from writing. Hemingway says, "He would start to work and as soon as he was working well Zelda would begin complaining about how bored she was and get him off on another drunken party."[18] Later, Hemingway accused Zelda of using the jealousy of suitors against Scott to sabotage his work. Rather than alcoholic binges, Nicole used her money as a way to make Dick soft.

Dick and Nicole carry out opposing trajectories in *Tender*. Surprisingly, however, she is not willing to rescue him in the end, like he did for her. The marriage saves her but destroys him. Nicole carries on as a full-fledged Warren, traipsing around the globe with Tommy Barban, the Barbarian he-man lover she takes on as her protector. Dick, though, grows increasingly obscure in small-town America, not even recovering enough to assume the mantle of "big fish in a small pond." The cycle is complete.

Nicole's gradual loosening of Dick and her budding independence certainly make it difficult to pin too much of the autobiographical label on the Diver marriage based on the Fitzgerald union. Instead, the Diver marriage (and Nicole's character, in particular) may better be viewed as a composite of many individuals the author encountered, not least of whom are Gerald and Sara Murphy, who are acknowledged by Fitzgerald as the models. In writing *Tender* over a seven-year span with several complete overhauls of the plot, it is reasonable to consider that Fitzgerald simply worked pieces of Zelda and her illness into the story, just like he did with the Murphys and other friends and acquaintances from his days in Europe and on the Riviera.

Clearly, the novel's intricate plot, philosophical and historical themes, and flashback chronology influenced several decades of reviewers, who were quick to judge the book as subpar or average. However, *Tender* has enjoyed more favorable critical and scholarly attention over the last several decades. Some old myths about the book still remain, such as the notion about its level of autobiographical detail. A close reading of Dick and Nicole's marriage reveals that there is more to the union than a replica of the Fitzgeralds, yet it is also unmistakably a model of sorts.

HOLLYWOOD DREAMS AND DEFEATS

Fitzgerald spent the last eighteen months of his life in chaos, near collapse psychologically, physically, and financially. The most pressing day-to-day concern was money. Once his scriptwriting assignment for MGM ended in late 1938, he had no reliable income. With little advance knowledge from MGM that they were dropping his contract, Fitzgerald's income plummeted from $1,250 a week to virtually nothing. The situation forced him to scramble for bit studio writing gigs that were far below his former salary. He also resorted to begging friends and acquaintances for money, an old tactic that humbled him and would later feed rumors of his hand-to-mouth existence and carelessness with money. Given his deteriorating health conditions, which prevented him from holding any kind of traditional job, Fitzgerald had little choice but to attempt to write his way out of the turmoil.

Fitzgerald moved to Hollywood in July 1937 to break out of debt on the back of the studio system. When he arrived, the MGM contract made him one of the highest-paid writers on the lot. Working and reworking the figures, Fitzgerald made progress in whittling down his obligations. However, his creditors, including the Internal Revenue Service and Zelda's North Carolina sanitarium, continued to demand payment. The bleak situation necessitated that he take extreme measures, including haranguing editors over the phone while drunk, which simply perpetuated the common notion that he was on a never-ending bender.

At one point in September 1939, Fitzgerald pleaded with Zelda's doctor because he could not pay her bills. Describing his dire situation, including a recent recovery from tuberculosis, he claimed, "It is simply impossible to pay anything . . . when one drives in a mortgaged Ford and tries to get over the habit of looking into a handkerchief for blood when talking to a producer."[19] Showing his deep concern for his wife but realistically examining the situation, Fitzgerald hoped "that this does not mean Zelda will be deprived of the ordinary necessities . . . [but] if things go as bad as they have for another month, the hospital can reimburse itself out of life insurance. This is a promise."[20] Foreshadowing actual events, fifteen months later, the author died of a heart attack in December 1940.

If there were a positive to be drawn from standing on the edge of financial ruin, Fitzgerald found it in the ready market of *Esquire* magazine under the editorship of Arnold Gingrich. Long a Fitzgerald admirer,

Gingrich accepted almost everything Fitzgerald sent for a base fee of $250 per piece. Both out of necessity (for money) and to exercise his creative writing skills after almost two years of doing almost nothing but screenwriting, Fitzgerald created Pat Hobby, a character unlike any he had produced before.

Some seventeen Pat Hobby stories appeared in *Esquire* between January 1940 and May 1941, despite Fitzgerald's death. Payment for the Hobby stories helped Fitzgerald remain solvent, but even still he fought with Gingrich over pay, often nearly to the point of destroying that relationship as well. In October 1939, Fitzgerald sent a telegram threatening to send the Hobby stories to magazines back east if Gingrich could not increase the per story price by $150. In a reply telegram—after a lengthy collect telephone call from Fitzgerald, which included profanity—the editor replied by telling Fitzgerald not to "jeopardize old reliable instant payment market like this by use of strong arm methods . . . next move is up to you but on bird in hand theory believe you would be better businessman to regard it as advance against another story."[21] Fitzgerald's desperation kept the Hobby stories coming, even if he could not convince Gingrich to increase his pay.

***

Two or more Fitzgeralds emerge in just about every instance, which makes assessing him problematic. One could claim that the last decade and a half of his life was a roller coaster of good and bad with the negative sucking up more of his time and energy. Yet, at the same time, I wonder how many people would trade just about any possession they own to author a great work of literature like *Tender Is the Night*? Was he really breaking at the same time he had the wherewithal to write that novel? These kinds of questions bedevil the researcher but also serve a level of intrigue and mystery to the narrative. I think these questions and others like them go a long way toward supplying a more complete picture of this complex individual, even though some of the ideas about him prove to be little more than speculation. Despite half a century of scholarly study about Fitzgerald and his work, mountains of published primary documentation, and the memoirs of those who knew him well, as well as his own writing, there is still much room for engaging with the author.

Eminent literary critic Alfred Kazin, writing just two years after Fitzgerald's untimely death, attempted to place the writer within his times, explaining, "Fitzgerald was a boy, the most startlingly gifted and self-destructive of all the lost boys, to the end."[22] But even granting Kazin's understanding of the era, such a pithy rationalization comes up short. The notion of Fitzgerald being a "boy" genius persisted in the early days of his postdeath revival. Not enough time had passed for him to adequately separate the myth from the real-life writer crafting the work, nor had the pioneering scholarly work been undertaken by Matthew J. Bruccoli. As a Fitzgerald champion, Bruccoli researched the author from a textual analysis perspective, which revealed the detailed revision he did, and scoured the Fitzgerald papers and then published what he found, which profoundly transformed the way people assessed Fitzgerald.

Writing in the twenty-first century, critic Clive James takes a different position on Fitzgerald, concluding, "It takes a great artist to have a great failure, and F. Scott Fitzgerald was so great an artist that he could turn even his fatal personal inadequacies into material for poetry."[23] The difference between Kazin's and James's interpretations of Fitzgerald demonstrates the way the academic study about the author has changed people's observations. Now that we have a more complete picture of Fitzgerald's challenges late in life—both from the outside and the ones he created for himself—we can still appreciate the tragedy of his early death, but also better place his life within its cultural and socioeconomic times.

Part II

Gatsby in the American Century

3

GATSBY REBORN, 1941–1963

Through all he said, even through his appalling sentimentality, I was reminded of something—an elusive rhythm, a fragment of lost words, that I had heard somewhere a long time ago . . . what I had almost remembered was incommunicable forever.—Nick Carraway, *The Great Gatsby*

History is filled with events that initially seem like accidents but ultimately transform from calamity into a significant innovation. In a similar vein, certain people find themselves falling into great crisis situations and then performing heroically. Sometimes, in a world filled with unintended consequences, a confluence takes place that leads to a future tidal wave. When the unanticipated outcomes are positive, we attach positive labels to them, such as luck, serendipity, or destiny. Such is the case with Fitzgerald's revival, which began on several (often unrelated) fronts relatively shortly after his death and gained steam as the 1940s and 1950s rolled on. The micro- and macrolevel catalysts sparked a Fitzgerald wildfire that not only established him as one of America's great writers, but also led to the reexamination and exaltation of *The Great Gatsby*.

Undeniably, many aspects of the Fitzgerald revival took flight based on deliberate efforts on the part of his proponents to elevate him, so we certainly cannot claim that the resuscitation occurred solely based on luck. However, analyzing the many fronts taken together as a whole, it does look like destiny played a role in the revival. Reassessing his work, critics, commentators, and scholars could not overlook *Gatsby*'s magnitude or Fitzgerald's word-by-word and line-by-line skills. As the old saying goes, "the cream rises to the top," so one can imagine some form of Fitzgerald restoration occurring at a future point, but certainly the concentrated efforts of many key players hastened the outcome.

Examining the series of serendipitous events and cultural changes taking place in the 1940s and 1950s, we see that these unintended consequences sprouted up in odd places. For example, if it were not for the need to ration paper in the 1940s, the publishing industry may never have figured out the public's interest in buying mass-market paperbacks. At the same time, if American GIs during World War II did not have so much free time on their hands on bases at home and abroad, then they might not have turned to reading to fill idle hours. Luckily, however, these disparate sparks came together to ignite the rise of cheap paperback copies of great books. Simultaneously, publishers realized the sales potential and pushed mass-market renditions as a method for making money on products without having to expend funds on new content. As a result, many books stayed in print that otherwise may have been lost to history's dustbin.

During the latter stages of the Second World War, for instance, servicemen could read the Armed Services Editions of both *The Great Gatsby* and a story collection that featured "The Diamond as Big as the Ritz," one of Fitzgerald's best short stories. The military distributed about two hundred thousand free copies, which promoted Fitzgerald's reputation beyond measure. For other important writers, such as Hemingway, the military versions opened up their works for new generations of readers and book purchasers, but given Fitzgerald's untimely death, he needed the boost to stay in the limelight. The exposure to reading swelled book club memberships after the soldiers returned from the war, as did the push for attaining an education based on the GI Bill. One could argue that reading for pleasure probably reached its all-time pinnacle in the mid to late 1940s before television burst onto the scene.

Perhaps for the first time in American history, publishers had to devise new ways to get books into the hands of literature-starved readers. The postal system had the capacity to handle a book order business, so publishers set up book clubs that mailed books to readers based on their specific interests. Soon, more than a million books a month were sold through the dozens of book clubs across America. At the same time, the rising affluence of American households and the establishment of life in the suburbs pushed young parents to not only buy books for themselves but also to invest in their children's education by purchasing book sets. What one sees is that books developed into a kind of showcase for suburban couples and a form of decoration for filling wall space in formal living rooms, family rooms, and dens.

For example, the Great Books Program, an intensive reading course devised by University of Chicago president Robert Maynard Hutchins and professor Mortimer J. Adler, promised to teach the reader everything that the "well-read" person should know, from Aristotle and Plato to Milton and Shakespeare. Whether people were actually diving into Dante's *Inferno* or the political writing of Rousseau, the hardback or leather-bound sets soon became accessories in the stylish living rooms of 1950s homes. Book sets enabled suburban couples to make a statement about who they felt they were or imagined themselves to be.

Moving from war rationing to publishing inexpensive paperbacks and the influence of the suburbs and push toward higher education in the postwar nation seems somewhat scattershot, yet these examples comprise just a small sliver of the impulses that converged to launch Fitzgerald's comeback. We also cannot undersell the author's early death and roller-coaster ride with fame in determining how and why his work came back into vogue.

The United States emerged from World War II in a different place, physically and emotionally stronger. Technology, education, military and economic power, and new ways of living led to an era that demanded more. Fitzgerald became part of this call. *Gatsby* helped literature professors and high school teachers explain the nation to their growing classes, filled increasingly with returning war veterans and the first glimpses of the baby boom. Readers yearned for great books. The slim novel seemed the perfect fit—it even had the word "great" in the title. *Gatsby*'s timeless themes worked in a world emerging from the horrors of world war and nuclear carnage and transitioning to a new brand of military strength and economic prosperity.

In addition to the needs of readers and publishers, the entertainment industry also demanded content as film, radio, and television fought for audiences. The great Fitzgerald scholar Matthew J. Bruccoli is an example here. Publishing scion Charles Scribner III recounted Bruccoli's story of his first interaction with Fitzgerald, as a high school student listening to a 1949 radio broadcast of the sci-fi fantasy "The Diamond as Big as the Ritz" as he and his parents drove between Connecticut and New York

City.[1] Hearing the rendition on air of the famous short story first published in 1922, the young man experienced an epiphanic moment. He immediately set out to find more about the mysterious author, which set off a lifetime of scholarly work on Fitzgerald. As the Bruccoli case reveals, radio, film, and the stage helped deliver Fitzgerald to countless new readers in the two decades under review in this chapter.

Taken together as a whole, from the scholarly and general interest in Fitzgerald's work to the cultural and technological changes transforming the nation, one sees a nation casting about for ways to reinterpret and reimagine itself. The ambiguity of the novel seemed right for the times, enabling readers to either see themselves and their country reflected in its pages, or experience it as a way of questioning the new era. Quite frankly, as America rebooted in the postwar age, *Gatsby* became an important part of the cultural imprint.

***

This chapter demonstrates how Fitzgerald's untimely death sparked a revival of his work, particularly *The Great Gatsby*. A number of the author's friends and other supporters initially orchestrated a campaign to solidify his place in American literary history simply by remembering his work and pointing to its value. As momentum toward this effort expanded and intensified, soon readers, commentators, critics, and scholars responded. At the same time, the changes affecting the nation helped spur interest in the book.

The arrival of the United States as a military and economic superpower in the post–World War II world fundamentally altered the nation. These changes impacted every facet of life, from the number of children young couples produced to the way people spent their newfound leisure time and discretionary income. Many of these parallel influences converged to utterly transform the way people thought about spending. Suddenly, emerging from the scarcity of the Great Depression and the rationing of the Second World War, people had more time, extra money, and the willingness to spend it on shiny new things. No small percentage of time or effort went into self-improvement efforts, which included expanding the national education system and offering more opportunities via nontraditional education programs, like television talk shows and community-based curriculums.

What the evidence reveals is that during this tumultuous period, both Fitzgerald and *Gatsby* took root in our national culture. "Along with Hemingway and Faulkner he became the writer's writer for the post–1945 generation, revered and widely imitated," explains scholar Morris Dickstein. "*The Great Gatsby* was canonized not simply as a document of the Jazz Age but as a key to the American psyche and the national experience."[2] As the nation emerged from the Second World War and confronted a new epoch, people searched for tools that might help them make sense of the quickly changing world. Based on the concerted effort by a handful of critics, admirers, and friends, therefore, *Gatsby* grew into an instrument for examining and comprehending society, not only for rethinking the 1920s, but for reexamining the postwar time frame as well.

THE INITIAL COMEBACK, *THE LAST TYCOON,* AND *THE CRACK-UP*

The most surprising aspect of the "Fitzgerald revival" in the 1940s is that the author never really slipped out of the public eye, at least an informed reader's eyes, in the years leading up to his death. In other words, many scholars and commentators conflated the fact that his novels no longer sold well with his general decline and disappearance from the literary scene. It is true that his novels were not selling, but that does not automatically mean that the part of the public one would call "literary" had forgotten him or his work.

Taking a contrarian position, I posit that Fitzgerald remained both a public figure and in the cultural mind-set throughout the 1930s and definitely through the first major events of the revival, most often dated to the 1945 publication of *The Crack-Up*, edited by Edmund Wilson. This is not just idle speculation or a desire for revisionist history. Instead, today's researcher simply must use the tools at one's disposal to get a fuller picture of the cultural scene in these years and then look at the archival records.

Taken all together, research demonstrates Fitzgerald's continuing ubiquity among the nation's educated readers. Obviously, his star did not shine as it did in his 1920s heyday, but ever since the publication and disappointing sales of *Gatsby* in 1925, Fitzgerald's iconic status went into slow descent. In contrast to the washed-up portrayal usually put forth to account for the late 1930s to his death at the end of 1940, however, we see that he never fully disappeared, though the common perception is that he rotted away on some gin-soaked Hollywood side street just inches from the gutter.

We cannot discount the pressures Fitzgerald faced, from paying for Zelda's care to his own (often self-induced) medical maladies and constant financial strain. These difficulties, though, do not equate to a skid row existence. By some measures, one could ably argue that Fitzgerald had turned a corner as the 1940s began, if only his failing health could have been averted.

A search of the *New York Times* database from the mid-1930s to the late 1940s reveals that Fitzgerald often served as an intellectual fulcrum for reviewers and critics as they assessed other authors. This initial search is supported by the clippings in Fitzgerald's own scrapbooks, *The Romantic Egoists*, published by Bruccoli and Scottie Fitzgerald Smith in 1974. Here we see Fitzgerald and his work being compared to that of John O'Hara, Louis Bromfield, and others. Most frequently, the critics use Fitzgerald as a stand-in for coming-of-age novels (reminiscent of *This Side of Paradise*) or as a counter to those novelists trying to capture the meaning of an age (like *Gatsby*).[3]

Looking at the *Times*, one finds that there were at least half a dozen mentions of Fitzgerald in 1940 alone prior to his late December death, which is a pretty good showing for a writer thought to be obscure. Of the six articles, two are Hollywood reports. The second, published in the *Times* on August 27, 1940, announces that Twentieth Century-Fox hired Fitzgerald to work on the screenplay for the Emlyn Williams play *The Light of Heart*. According to Bruccoli, he worked on the screenplay until October 15, producing three versions, but ultimately the studio rejected it.[4] He did not receive credit in the film version, retitled *Life Begins at Eight-Thirty*, released in 1942. Most of the other *Times* articles use Fitzgerald as a point of comparison in book reviews examining the work of Philip Atlee, Martin Flavin, and Katharine Bush, all popular novelists and writers of the era. Flavin went on to win the Pulitzer Prize in 1944 for his novel *Journey in the Dark*, while Atlee went on to great fame writing detective and mystery novels.

Although some of Fitzgerald's obituaries undercut his lasting significance by focusing on the celebrity aspects of his life or recent difficulties, his death (like the deaths of all celebrities in our celebrity-obsessed world) got people talking about him again. The flurry of activity related to his death led to tributes published in the *New Republic* in March 1941 by some of his most famous colleagues and friends, including John Dos Passos, Malcolm Cowley, and others. According to scholar Jackson R. Bryer, "This flurry of attention . . . was not only a harbinger of what was to come; it also was a reprise, if abbreviated and more limited, of the sort of coverage Fitzgerald and his wife Zelda had received during the 1920s and early 1930s."[5] While the hyperbole surrounding the restoration of Fitzgerald's place in literary history may have gone a bit too far, one could certainly argue that the revival may have never taken place without the intensity of his early proponents. At the very least, it needed the spark from these supporters to really catch hold.

The *New Republic* essays were followed later that year by the publication of *The Last Tycoon*, Fitzgerald's unfinished novel, edited by Wilson. Although the book was not a hit in terms of sales, some observers deemed it Fitzgerald's best and most mature work. The critical spotlight kept Fitzgerald on the mind of the nation's intelligentsia. *The Last Tycoon* also featured several outstanding Fitzgerald short stories, which enabled readers to once again assess his significance in that genre. In an often-quoted review of *The Last Tycoon*, writer Stephen Vincent Benét noted, "This is not a legend, this is a reputation—and, seen in perspective, it may well be one of the most secure reputations of our time."[6]

An interesting aspect of the Fitzgerald posthumous comeback is that it almost immediately cut across academic and general readership lines. This is due, at least in part, to the prominent role of public intellectuals in that era. Writers like Wilson and John Peale Bishop served as the nation's literary and artistic arbiters, keeping the public informed via national magazines and newspapers. In the pretelevision age, public intellectuals had great influence. In Fitzgerald's case, many used their power to resurrect his reputation.

The consensus, however, did not fall wholly in support. In those early years, critics wrangled over his place among the other writers of his day. Not everyone agreed that Fitzgerald stood among the greats. For example, in an April 1944 essay in *College English*, Leo and Miriam Gurko built a case for Fitzgerald's "minor" status relative to Sinclair Lewis, Ernest Hemingway, and John Dos Passos.

The Gurkos admit to Fitzgerald's skill as a stylist, but find his world-view stifling and debilitating. They surmise:

> Yet, for all the peculiar excellence of the style, the range of his ideas remains hemmed in by the singular negativism of his view of the world and the dogged, unvaried way in which this is repeated from story to story—which further tends to pin Fitzgerald in the ranks of the minor writers.[7]

Surprisingly, in this example, the authors do not distinguish very much between Fitzgerald's first three novels, essentially lumping them together, since they featured "adolescents in sequential stages."[8] From the perspective of Leo and Miriam Gurko, Gatsby bears close resemblance to Fitzgerald's earlier protagonists and is a lesser character than Dick Diver of *Tender* or Monroe Stahr of *Tycoon*. With the latter, the Gurkos conclude, "Before this, Fitzgerald never attempted anything half so difficult and never succeeded in welding a full-grown adult into a full-grown, man-sized adult world."[9]

On the other hand, in 1942, critic Alfred Kazin, who would soon become one of the nation's preeminent literary authorities, pointed to the author's style and perception, explaining, "Fitzgerald always saw life as glamour, even though he could pierce that glamour to write one of the most moving of American tragedies in *The Great Gatsby*."[10] If Fitzgerald and his work served as intellectual fodder in the early 1940s, however, the arguments for or against took place in the background of World War II. The chaos and desperation of the war took precedent over literary battles and pushed most other topics to the background. Not until after the war's end would a major volley be fired in support of Fitzgerald and his long-term reputation, again at the hands of Edmund Wilson and the edited collection, *The Crack-Up*.

In 1945, while the military gave away a couple hundred thousand copies of *The Great Gatsby*, both Wilson's *The Crack-Up* and Dorothy Parker's *The Portable F. Scott Fitzgerald* appeared. Together, these books sparked a more intense reaction to Fitzgerald, not only putting his work on full display, but placing it within its historical context. Surely, too, postwar readers found something in Fitzgerald that helped them better comprehend their current struggles, whether it centered on a new version of the American Dream or how individuals might live ethically in a consumer society.

The sales of both *The Crack-Up* and *Portable* were strong. *Portable* sold some twenty-nine thousand copies, according to scholar Elaine P. Maimon, who conducted pioneering work on Fitzgerald's sales in the early 1970s. Exact sales for Wilson's volume are not available, but the book sold out its first edition in three days and its second in advance of publication. Maimon indicates that in addition to these formal sources, the 1945 to 1950 period also witnessed various inexpensive paperbacks by publishers other than Scribner's. Also, many of his short stories and novel excerpts appeared in numerous anthologies. Altogether, these many channels for buying or accessing Fitzgerald's work must be assessed as a whole to give the contemporary reader a full understanding of the early revival.[11]

THE GREAT GATSBY AS FILM NOIR

Playing up the gangster element and violence popular in movies of the late 1940s, Paramount released a new adaptation of *The Great Gatsby* in 1949, starring Alan Ladd as Gatsby and Betty Field as Daisy. Cyril Hume and Richard Maibaum wrote the screenplay, an amalgamation of Fitzgerald's novel and the play version written by Owen Davis. For clues about the film's direction, one needs look no further than the marketing poster, which signals its focus. In it, a realistic painting shows Ladd front and center in a tan trench coat. Ladd's Gatsby looks more like a private eye or criminal than the suave character from the novel. As he stands tensely looking off to his right, a quartet of scantily clad women surrounds him, each looking up eagerly. At the bottom right, a small picture of a large car slamming into a woman is presented, though a blink of an eye before impact.

The opening scene deviates from the novel, picturing Nick twenty years older and placing a bouquet of flowers at Gatsby's gravestone with Jordan on his arm. She remarks at how small the gravestone is, with Nick replying that it would not be his style at all—"He'd have fancied something more like Grant's tomb." Immediately implying that Gatsby is the kind of person who needs a large, showy tomb sets the movie off on bad footing and demonstrates that the film is not going to be faithful to Fitzgerald's central character, who took little interest in wealth outside of how Daisy would interpret it.

Even more egregious for an audience that might actually desire an adaptation more attuned to the novel, in one of the first scenes that we see Gatsby, he is shown in a car chase with guns blazing. While a machine gun fires at his car from close range, Gatsby calmly sits in the front passenger seat and kills the two men firing at him, forcing their car off the road and headfirst into the side of a building. Such looseness, according to eminent film historian Wheeler Winston Dixon, leads to "a curiously tedious, flat, and unimaginative film, with little visual or thematic resonance."[12] Ladd's Gatsby is a man surrounded by henchmen and is much more sinister than the novel version. And since the 1949 film is a star vehicle for Ladd, director Elliott Nugent focuses on him at the expense of the story.

Reviewing the film for the *New York Times*, Bosley Crowther pointed to its inherent weaknesses, but did so without fully comprehending the power of the Fitzgerald revival about to be in full swing. He explains, "Paramount selected this old tale primarily as a standard conveyance for the image of its charm boy, Alan Ladd. For most of the tragic implications and bitter ironies of Mr. Fitzgerald's work have gone by the board in allowing for the generous exhibition of Mr. Ladd."[13] Subsequent film versions of the novel would repeat the mistake in the 1949 film—not realizing that *Gatsby* is a novel of ideas, not characters, thus rehashing it as a star vehicle for a male lead necessitates that any faithfulness to the novel must go by the wayside.

Although the 1949 *Gatsby* looked and felt more like one of its era's gangster flicks, the Ladd vehicle kept the Fitzgerald train rolling regardless of its comparison with the novel. As a matter of fact, the movie even featured some modern marketing efforts that bolstered Fitzgerald's newfound ubiquity. For example, the publisher Grosset & Dunlap issued a 1949 edition of *Gatsby* that featured a "wraparound band" advertising the film. The cover of the book shows a flapper dancing wildly as a group of partygoers watches. The back cover reveals a still from the film of Daisy, Nick, and Gatsby. Bantam Books also put out a dust jacket featuring Alan Ladd in a scene from the film.[14] In addition to typical press materials, like photo stills from the movie and a press book, the film also had international marketing materials, including a British edition with a special dust jacket and an Australian poster featuring "head and shoulder portraits of [the] three main characters."[15]

GATSBY IN THE GRAY FLANNEL SUIT

One may not be able to find a starker contrast than the eras before and after the Second World War. In the 1930s, people battled a series of ills, beginning with financial misery and ending with global anxiety caused by the military turmoil and ensuing warfare in Europe. As the unrest overseas mounted and seemed more and more likely to include the United States directly, Americans turned to President Franklin D. Roosevelt to lift them from the economic chaos and guide them militarily as the nation prepped for war via its industrial base. Ironically, the answer to people's Depression-era prayers came in the form of firing up the arsenal of democracy to win World War II. Despite the misery it caused, the war also righted the nation economically and initiated the shift to a thorough and comprehensive consumer culture.

The Great Depression and the war fundamentally altered American society and forced changes in its culture as well. The national popular culture machine responded to the twin crises on a number of fronts, from the use of advertising and marketing as a tool to increase nationalistic feelings to creating entertainment that alleviated the stress felt by workers at home and soldiers abroad. These efforts were especially fruitful at a time when people thought their darkest days still seemed ahead of them.

Hollywood, for example, responded to World War II by producing films that emphasized American heroism and patriotism. Although these efforts seem overly propagandistic to contemporary eyes, the movies gave people hope in an era filled with darkness. The film industry also kept citizens informed by creating a variety of newsreels, special reports, and documentaries about the day's issues. Although films had always fascinated American audiences, the attraction deepened in the 1940s. In 1946, for instance, more than one hundred million people went to the movies each week, about two-thirds of the total population.

The 1950s symbolized a new beginning for the United States, but many of the primary tenets of the decade evolved from the previous decade, including the move to a consumer-based economy. The launch of the "American century" delivered unprecedented prosperity for much of the nation. When soldiers returned from the war, they had money to spend, as did those who worked on the home front during the war and had little to purchase because of rationing programs. Driven by innovation and new technologies, the subsequent abundance of consumer goods transformed life.

The cause of national anxiety changed dramatically in the two eras, from real war in Europe to Cold War across the globe, primarily fought in the minds of politicians and diplomats in Washington, D.C., and Moscow. Yet, at home, Americans looked to establishing lives much different than their parents and grandparents. The booming economy and college aid programs gave young people—particularly returning veterans of World War II—opportunities to either work at high-paying jobs or go back to school for little or no money.

While changes were underfoot in the 1950s, there were large segments of the population denied its benefits. Certainly, the nostalgic feelings later generations held regarding the 1950s glossed over a darker, troubling time, fueled by rapid cultural changes and emotions still fresh from World War II. As writers William H. Young and Nancy K. Young conclude, "Depending on one's focus during the fifties, the decade could seem complacent and conformist, or it could be filled with threatening change and shrill individuals who turned their backs on anything held dear by generations of Americans."[16] Many of these challenges would explode to the surface in the 1960s. However, for those willing to view the postwar world as a new beginning, particularly in the growing middle class, the future looked dazzling.

In terms of the burgeoning Fitzgerald revival, the momentum gained in the decade since his untimely death gained speed in 1950 and 1951. Arthur Mizener's biography, *The Far Side of Paradise*, for example, sold some 20,000 copies in just five days and 42,287 by the end of 1951, according to scholar Elaine P. Maimon, whose early work on Fitzgerald's sales statistics and those of authors writing about him served as the foundation for understanding the author's reach and budding importance. The era's book clubs also played a pivotal role in expanding interest in Fitzgerald. An additional 30,000 copies of Mizener's biography went out via the Book Find Club.[17] Ironically, the resurgence in Fitzgerald led to his biographer selling many tens of thousands more copies than the author did when *Gatsby* first appeared some twenty-five years earlier.

The 1951 study *F. Scott Fitzgerald: The Man and His Work*, edited by Alfred Kazin, also helped establish the tone for studies regarding Fitzgerald. The collection featured reviews and other pieces that demonstrated Fitzgerald's place in the literary canon. The growing "rediscovery" of

Fitzgerald and his work in the early 1950s served as a kind of self-fulfilling prophecy. The more scholars and critics wrote about discovering Fitzgerald all over again, the more that work served as news itself. Each story or article that approached Fitzgerald served as kindling for the larger fire set ablaze by each successive critic. New books and stories about Fitzgerald in turn led to even more coverage.

Mizener's biography, along with Budd Schulberg's novel *The Disenchanted* (1950) helped keep Fitzgerald in the spotlight. However, Fitzgerald's own work went into relatively soft mode through 1958. The appeal that later year, as with the sales increases in the early years of the decade, was spurred by another biography, this time Sheilah Graham's *Beloved Infidel*.[18] Graham, Fitzgerald's girlfriend during his later era in Hollywood, would later go on to write several other best-selling memoirs of her time with him. The 1950s ended on a positive note in terms of Scribner's sales of Fitzgerald works, with nine editions available in 1958 and 1959, selling 57,351 and 56,063 copies, respectively.[19]

In addition to the work of specific individuals in bringing Fitzgerald back from obscurity, one cannot overlook how both Scribner's and Harold Ober Associates orchestrated the revival as well. Fitzgerald's publisher, according to scholar James L. W. West III, "continued to manage his work responsibly, keeping the already published writing available and bringing out, from time to time, editions of Fitzgerald's letters, his nonfiction, and his better uncollected short stories." Indeed, West notes, Scribner's worked with Ober's agency "hand-in-glove" to manage Fitzgerald's literary estate.[20]

GATSBY IN CAMELOT

The news on the mind of many Americans as the new decade of the 1960s came into focus centered on the dramatic changes in everyday life during the preceding decade and how that transformation set the nation on a course for further growth. In a fascinating article contrasting 1900 versus 1960, for example, writer Bruce Bliven revealed the great strides the nation achieved, from its percentage of the production of the world's total goods to the vast increase in the number of people who received a high school and college education. While acknowledging a great deal of inequity still existed, he nonetheless concludes that the United States in late

1960 is basically a "classless society" featuring a "homogenized population."[21]

Certainly, in Bliven's estimation, increased overall wealth across the country raised the lot of the emerging middle class. He cites a significant increase in median income from 1950 to 1960, from $3,300 to $5,050 annually. As the economic outlook brightened for the growing middle class, the newfound wealth then fueled cultural change. Bliven saw many concrete shifts occurring that essentially recreated the nation physically and mentally, from the mass migration of fifteen million people to the suburbs after World War II to the three million students in college in 1960, a figure that he estimated would double by the end of the decade. The latter, which established the United States as the world's leader in "self-improvement," Bliven calls "one of the wonders of the world" and "without precedent." Part of the self-improvement trend meant that more Americans were watching television—possessing both good and bad in Bliven's mind—and that sales of paperback books reached 333 million, some of it dreck and some of it classic. For example, he claims, "Shakespeare's plays sell more than a million copies annually."[22]

The reason for concentrating on Bliven's thinking and its consequences is that it helps unravel the reasons why Fitzgerald's sales of *Gatsby* grew so astonishingly over the course of the 1960s. Numerous economic and societal threads came together in the late 1950s and early 1960s that pushed *Gatsby* from the status of admired novel to cultural lynchpin.

Some of these impulses might be difficult for contemporary readers to comprehend given the popular culture portrayal of the 1960s as a transition from Camelot to Kennedy's assassination to the summer of love and hippies. This vision of the decade more or less obfuscates much of the foundational transformations that we now take for granted. Bliven identifies many of these strains, including the large increase in high school– and college-educated people and the huge number of paperbacks in circulation. Exploring these topics, for example, causes one to contemplate the increase in government funding for education, the outcomes of the GI Bill, the centrality of education linked to fulfillment of the American Dream, and others that demonstrate how a novel like *Gatsby* could get swept up in the sociocultural machinery of the age. Each piece of the puzzle in determining why the novel reached such mass approval and acceptance could be unraveled in a similar manner, given access to the right kind of data.

In addition, Fitzgerald's masterpiece developed into the kind of "classic" that people needed to know or be able to discuss as part of what was generally accepted as an educated person's intellectual framework. For example, also in 1960, on the thirty-fifth anniversary of *The Great Gatsby*, literary critic Arthur Mizener wrote a laudatory essay in the *New Yorker* that analyzed the way Fitzgerald's reputation changed over that time. Given its placement in one of the nation's cultural cornerstones, Mizener's piece set the tone for future Fitzgerald studies by offering new ways for readers, scholars, and critics to interpret the book as the Camelot era unfolded. Noting the important scholarship of Fitzgerald's supporters, like his college friend Edmund Wilson and critic Malcolm Cowley, to firmly establish the book's reputation, Mizener turned to thematic concerns, which he felt were important in the next wave of studies. [23]

Two areas the critic identified centered on "the book's realization of the fluidity of American lives" and Fitzgerald's "voice." The latter, Mizener explains, enabled Fitzgerald to create "an image of The Good American of our time in all his complexity of human sympathy, firm moral judgment and ironic self-possession." Tying these ideas together produced a profound vision of the "American experience." For decades, critics and other commentators both argued and confirmed Mizener's early verdict on Fitzgerald, setting the tone for the wave of academic criticism that soon followed the commercial revival. [24]

As mentioned earlier, Mizener's Fitzgerald biography *The Far Side of Paradise* contributed greatly to the renewed interest in the previous decade. More importantly, though, Mizener's book and several other key texts had a cumulative effect and were being read by new readers as they engaged with Fitzgerald's writing as high school and college students. As a result, sales of Fitzgerald's novels and short story collections skyrocketed in the 1960s.

The reach of the revival can be seen in sales data obtained from Scribner's by Elaine P. Maimon. The 1950s began with one volume of Fitzgerald's work selling 866 copies, but ended with nine editions in print, selling in excess of 56,000 copies. Clearly the 1950s solidified Fitzgerald's place in literary history. Ever since Fitzgerald died, a small but growing number of supporters, friends, critics, and scholars worked to keep the author's legacy alive and thriving. Over the years, the renaissance took hold as the level of critical attention increased and then drove rather respectable sales. By the mid-1950s, one could be relatively certain that Fitzgerald's place among American greats had been secured.

Andrew Turnbull played a significant role in Fitzgerald studies in the age of Camelot by writing a biography, *Scott Fitzgerald* (1962), that countered Mizener's earlier work by focusing on the writer's personality and adding information about his friendship with Fitzgerald as a young boy (the author rented a house on the Turnbull estate in Baltimore when Fitzgerald was thirty-six and Turnbull eleven). He also helped build the critical reputation by editing *The Letters of F. Scott Fitzgerald* (1963), which provided scholars with the primary source material to further explore the writer and his work.

What no one could have foreseen, however, is how central *Gatsby* would become in the 1960s, which cemented Fitzgerald as both a critical favorite and a sales force. Maimon's statistics reveal that from the 56,000 figure at the end of the 1950s, sales more than tripled in 1960, reaching 177,849 copies. This tidal wave only grew, though, with 1968 sales hitting 448,420, the last year included in her study.[25] The overall increase from 866 copies in 1950 to almost half a million in 1968 is mind boggling and must be attributed to many influences, both on a personal level and as society and culture evolved.

Writer Richard Anderson explains that increased sales and readership resulted from "the combination of paperbound technology and the growth of school-age readers during the post–World War II baby boom [which] led Scribner's to concentrate on reprints aimed at students." The company published a reprint edition in 1957 that prompted additional versions. Three years later, *Gatsby* served as the first volume in the Scribner Library series, which the publisher aimed at the high school and college market. In 1961, another high school edition appeared, this time with reader's guide materials focused on helping young people comprehend and assess the novel.[26] These efforts on the part of Scribner's to get *Gatsby* into America's classrooms played a critical role in getting the book into the literary canon. The millions of future teachers and college faculty reading the novel as students in the early 1960s virtually guaranteed that it would be a mainstay through the present day.

Another point that cannot be overlooked is that the Fitzgerald rebirth had significant financial and reputational aspects as well. On one hand, once the revival took form, the sales figures skyrocketed, which had real bottom-line consequences for Scribner's and other publishers who put out inexpensive paperback editions of Fitzgerald's back catalog. The other factor is that commentators, scholars, and critics had a stake in the Fitzgerald rejuvenation taking hold. In many cases, careers were launched or solidified on the basis of one's writing and research about the author and his work.

For example, in early 1960, Scribner's launched "The Scribner Library," a collection of twenty-one "great modern works" that included *Gatsby* and *Tender Is the Night*. In the promotional copy that covered a page of the *New York Times*, the publisher claimed, "Unprecedented public demand has caused us to release this select list . . . in inexpensive paper-covered editions." With a fancy logo and uniform spines, Scribner's intended the collection to both sell books and serve as a kind of cultural indicator for those who wanted to demonstrate themselves as well read and trendy. One wonders how the publisher determined "unprecedented pubic demand," and if that claim merely served as convenient marketing copy to sell the collection, priced at a little more than $30 in total, or about $230 in 2012 dollars. [27]

The twenty-one-book collection, then, targeted those middle-class homeowners with discretionary spending who were interested in cultural tastes and a certain degree of sophistication. Selling *Gatsby* for $1 to $1.50 a copy not only ensured that more people would buy the book, but tying the novel and other works to decorating one's home meant sales would increase whether the buyer planned to crack the spine or not. Scribner's also published several Fitzgerald collections in the early 1960s that expanded the amount of material by Fitzgerald in the marketplace, including *Six Tales of the Jazz Age and Other Stories* (1960) and *The Pat Hobby Stories* (1962).

For those scholars and commentators who were reading *Gatsby* and Fitzgerald's wider catalog, the revival provided new ground to cover. Certainly, Mizener's fame grew as interest in Fitzgerald germinated. In the mid-1960s and through the end of the decade, Mizener would be joined by a handful of others who had more or less staked out Fitzgerald as their primary research topic.

In 1961, *New York Times* columnist Lewis Nichols also sparked a bit of Fitzgerald mania by mentioning the existence of a *Fitzgerald Newsletter*. He received mountains of mail on the subject, so in a follow-up piece, he explained that the four-page quarterly was published by Matthew J.

Bruccoli, then a young scholar at the University of Virginia. The story contradicts Bruccoli's famous tale of hearing a short story performed on radio as a teen, rather pinning it to him seeing a film version of *Gatsby*, which then led to his interest. As a side note, for those who would come to know, appreciate, and be thankful for all Bruccoli would later do to promote Fitzgerald scholarship, Nichols notes that the young man "thinks that in its depth, his collection [of Fitzgerald material] may be the best in the world."[28] Readers may be interested to know that Bruccoli did, in fact, continue to build the greatest private collection of Fitzgerald materials in the world, estimated to be worth millions of dollars. The Matthew J. and Arlyn Bruccoli Collection of F. Scott Fitzgerald is housed at the University of South Carolina, where Bruccoli spent his later career.

As early as July 1963, commenting on this seeming army then following Fitzgerald, critic Charles Poore explains, "A thousand and one criticasters are forever contemplating the spectacle his life presents: they alternately wail over his wasted genius—and proclaim its lasting excellences." Much of the work, he concludes, "[An] inky comet's tail of commentary masking as biography and biography masking as commentary now follows the Fitzgeraldian orbit. It, too, helps keep writers, critics, lecturers gainfully employed."[29] Furthermore, evidence of Fitzgerald's place in academe is noted by his inclusion in *American Literary Scholarship* in 1963, an annual published review of the topic by the American Literature Section of the Modern Language Association.[30]

***

Beginning almost immediately after his death in 1940, the Fitzgerald rebirth launched when his friends, supporters, and other commentators publicly reassessed his writing. The entire episode could not have gone better if Fitzgerald himself had orchestrated the event. One can only imagine how vindicated the author would have felt at finally seeing his work widely read and studied—not only his novels, which he loved, but also many of the short stories, even the ones he claimed were written for a fast dollar.

Soon, the confluence of critical praise and general interest in Fitzgerald's writing led to innovative avenues—many linked to new technologies—for extending the revival, from the 1949 film starring Hollywood icon Alan Ladd to the improvement in mass-paperback quality, which gave countless readers the opportunity to purchase the novels at afford-able prices.

In addition, there were able managers at the lead of the Fitzgerald rejuvenation. These included executives at Scribner's and Harold Ober's literary agency, who quickly realized that the interest could be marketed until it became a kind of industry in and of itself. Countless people be-came cogs in the Fitzgerald machine, from scholars and professional literary critics to teachers and faculty members. The revitalization could not have taken hold the way it did if not for the way *Gatsby* served high school and college curricula. In addition, many careers were established and reputations solidified as Fitzgerald mania swept the 1960s as both academics and critics spent time and effort reassessing the writer and his work.

At the heart of the Fitzgerald revival stood the author's brilliant writ-ing, which any sustained interest in his work would demand. However, to experience the kind of rebirth that took place in the four decades since *Gatsby*'s publication and twenty-five years since Fitzgerald's early death, the author and the novel needed help that in retrospect one wishes he had received while alive. Numerous individual and connected sociocultural influences merged and spread, many on the strength of the growing na-tion and its transformation economically and culturally. Taken together, these trends enabled *Gatsby* to pave its way into the national conscious-ness.

4

A GRAND ILLUSION, 1964–1980

Again the old ache of money. Again will you wire me, if you like it
[short story, "Pat Hobby's Christmas Wish"]. Again will you wire the
money to my Maginot Line: The Bank of America, Culver City.
—F. Scott Fitzgerald, in a letter to *Esquire* editor Arnold Gingrich,
October 14, 1939

Some ironies are so devious that they are nearly impossible to contemplate. Fitzgerald's life and afterlife seem filled with these incidents, like the revelation that the film rights to the 1974 movie version of *The Great Gatsby* sold for $350,000 or that the movie spurred book sales to about one million copies that year, up from about three hundred thousand in 1973.[1] Any one of these figures would have been incomprehensible to the author.

However, the saddest aspect of the Fitzgerald renaissance is how it contrasted with his life, which in his later years proved so much darker. He spent a great deal of time and energy begging friends and acquaintances for money, trying to cobble together funds to keep his extended family running. In the years after the commercial failures of both *Gatsby* and *Tender*, he often wrote and wired his agent, Harold Ober, and Scribner editor Max Perkins with urgent pleas for advances just to get by and pay his daily living expenses, just as he had when his fortunes were more promising and the glossy magazines frequently bought his short stories. The situation turned dire toward the end of Fitzgerald's life when the big circulation market evaporated. Eventually, his persistent appeals damaged the relationship with Ober, though they kept an uneasy alliance until the end.

The level of groveling and pleading makes the sensitive reader more than a little uncomfortable when examining Fitzgerald's collected letters. The documents reveal his complete disregard for either saving money or budgeting himself. The constant state of financial insecurity and mounting debt constantly weighed on the author's mind, as well as the real-world consequences of facing eviction, having little money for food, or facing down the bill collectors and administrators looking for payment for Zelda's care. To his credit, though his wife's stays in top facilities taxed him to no end, Fitzgerald always took pains to ensure that she received the best treatment possible.

A professional writer, Fitzgerald could only attempt to write his way out of these troubles, which became increasingly more difficult as the years progressed. The tough economic days of the Great Depression were not kind to freelancers, which forced him to turn to low-paying gigs, like Arnold Gingrich's *Esquire*. If it were not for Gingrich, Fitzgerald may have withered away in the late 1930s, particularly after the movie studios cut their losses and did not renew his contracts. Although the initial work paid handsomely, an enabled Fitzgerald could not stay in the game. Eventually, the studio managers got wind of his drinking or rumors of his binges. Coupled that with his basic inability to work in the studio system that by its very nature necessitated many hands working on scripts, not the lone auteur he fancied himself, and one realizes that the end of his work life was not satisfying. Maybe Sheilah Graham would have supported him, but without selling his work, he may have instead died of a broken spirit.

Imagine, then, that this broken-down, old-before-his-time author actually lived to 1974, the year the Robert Redford version of *Gatsby* came out, when he would have been seventy-eight years old. Fitzgerald would have been rich and perhaps as famous as his brightest heyday of the early 1920s. The burgeoning celebrity industry and mass communications system would have catapulted Fitzgerald to new heights. He could have afforded multiple financial managers to ensure that his money got socked away for potential darker days.

Imagine . . .

There would have been spiritual rejuvenation as well, because Fitzgerald would have seen his work earn the acclaim it deserved. In addition to selling about five hundred thousand copies of all his books collectively each year, according to *New York Times* reporter Richard Severo, Fitzgerald would have benefited from knowing that some 2,400 colleges in the United States had his work as required reading, in addition to the eight to ten thousand high schools. From the figures that Severo gathered, it is certainly clear that the revival of Fitzgerald studies that took place and steadily gained momentum had worked. In the early 1970s, Fitzgerald and *Gatsby* were firmly entrenched in American popular culture and in the K–16 education system. As a result, Fitzgerald's famous phrase about writing for the youth of one's generation and the schoolmasters ever after turned out to be prophetic. Within thirty years of his death, a case could be made that Fitzgerald stood as one of America's widest-read authors, if not at the very top of the chart.[2]

The rationale for making the new film version of Fitzgerald's masterpiece, according to then president of Paramount, Frank Yablans, revolved around the connections between the 1970s and the 1920s. "We thought people were quite fatigued with the pressures of contemporary living," he explained, "and that nostalgia was a safety value . . . the only way of getting perspective."[3] Given the state of the contemporary world in the early 1970s, from the horrors of Vietnam to the national morale-destroying tales of Watergate, it is not difficult to understand the need to break from the stress and strain of everyday life. However, approaching *Gatsby* as a nostalgia piece is taking liberties with Fitzgerald's vision.

Looking at other major motion pictures from the early 1970s, one sees a pattern of nostalgia-based films, though not all dealt with uplifting subjects or themes. In 1970, for example, *Patton* won the Academy Award, featuring George C. Scott as the all-American military hero General George S. Patton. Clearly, *Patton* served as a kind of boost for the country's morale, given the hangover of the 1960s and the increasingly unpopular war in Vietnam. From a much different perspective, *The Godfather* (Academy Award 1972) and *The Godfather, Part II* (Academy Award 1974) operated in a nostalgic framework, though presenting a distorted version of the American Dream via the criminal underpinnings and brutality of the Mafia. Interestingly, famed film writer and director Francis Ford Coppola is connected to all three films mentioned above, as well as the *Gatsby* adaptation. He wrote the screenplays for *Patton* and *Gatsby* and wrote and directed the *Godfather* films. Not a bad few years for Coppola in terms of filmmaking history.

Scottie, Scott and Zelda's daughter and caretaker of her father's work, approved of the 1974 film and had glowing comments about its stars Robert Redford and Mia Farrow, particularly after visiting the set in Rhode Island. In a magazine article, she discussed the way the film represented the present day, saying:

> There seemed to be a hint of violence in Coppola's version, above and beyond the book. *Gatsby* is so subtle, and today everything is sex and violence. There is lots of implicit sex in the book, but I have an old-fashioned horror of what's going on in movies today. And I surely didn't want *Gatsby* turned into that sort of thing.[4]

Certainly, Scottie's reaction could have just been a generational difference, but she had faith in director Jack Clayton to create a wonderful film. She lamented that films in the era were driven by violence, noting that her father would have been aghast at the content of another big movie of the time, *The Exorcist*.

***

This chapter explores a pivotal era in American history that spans from post-JFK to pre-Reagan. At the center of the time frame are both the Vietnam conflict and the battle for civil rights, but the era also includes the malaise of the 1970s and Watergate. Given the tumult of this period, one might imagine that the nation had little time or concern for a fifty-thousand-word novel published in 1925 by a long-dead author. Yet, amid the chaos and uproar, what the researcher discovers is that *Gatsby* solidified and broadened its place in the cultural milieu during this time.

The central question this chapter addresses is this: How did the *Gatsby* revival transform from a primarily academic event to a part of the broader culture that swept through the national psyche in the mid to late twentieth century? What we find, I contend, is that numerous threads must be explored to fully answer this query, some more evident than others, but all combining to fuel the novel's magnitude. If there is a central facet from a thematic perspective, one could argue that *Gatsby*'s ambiguity is key, since this trait enables readers, teachers, instructors, and others to constantly reevaluate and reinterpret the novel, even though the country continues to change. One also cannot overlook the novel's brevity, which makes it more palatable within K–16 curricula.

Together then, I believe, *Gatsby* is like a concentrated dose of history, literature, and culture wrapped in a tight little package that virtually explodes with meaning when unwrapped. As the initial readers and audiences grew to understand as they were exposed to the novel in the 1950s, many pertinent questions on the national consciousness could be addressed in Fitzgerald's work. As these early groups became teachers, professors, and cultural influencers, they passed on this knowledge to the titanic generation following them. The cycle continued over the decades, punctuating *Gatsby*'s importance.

GATSBY AND THE HIPPIES

Although the most common popular culture representation of people in the 1960s probably centers on anti-Vietnam protesters and those battling for civil and equal rights, in reality many aspects of the decade seemed just like those that preceded it and would later follow. It is not as if the 1950s were as dull and devoid of controversy as some commentators and historians might have us believe, but many disparate strains of unease came together in the 1960s that taken in total fundamentally changed American society. When the 1950s gave way to the next decade, however, a handful of transformations could not be denied. These included the emergence of a more critical examination of society and the blossoming of the baby boomer generation that would soon enter college in great waves.

The critical and sales revival of Fitzgerald and his 1925 novel in the early and mid-1950s led to further interest in the book in the 1960s. Academics assigned *Gatsby* in college courses swelling with students from the combined tsunami of the post–World War II baby boom and those who hoped to stay in school to keep out of the Vietnam draft. As the opportunities for acquiring education expanded, particularly at the college level, more young people used their budding critical and contextual thinking skills to question American society, particularly the ethical consequences of being a global superpower and the nation's place in Southeast Asia.

The sheer size of the population between fifteen and twenty-four years old in the 1960s had profound effects on just about every aspect of daily life. Some people found this growth terrifying and either urged or enacted

official and unofficial rules for both institutions and parents to use to keep
them under control. Others saw the enormous size as an opportunity and
created new ways for consumer goods to be marketed and advertised to
young people.

While this bulging demographic transformed mass culture with its size
and purchasing power, it had a similar effect on higher education. The
federal government, furthermore, acted as a catalyst in this regard, urging
more young people to college as a means of combating the perceived lead
by Soviet students in math and science. As a result, in the United States
the number of young people in higher education degree programs more
than doubled from about 3.5 million to almost 8 million by decade's end.[5]
The student growth caused increased demand for faculty and resources.
Many of these changes were curriculum based, which necessitated that
canonical texts like *Gatsby*, already widely available because of the im-
provements in paperback publishing technology, be purchased in even
greater numbers.

Although one could argue about the quality of Fitzgerald studies in the
1960s versus the 1950s, there is little doubt that scholars in the latter
decade used the era's challenges to place *Gatsby* in a broader context. For
example, writing about the novel in the late 1960s, scholar David F. Trask
sees the failure of the American Dream as a battle between the nation's
agrarian past and urban future. He claims that the billboard Eckleburg
with the haunting eyes represents "none other than a devitalized Thomas
Jefferson, the pre-eminent purveyor of the agrarian myth."[6] The valley of
ashes, then, is the dream defiled and destroyed, burned out and blurred
beyond all reality. "Fitzgerald," Trask explains, "thus presents a remarkably evocative description of the corruption that had befallen Jefferson's
garden."[7] Nick, who witnessed the carnage of World War I battlefields
and returned restless, needed the pace of New York City, but in Gatsby
and his dreams found a representation of all that he left behind in the
Midwest.

This loss of innocence and its tie to the nostalgic past propelled some
of the late 1960s' most important popular culture works. Although it is
difficult to prove a direct correlation between *Gatsby* and some of these
creations (for instance, the hit film *Planet of the Apes*), the popularity of
the novel and its broad readership did mean that such ideas were part of
the mainstream. People were contemplating these issues in their entertainment and simultaneously addressing them in the broader experience

of America's intervention in Vietnam and Southeast Asia within the larger backdrop of the Cold War with Soviet Russia.

Given the domestic challenges of the 1960s, from violence and civil rights to inequality and radicalism, many people also began questioning how the nation should address these issues. *Gatsby*'s link to status, wealth, aristocracy, and the place of the American Dream in the contemporary world made it a worthy tool in examining how the country should proceed. Again, it is not as if commentators were announcing, "I just read *The Great Gatsby* and now I understand how to fix [insert social problem]," but the fact that the novel was read by hundreds of thousands of people as a part of high school and college courses meant that its themes and designs resided within their mental toolboxes as they searched for answers.

The revolution in college education played a critical role in how young people learned to question authority. The number of people studying grew beyond capacity, thus the search for texts that could be used to teach higher-order thinking skills would ease some of the burden for professors and instructors faced with enlarged classes bursting at the seams with students. In this respect, *Gatsby* served as a kind of literary protein bar—small and edible quickly, but carrying a great deal of nutrients to keep one's mind racing. The movement toward standardization also played a role here. As standardized tests became more of the norm for high school students, a simultaneous effort had to be put forth for developing a curriculum that had similar aspects nationwide. Again, *Gatsby* fit here. Fitzgerald's reputation and utility grew up alongside the standardized test industry and within the growing high school and college student populations. [8]

Writing in July 1967, Andrew Turnbull explains how Fitzgerald, Hemingway, and Thomas Wolfe each experienced highs and lows in their lifetimes but established literary reputations within the handful of American greats. [9] Yet, though Hemingway and later William Faulkner were the ones anointed as artists through the late 1930s and 1940s, it is Fitzgerald after his death whose reputation and personal life mixed in a way that sparked interest in his work that his literary colleagues could not match. One could see that even in the 1960s, when Hemingway's death was still fresh on the minds of the general public, he would never strike the same nerve as Fitzgerald, even as mythic and important as Hemingway's legend eventually became. Hemingway's writing style might be widely imitated, but few are referencing him or using his ideas in the classroom like they do with Fitzgerald and *Gatsby*. Both men sprouted veritable academic industries focused on every bit of minutiae that could be unturned and mountains of scholarly analysis and criticism, yet within the broader culture, Fitzgerald has bested his old friend and rival.

Although Hemingway and Wolfe both consistently outsold Fitzgerald by huge margins when they all lived, by the mid to late 1960s, Fitzgerald pulled ahead when one considered *Gatsby*'s sales over time. In 1966, for example, when Fitzgerald and Hemingway were published as slightly higher-priced paperbacks, *Gatsby* sold 300,000 copies. In contrast, *The Old Man and the Sea* by Hemingway sold 220,000. One might also note that Hemingway had two other novels on the list: *A Farewell to Arms* (140,000 copies) and *The Sun Also Rises* (135,000 copies). Thus, while I contend that *Gatsby* had more effect on mass communications and greater sales as an individual title, Hemingway still bested him if total paper-backs sold are calculated. [10]

For comparison's sake, that same year there were forty-three lower-priced paperbacks that sold more than five hundred thousand copies, ranging from the top-selling novel *Up the Down Staircase* by Bel Kauf-man (2.45 million copies) to the semifictional *The Green Berets* by Robin Moore (3.1 million copies). The book would later be turned into a movie starring Hollywood legend John Wayne and feature the No. 1 *Billboard* hit "The Ballad of the Green Berets," which Moore cowrote with Staff Sgt. Barry Sadler, a medic wounded in Vietnam. Not only did the most popular titles dwarf *Gatsby*, but these top sales figures seem stunning, since they provide hard evidence regarding people's reading habits during that era. [11]

The next year, *Gatsby* sales jumped to 350,000; however, *The Old Man and the Sea* also climbed to 275,000 copies. Even in the higher-priced paperback category, however, these masterpieces of American fiction could not compete with lesser works that caught the popular fancy. For example, *My Secret Life* by Anonymous sold 800,000 books, while *Psycho-Cybernetics* by Maxwell Maltz sold some 495,000. The former, a frank memoir and exploration of sex in the Victorian age (though prob-ably fictionalized to some degree), appeared after being suppressed as obscene, published by the notorious Grove Press. More or less at the other end of the spectrum, Maltz's book served as a form of self-help tome, stressing the importance of positive self-image and goal setting as a means to a better, healthier life. [12]

In 1968, *Gatsby* dropped to sales of 286,000, a sharp decline from the previous year. Conversely, each Hemingway title increased: *A Farewell to Arms*, 160,000; *The Old Man and the Sea*, 240,000; and *The Sun Also Rises*, 153,000. Despite the fall, *Gatsby* still placed second in its category, behind Albert Camus' *The Stranger* (295,962 copies). Like 1966, the next report witnessed popular paperback titles trounce these numbers. For example, *Rosemary's Baby* by Ira Levin, on the strength of its box office success, sold 4.2 million copies in 1968, while *The Arrangement* by Elia Kazan rang up 2.58 million. Again, although these figures are mind boggling, even they pale in comparison to the publishing juggernaut of Charles M. Schulz. The *New York Times* reported that four of his books published in 1968 had print sales of at least seven hundred thousand copies. However, when looking at all eighteen "Peanuts" books put out in the 1960s, the total sales reached thirty-six million. [13]

What these sales figures reveal is a fascinating portrait of the United States in the midst of all the global and domestic turmoil that plagued this era. For a literary text, *Gatsby* clearly sold well, but merely hit humble figures compared to the biggest of the best-sellers. Topical books, those tied to hit films, and the cartoon antics of Charlie Brown and Snoopy reached sales figures that are astounding, similar to the seemingly unprecedented numbers of current juggernauts, including the Harry Potter series by J. K. Rowling and the last several Dan Brown novels.

From my perspective, the most telling ideas to emerge from the sales information is that American readers—much like they always have—turned to reading material that either shielded them from the day's socio-economic or political chaos, or conversely, dug into books that provided deep detail on these events. What I posit is that these two groups probably had very little overlap. A self-categorization took place based on the types of books a person selected and read.

Second, while many titles in both categories dwarfed *Gatsby* sales, Fitzgerald's novel remained relevant and influential long past these work's expiration dates. So, while for decades kids have had Peanuts sheets on their beds or watched Charlie Brown holiday television specials, no one is using the characters to establish their worldview or understand their cultural world. Again, we must point to *Gatsby*'s classroom usage, which elevates its status, more or less serving as a validation of its importance. The themes Fitzgerald addressed continued to be the ones that teachers and faculty members wanted to assess and evaluate; thus, the nifty little book provided a natural avenue for accomplishing this task.

THE GREAT GATSBY: THE FILM

In March 1974, a little more than three decades after Fitzgerald's death and nearly fifty years since the publication of his masterpiece, a third film version of *The Great Gatsby* debuted. Unlike the earlier films, however, this installment burst onto the scene, demonstrating the vast changes in the entertainment industry since Fitzgerald's death. In the early 1970s the growth of Hollywood and its reliance on national marketing campaigns meant that *The Great Gatsby* would have product tie-ins designed to play off the film's hype and be a catalyst for launching waves of *Gatsby*-related merchandise.

A behind-the-scenes article in the debut issue of *People* magazine revealed that the Paramount picture served as the fulcrum for a broad campaign, which the studio felt it would deliver on, given that advanced bookings reached $19 million. According to the piece, "big-business marketers" also bet on the film's success, putting $6 million into promotion of numerous products, including "a Gatsby-linked line of sportswear, whisky, beauty products and even cookware."[14] The new adaptation, in the minds of marketing execs, had all the hooks necessary: major Hollywood stars, a universally known story with large themes, and a kind of glamour that both carried on and set new trends.

The film served as a star vehicle for Robert Redford, who played Gatsby, and who stood at the time as one of Hollywood's top draws. His fame grew in the late 1960s, certainly after starring with Jane Fonda in *Barefoot in the Park* (1967) and pairing with Paul Newman in *Butch Cassidy and the Sundance Kid* (1969). Redford's star rose even higher with *Jeremiah Johnson* (1972) and teaming with Newman again in the 1930s caper picture *The Sting* (1973), then one of the highest-grossing films of all time.

Fitzgerald himself may have found the $6.5 million budget for the production ludicrous, if he could have even fathomed such an outlandish figure in his own day. However, he may have found a home away from home among the mansions of Newport, Rhode Island, where production began in early June 1973.[15] Producers combed the surrounding area for people who owned antique automobiles and lined up a brilliant mansion to serve as stand-ins for Gatsby's West Egg enclave.

What Fitzgerald might have found most humorous focused on the extras casting call that took place early in production. Director Jack Clayton and his assistants picked out potential extras; each paid the whopping sum of $1.65 an hour for a guaranteed twelve hours minimum daily. According to Bruce Bahrenburg, the author of an insider's account of the film's creation, the wealthy sophisticates of Rhode Island clamored to attain these positions: "It has become a matter of social prestige to get into the film, especially among the summer colony in Newport, and those rejected look as if they had been handed their walking papers from the Newport Country Club."[16]

The important role of turning the novel into a screenplay initially fell to Truman Capote, but Paramount executives found the writer's work too scattered to be used. In response, Robert Evans, the company's production boss, asked Coppola to write a screenplay, particularly since he experienced such great success with *The Godfather* in 1972. Evans tasked Coppola to write a more faithful screenplay, which he turned out in about five weeks. Clayton then used Coppola's work with little modification, except to add additional scenes from the novel.

In Coppola's view, the additions hurt the film at the box office, making it seem "interminable."[17] According to scholar Gene D. Phillips, the changes Clayton made "eventually resulted in a motion picture that in the last analysis seems at times slow-paced and overlong."[18] Ironically, though, the film was deemed a commercial success based on Redford's star appeal.

THE FILM AND FITZGERALD

There is no doubt that the allure of the Redford-driven film sparked new interest in Fitzgerald and the novel. In an early 1974 essay for the *Saturday Evening Post* prior to the movie's release, journalist George Frazier wrote a glowing assessment of the author and the book's important place in American history. He examines the dichotomy between Fitzgerald as writer and celebrity, explaining, "A perfect sentence would go unnoticed by all except admirers of his prose, while the whole of sophisticated New

York would be titillated by his and Zelda's midnight dips in the pool in front of the Plaza." No other literary celebrity ever had the charisma and public's eye quite the way Fitzgerald captured it, or as Frazier says, "Fitzgerald was sui generis, which is to say that, for all the wallowing in the gutter, there was a certain fashionable playboyishness to his drunken disorderliness."[19]

Accompanying the article (representative of the *Gatsby* craze the movie stirred up) were large, full-page, color photographs taken of a Nashville, Tennessee, couple dressed in the clothes from a themed Swan Ball held in a 1920s mansion, later donated to the community to house the Tennessee Botanical Gardens and Fine Arts Center. In one photo, the couple looks confidently at the camera, the wife sitting in a 1920s convertible, while her husband holds the door open, white summer pants and white patent leather shoes showing his Jazz Age style. In the other, she sits atop a grand piano, adorned in a feathery white shawl and clutching a cigarette in a long holder. Perhaps attempting to emulate Zelda, she looks off into the distance, disinterested in the man. He, however, gazes up at her lovingly, decked out in a tuxedo and with a dainty pinkie ring on his hand.

The cultural symbols at work in the *Saturday Evening Post* article (once Fitzgerald's highest-paying short story market) portray the common idea of how the wealthy lived in the Roaring Twenties. Whether they understood what they conveyed in the photos, the couple (listed as Mr. and Mrs. Joseph Darling Pickslay Cheek Jr.) definitely seems more like Tom and Daisy than Gatsby. There is a smugness about them, as if they are wealthy and thus can make the effort to dress up for a charity ball. An editorial note at the beginning of the article notes that the mansion is the former home of the couple's family, dubbed "Cheekwood."[20]

Frazier acknowledges the impact of the movie and renewed interest in the author and era, saying that it stands "more than a mere novel . . . almost fifty years after its publication, a way of life among the young." He notes that "elegance" is becoming fashionable based on the excitement surrounding the film, ranging from *Gatsby*-style haircuts to "the soft Southern Belle type."[21]

Notwithstanding the great care that Clayton and his team took in creating the film, *The Great Gatsby* stirred up quite a bit of interest in Fitzgerald and his era but did not meet the level to be considered a great film. Roger Ebert, one of the nation's major film critics, called it "a superficially beautiful hunk of a movie with nothing much in common with the spirit of F. Scott Fitzgerald's novel." From his perspective, the film version got the look right but failed in "penetrating to the souls of the characters."[22]

Ebert, perhaps speaking to the cultural tone of the early 1970s, criticizes Clayton for not getting top performances from his stars. The critic views Redford as too stilted and formal, rarely connecting with the audience or the novel's emotional core. Even worse, Farrow plays Daisy as "all squeaks and narcissism and empty sophistication," according to Ebert. The performance diminishes the audience's comprehension of why Gatsby would risk so much for her.[23]

Reducing the 2013 and 1974 film versions of *The Great Gatsby* to one word each would result in "action" and "romance," respectively. With Leonardo DiCaprio as star, the film is exploding fireworks, violence, and intensity, all operating under a pulsing, beat-driven twenty-first-century sound track. On the other hand, the earlier version centered on scenery and authenticity. In this instance, the relationship with Daisy is at the fore. Plot took a secondary place behind the chemistry between Redford and costar Farrow. In both cases, however, a reader who has enjoyed the novel is left with a sense of longing or wanting more due to the change in emphasis from page to moving picture. Either film would be more enjoyable if one had never actually read the book, which is a common refrain among readers, but particularly apt in the case of Fitzgerald's novel.

The great film critic Vincent Canby cut to the heart of the problem with the 1974 screen version of *Gatsby*, explaining that by filling the holes in the plot with sentimentality, the filmmakers failed to address the novel's intensity and why the young man would so obsessively pine for Daisy for all those years. Instead, Canby says, "The movie . . . treats us to shots of Gatsby and Daisy picnicking, holding hands, behaving like models in a soft-focus hair dye commercial."[24] In its attempts at authenticity, the film emerges as overly sentimental, without the heft at the core of Fitzgerald's work.

As a result, the film looks beautiful and is shot brilliantly, yet still collapses in on itself as the depiction of romance takes precedent over the idea of romance. The former is what filmmakers create in an assessment of what filmgoers want to see, but the latter is what Fitzgerald actually produced and has kept readers returning to the novel. Certainly the Hollywood star system has an impact here. Movie producers cannot hire actors like Robert Redford and Leonardo DiCaprio for millions or tens of millions of dollars to play iconic roles and then keep them offscreen for two-thirds of the film, as Fitzgerald does in the novel. Thus, adapting the book to film necessitates that Gatsby become the central figure in the story, much more concrete and "real" than the author ever intended.

The distance between a novel of ideas and a novel of action is what makes Fitzgerald's masterpiece so elusive and difficult to film. Gatsby's place in the action is at the core here. Fitzgerald keeps the titular character submerged, while Hollywood requires that his story be central. For some readers, too, this dichotomy either results in one loving or hating the book. People simply do not realize that *Gatsby* is a novel of ideas masked within a novel of action. The cloaking that occurs is the result of Fitzgerald's ability in managing the intricacies and his beautiful writing style. Using Nick as a narrator enables Fitzgerald to emphasize the storytelling aspects, while concurrently casting the unreliability in that recounting. Because Nick is all over the place in retelling the story and weaving it with his own judgments of the action, the reader finds room for interpretation that other novels try to force. Thus, *Gatsby* lives on into the twenty-first century in a way that other books of that era have not.

***

The launch of a Fitzgerald revival shortly after his death gradually gained steam, keeping him in the public eye through the first wave of biographical work published in the early 1950s. After that, Fitzgerald studies took on a life of its own as more readers and more academic studies combined to transform the author and his work into something larger and more significant than 99.9 percent of the writers and books ever published. As a matter of fact, one reviewer claimed in 1965, "The general interest in the person of Fitzgerald has persisted to such a degree that it can be said today that he is the most intimately known of American writers."[25] The key phrase here is "intimately known."

Many writers are brand names in a nation that commoditizes knowledge, yet few people could provide a brief sketch of a writer's life and era. While many authors have had exciting or interesting lives throughout literary history, Fitzgerald came to represent an era and idea that people could employ to make sense of their own time. No other writer could mirror this synergy, not even greats who became public or popular culture figures as well as authors, such as Mark Twain, Edgar Allan Poe, or Ernest Hemingway. The latter, as accomplished and prolific in output and sales as he was, could not stake out a place in people's hearts like Fitzgerald did.

Even writers and books that had more policy implications, such as Upton Sinclair's *The Jungle*, could not sustain their influence like *Gatsby*. Since Theodore Roosevelt and other politicians used Sinclair's work to reform the meatpacking industry and transform the way people ate after 1906, one could argue for *The Jungle*'s importance over *Gatsby*. Yet, despite the sensationalism of the former and its use in creating policy, Fitzgerald's book seeped deeper into mass culture.

As this intimacy with Fitzgerald and *Gatsby* persisted, the images and ideas represented by the writer and his novel spread across popular culture. As a result, both were used to symbolize a variety of positions, mind-sets, and concepts, whether contextually in a newspaper or magazine article or on television as a story arc. Therefore, one is not surprised (necessarily) to find that Nick Carraway is used as a lead in a 1966 financial story about surging bond interest rates in the *New York Times* or that novelist C. D. B. Bryan satirizes *Gatsby* in his 1970 novel *The Great Dethriffe*, a kind of 1960s version of *Gatsby* that constantly references the novelist and work as a way of paying homage. Bryan's version of Nick, a successful writer named Alfred Moulton, explains the premise at the beginning of the story, saying, "What was important to me about Fitzgerald was the myth. And when one was used to dealing with myths, one seldom let truth stand in the way."[26] For Moulton, Fitzgerald and *Gatsby* dictate the way life should be lived in the 1960s. Fitzgerald's 1920s is his past and his family's past, which he reveres and respects.

If sales figures alone do not convince the reader that Fitzgerald mania had hit the nation by the 1960s, then the release of the 1974 film starring Redford and Farrow certainly adds credence to that declaration. As a result of all these individual threads weaving in and out, *Gatsby* grew in significance as the novel and its author also zigzagged through people's lives. Exposure to the novel might come in the form of it being forced on a person within a high school or college curriculum, which could also include using any number of scholarly studies to decipher the text and its symbols. Yet this did not end the interaction, which might also include reading about or seeing the film and purchasing products that resulted from its popularity and role in making the Jazz Age fashionable again.

Through the chaos of the 1960s and the anxiety of the 1970s, *Gatsby* prospered, even though the heady days of the Roaring Twenties had slipped into the distant past. As the generations of students who studied the novel in the 1950s and early 1960s moved on to family lives and careers, they may not have been focusing on the novel directly, but its meanings were part of their intellectual platform. Furthermore, as lesson plans were built and college syllabi created with *Gatsby* as a learning tool, K–16 students found themselves indoctrinated with the novel's ideas, themes, and images. All these cycles continue churning, thus creating a work that transcends its status and becomes a channel for multilayered thinking.

Americans have always been notorious for self-analyzing and exploring the inimitability of the nation. As such, scholar Robert Gorham Davis writing in 1969 reasons:

> Our public credos are not false or irrelevant. Insofar as they are in contradiction to reality they maintain a constant energy-creating tension that has been socially productive . . . between seaboard and frontier, paleface and redskin, European past and American future. . . . Somehow Americans nearly from the beginning have been able from this strange composite to achieve an underlying consensus that is more than verbal, that gives us our national character and makes us immediately recognizable despite the diversity of our backgrounds, almost anywhere that we go in the world.[27]

Davis identifies a key to *Gatsby*'s success in this regard—its tensions mirror those that individuals and organizations faced in this period stretching from Kennedy's assassination through the dawn of the Reagan era. We repeatedly come back to the ideas Fitzgerald presented: the dichotomy between the rich and everyone else, living an ethical life, the evolution of American Dream, and navigating personal experiences and relationships in the modern world. In essence, these topics are eternal. Fitzgerald presented them in such a moving portrait of his age that the beauty of the written language and the heady content merged to create a timeless work of art.

5

ALL THAT GLITTERS, 1981–2000

Nowadays when almost everyone is a genius, at least for awhile, the temptation for the bogus to profit is no greater than the temptation for the good man to relax . . . not realizing the transitory quality of his glory because he forgets that it rests on the frail shoulders of professional enthusiasts.— F. Scott Fitzgerald, in a letter to Ernest Hemingway, June 1926

"Greed is good."

The immortal phrase ushered from the lips of the fictional tycoon Gordon Gekko in Oliver Stone's masterpiece *Wall Street* (1987) drips with symbolic meaning for a nation in the throes of a capitalist orgy. But it is more than just the words themselves that sustained power. The image of Gekko as portrayed by Hollywood star Michael Douglas   impeccable suit, slicked-back hair, evil smirk—came to represent the economic offenses of both the 1980s "me" decade and the dot-com bubble that swelled and then burst in the mid-1990s through the early years of the next century.

The confidence and exuberance of these times, as a matter of fact, seemed to be an intricate replay of Fitzgerald's Roaring Twenties. Like the 1920s, mass media and popular culture encouraged the money mania, but whereas Gekko seemed to get his in the end, representative television shows like *Dynasty* and *Dallas* depicted worlds in which the rich routinely got richer on the backs of everyday, "good" people.

As is usually the case, the media and culture industries fostered a change in attitude. Soon, the general populace got caught up in the mania, which expanded geometrically when what had been dubbed the "Reagan Recession" of the early 1980s swung around to the "Reagan Recovery" later in the decade. Between 1982 and 1987, for example, some $20 trillion in new wealth flowed into the nation's pocketbooks.[1]

Reagan himself sounded a bit Gekko-ish a year before the film's release, asking in the 1986 State of the Union address: "The magic of opportunity—unreserved, unfailing, unrestrained—isn't this the calling that unites us?"[2] Ironically, the American Dream or some other blind allegiance to success must have been at work during this era. Despite cheerleading for Reagan and Gekko, the vast majority of the nation's workforce suffered through losses in real wages in the 1980s. Simultaneously, the wealthiest 20 percent of the population saw its income increase by 33 percent under Reagan's economic policies.

The president's "calling," however, soon transformed into the disaster of the Black Monday Wall Street market crash on October 19, 1987, when total stock value plummeted $500 billion in one fell swoop. Although the crash did not cause a global depression, as many commentators feared (and would have put the final exclamation point on the comparison between the 1920s and the 1980s), the tottering economy doomed the presidency of Reagan's successor, former vice president George H. W. Bush. Not until the good times heyday of President Bill Clinton would the economic gold rush again take hold, this time in the form of the Internet and other innovative technologies that sparked the "information age."

Returning to Gekko as a symbol of these economic upheavals and the potential consequences, however, it is not surprising that people found points of comparison between Stone's fictional mogul and Fitzgerald's Jay Gatsby. Film historian Jack Boozer sees Gekko as a "new version of the American dream." The character has similarities to Gatsby but has been remolded for the 1980s. Boozer explains: "The impossible romantic longing of a *Great Gatsby* . . . has become Gordon Gekko's tyrannical lust for financial adventurism and power in the era of Reagan-Bush." The move from idealism in the novel becomes the film character's "worship of the almighty dollar for its own sake. Idealism has been reduced to the raw omnivore of monetary power."[3]

With Wall Street shenanigans and economic power and intrigue as cultural backdrops in the 1980s and 1990s, the ostensibly all-purpose use of *The Great Gatsby* and its titular character also shifted. The use of the term "Gatsby" fluctuated across a number of themes, usually as a synonym for any wealthy person that rose from humble beginnings or perceived unassuming origins to economic or political power, extravagance, or over-the-top behavior that might better be laid at Fitzgerald's feet.

Gekko, in particular, served as a kind of contemporary Gatsby—what might have become of the character if he rose to power some fifty years later. For Gekko, the pursuit of wealth held no sacred mystery. Instead, one simply fulfilled the destiny of a corporate raider by using any means necessary to achieve fantastic wealth regardless of legalities that would stop a less-driven man. Although Fitzgerald kept the lengths of Gatsby's own underhanded dealings a mystery, there are many examples of a Gekko-like drive, from his connection to the Mafioso Meyer Wolfsheim ("He's the man who fixed the World's Series back in 1919") to hanging Tom Buchanan's friend Walter Chase out to dry on a bootlegging charge.[4] Gatsby and Gekko have different ends, but they willingly operate outside the law in hopes of getting what they want.

In the next decade, when the stock market seemed merely a conduit for wealth driven by the aggressive speculation around Internet startups and technology, *Gatsby* continued to be misinterpreted, mangled, and turned generic, as media types and others used the novel and its characters in an attempt to explain vicious, no-holds barred capitalism in simple terms.

As early as November 1990, a *New York Times* reporter conflated "Gatsby" with top executives in investment banking who faced declining salaries and potential downsizing based on the aftershocks of the Black Monday crash and withering economy. The mergers and acquisitions firms, which the writer claims "create[d] a legion of modern-day Gatsby's," essentially collapsed. Even a casual reader can see that this usage devalues the novel. Though some M&A executives got rich based on illicit junk-bond trading, the shorthand for opulent living and riches is far removed from what Fitzgerald wrote.[5]

***

The ideas contained in *Gatsby* remained important in the 1980s and 1990s, but the use of the terms around it were watered down to fit the sound-bite celebrity culture. For instance, why establish that Fitzgerald actually meant to chastise the rich for their self-centered behavior and willingness to smash up and destroy lives around them on a whim, when one could simply look on Microsoft founder Bill Gates's $100 million high-tech mansion and label its owner and the house itself "Gatsby-esque"? Based on one's perception, the manner in which people held *Gatsby* up as a cultural barometer in the 1980s and 1990s is either incredibly significant or a basic diminishing of the collective intelligence, which this chapter examines in greater detail.

This chapter examines a tumultuous era in American history that encompasses the era of the Reagan administration and ends with the nation in frenzy over the dot-com boom. Arguably, for the first time since the publication of *Gatsby* in 1925, the nation lived through boom times that resembled the 1920s, first in the "me" decade of the mid-1980s and later in the heady days of the Internet bubble in the late 1990s.

In response, reporters, commentators, and other media types needed terms to contextualize what the nation experienced, which had many of them leafing through or rereading Fitzgerald's novel, which so eloquently described the bacchanalia they witnessed and reported. And, since most people read *Gatsby* at some point in their high school or college years, the examples were convenient, since the lexicon around meta-*Gatsby* stood firmly among our most-used cultural references and symbols.

ALL THAT SHIMMERS: *GATSBY* IN THE 1980S

Sometimes historical periods get named after an individual because that person symbolizes or dominates a given age. At other junctures, it is a cultural or socioeconomic matter that defines an era. Sometimes, people are merely searching for a way to make meaning via a universally understood or convenient sign system. Various contenders spring to mind when examining the two-decade run from 1981 to 2001. These include the obvious political leaders, such as Ronald Reagan or Bill Clinton, to more sublime signals, like our burgeoning interconnectedness based on computer technology or the roller-coaster economic fluctuations that turned average people into stock market junkies and led to fortunes won and lost in what seemed like a blink of the eye.

As far as we know, Fitzgerald did not possess a crystal ball or clairvoyant abilities that enabled him to see into the future. Whether one believes he signed some kind of Faustian bargain exists only in the outer reaches of that person's mind. Yet, when reading *The Great Gatsby* in light of the twenty-year period from 1981 to 2001, it seems as if the author had his sights set on the era when writing the novel. Many of the narrative and thematic arcs of the book line up pretty well with the fluctuations in American history during the 1980s and 1990s. Over and over again, commentators, journalists, and others would invoke *Gatsby* in attempting to define the leaders and cultural themes that ran through these tumultuous years.

Looking back with history's twenty-twenty gaze, it seems clear that the ideas central to understanding the period mirrored the novel. Repeatedly, commentators and others attempted to use *Gatsby* and its topics to provide context for the chaos and uncertainty surrounding this period. *Gatsby's* utility as a way of explaining the issues at the head of society's churn is commensurate with scholar Arnold Weinstein's thinking when he explains, "A living work of art actually possesses a bare-bones practicality, indeed a *utility*, that we need to recover: it helps us toward a richer grasp of our own estate."[6]

Fitzgerald's novel is an interesting case study in proving Weinstein's point of "a living work of art." By the late years of the twentieth century, *Gatsby* surely had a strong foothold on the nation's imagination. On one hand, the novel had national distribution based on decades of high school teachers and college faculty forcing it on students, who themselves had been forced to read the novel while students in the 1960s. Whether these readers found that experience an irritation or pleasurable adventure, anyone paying attention could at least outline the novel's main concerns, more or less reinforcing its potential efficacy. As readership grew with the novel's centrality within the literary canon, its usefulness as a tool for understanding one's life and society broadened, too.

Simultaneously, social structures changed in the 1980s that enabled *Gatsby* to play an interesting role as a tool for interpretation. In that decade, the corporate structure took on a more central position as those working within and for large organizations found themselves in rigid hierarchies. The merger of corporate life with the wider culture had been taking place for as long as large business enterprises existed, but solidified and expanded during this era. Scholar Simon J. Bronner explains the melding of these two realities, saying, "The public has become more accustomed to hearing about the worlds of power, organized worlds that were creating cultures of their own. . . . The organizational model of business seemed more prevalent in society."[7] With the rise of corporate culture and its increasingly central position, more traditional aspects of organizing one's life, such as community, family, and region, took a backseat.

Perhaps this is why Reagan could gain broad support for "family values" while at the same time, the corporation gained power across society and in people's lives. This disparity between propaganda and reality enabled politicians to use culture as a touchstone. In these times, when truth seems elusive or murky, there is solace in knowing that texts exist that might help one establish insight, particularly when the national conversation is built around persuasion, rather than the search for veracity.

Weinstein's vision of literature's broader service to society played out in mid-1987, for example, when Reagan's top speechwriter Anthony R. Dolan penned a highly controversial and widely publicized op-ed for the *New York Times* in support of his boss. Although not altogether common in the *Times* because it was clearly such a proadministration puff piece, the article—written in an era when newspapers mattered deeply in establishing the nation's mood—touched off a national reaction. At the end of the essay, after Dolan spent considerable time explaining why Reagan would rebound (and arguably had already rebounded) from the controversy regarding the Iran-Contra hearings then taking place, he finished by comparing the president to Jay Gatsby.

Dolan singled out Reagan's "steady self-assurance" in making the point that the president shared this trait with the fictional character, who he deemed "inescapable" and a "symbol of American optimism." Another Reagan turnaround in fortune, despite appearing beaten down by the anxiety and bad press of his late second term, Dolan reported, "reminded [us] once again that we have always been Nick Carraways to his Gatsby."[8] In making the comparison, Dolan heightened the aspects surrounding optimism and used the literary reference to make Reagan seem more heroic.

Who, Dolan implied, could doubt a figure that held such optimism, particularly when it translated into policy? He cited several of Reagan's "historic moves" as examples, such as the Strategic Defense Initiative (the then-new formal name for the "Star Wars" missile defense system), the Grenada invasion, and the Republican view on taxes. In Dolan's mind, Reagan's ability to bounce back demonstrated "a President who sticks to his issues, keeps smiling, refuses to fade—the political matinee idol of the 80's not fussing about his disappearing fans but getting laughs; the President whose Teflon didn't crack."[9]

Columnist Anthony Lewis answered Dolan's essay with a scathing indictment of his use of *The Great Gatsby* to pump up Reagan's popularity. In countering Dolan (and in effect Reagan, too), Lewis pointed to the darker side of the Fitzgerald character, his ties to organized crime and desire to make money by any means necessary as a way to fulfill his dreams. Invoking famed social critic H. L. Mencken, Lewis highlighted the vacuity of Gatsby and the corruption of America in the 1920s.

From this vantage point, Lewis saw a very different set of Gatsby-like traits, explaining, "Of course Ronald Reagan is not Jay Gatsby. The comparisons are not to be forced. But there are themes—values—that echo." Among these, the columnist pointed to the president's willingness to fixate on an end, regardless of the means in attaining that goal. "Like Gatsby, too, Mr. Reagan has created his own world," Lewis says. "In it facts yield to fantasy and obsession. . . . Someone else will have to clear away the wreckage." The president also shared with the fictional character a falsity that privileged charm and "a marvelously winning personality" over substance.[10]

Splashed in newspapers all over the country, the feud between Dolan and Lewis continued when the former answered Lewis's rebuttal with a letter to the editor in the *Times*. While lambasting Lewis for his "hard-edged liberalism," Dolan also cautioned the writer to enjoy "the great sweep and excitement of modern conservatism" along with the "greatness of Jay Gatsby and Ronald Reagan."[11]

Clearly, the use of Fitzgerald's central character as a political football at the tail end of the Reagan administration speaks to the way literature and literary figures can be used to establish context in debates that seem far removed from the era in which the work appeared. Not only did Dolan and Lewis engage in a high-profile battle, they also demonstrated the ways *Gatsby* remained open to conflicting interpretations. Their spat revealed that the novel continued to move the nation's collective intellectual compass. The fight also showed, as Weinstein relates, "Great art lives in a way that transcends its moment, reaching something more universal, gesturing toward life experiences that are at once time-bound and timeless."[12] As a result, Jay Gatsby could inhabit a number of guises in the late 1980s—from optimistic rogue to inauthentic gangster—and each side invoking the character could provide quotes, bullet points, and other information to back their thinking.

NICK'S SHIFTY NARRATION AS A SIGN OF THE TIMES

There seemed to be a basic disconnect in the 1980s in the way people blurred the lines between illusion and reality. For example, large segments of the population simultaneously believed in the real-life Reagan (the former actor turned politician who spent a lifetime reciting other people's words) and the movie character Gekko (the evil antihero who business school students worshipped). This continual mixture between reality and illusion—mixed with widespread celebrity and fame obsession—resulted in the public developing conflicted ideas about trust, morality, and authenticity.

While one could argue that this divide always existed, I contend that the increase in mass media channels in the 1980s spawned by the rapid expansion of cable television and the growing film industry increasingly influenced and essentially transformed the way people behaved and made decisions about the world around them. As technology pushed into new areas in the 1990s, the resulting boom in communications not only expanded the potential interactions between people and institutions but also revolutionized the way people think. Discussing Marshall McLuhan's famous dictum, "The medium is the message," writer Nicholas Carr expands the idea, explaining:

> What both enthusiast and skeptic miss is what McLuhan saw: that in the long run a medium's content matters less than the medium itself in influencing how we think and act . . . a popular medium molds what we see and how we see it—and eventually, if we use it enough, it changes who we are, as individuals and as a society. [13]

For Carr and many other thinkers, the Internet as it has developed since the mid-1990s has fundamentally altered the way people (an "engrossed and compliant audience") approach the world. The screen has won, according to Carr, and while his statement takes us slightly beyond the chronology of this chapter, such ideas were birthed on the technology and tabloid culture that developed in the 1980s and early 1990s. He concludes: "The computer screen bulldozes our doubts with its bounties and conveniences. It is so much our servant that it would seem churlish to notice that it is also our master."[14] The Internet, then, from my perspective, is the latest tool in the merger of technology and communications. With cell phones, tablets, and other handheld devices, its ubiquity is established.

Looking back on the origins of the merger of reality and illusion, one sees examples in the political world, which has a long history of its denizens making rash, insensitive, or ignorant comments. The 1980s certainly seemed rife with obtuse statements by politicos who seemed utterly clueless to the realities people faced in the broader society. During the Christmas holiday season in 1983, for example, Reagan administration counselor Edwin Meese III, the future attorney general, raised the nation's ire when he told reporters that there are no hungry children in America. When pressed on the issue, Meese responded that some anecdotal evidence existed, but "I haven't heard any authoritative figures . . . we've had considerable information that people go to soup kitchens because the food is free and . . . that's easier than paying for it."[15] A photograph in this writer's possession taken within days of Meese's comment shows a homeless man sleeping at the White House front gate. Furthermore, several blocks away, a soup kitchen served the poor in the nation's capital, including entire families who had been swept under the rug in Reagan's trickle-down economy.

Writing in 1983 about the neoconservative rise in politics embodied by the corporatist Reagan administration, literary critic Alfred Kazin wrote about a conservative conference held at Fitzgerald's favorite New York City haunt, the Plaza Hotel, which has a prominent role in *Gatsby*. One session Kazin attended, titled "Politics and the Arts," featured several thinkers who criticized the contemporary literature of the decade for its anti-American attitudes. Since this panel served as a snapshot of conservative literary criticism, Kazin lamented the decline of satire, which the group (Kazin calls them "Plaza patriots," which foreshadows the Tea Party rise some three decades later) equated with anti-American views. Sitting in Fitzgerald's old stomping ground, Kazin recalls talking with one panelist about the Plaza scene in *Gatsby*. To his surprise, the person responded, "What's a Gatsby?"[16] The irony is staggering, but that more or less encompasses the 1980s.

The long history covering the era spanning the 1980s through the 2010s taken as a whole demonstrates the ubiquity and growing importance of popular culture and mass communication vehicles on the way people create their individual worldviews and engage in their cultures. If one then accepts the notion that *Gatsby* is a mainstay in mass culture, not only as a novel, but also as a referent for multiple ideas encased in that wider socioeconomic system, then the blurry line between reality and pseudoreality has significance on the way the book is understood and applied. Nowhere is this intersection of *Gatsby* as an idea and a tool more vivid than in Fitzgerald's construction and portrayal of the wily, erratic, and deceptive narrator, Nick Carraway. His trickster persona, enveloped in a cloak of self-delusion and self-righteousness, seems perfectly suited for contemporary America as it unfolded in the late twentieth century.

Writing in 1984 about Nick's unreliability as a narrator, scholar Kent Cartwright distinguishes between an earlier group of critics who assumed that Nick merely served as Fitzgerald's fictional surrogate, a kind of stand-in that enabled the author to harshly criticize the flagging American Dream. This initial set came under fire as later literary critics and commentators took Nick to task for any number of character faults, from being a hypocrite to a sycophant.

Instead, Cartwright finds Nick not a double for Fitzgerald, but a character with multiple flaws that make his telling of the story unique. "Such a view of Nick's weaknesses," Cartwright explains, "must challenge the traditional assumption that Nick generally doubles for Fitzgerald." He continues, "It might, indeed, reveal that Nick's closing asceticism is more a preference than an imperative, that his assessment of the dream is not conclusive, and that the novel is far more open-ended than some critics have suggested."[17] Nick's confusion, in a sense, mirrors the bewilderment of his own age, as well as the later twentieth century.

The narrator's ideas about the distinction between the old America and the new, as personified by New York City, continued to demarcate the intellectual and spiritual lines running through the nation. One could witness this disparity most clearly in the way presidential elections unfolded. When Democrats won, for instance, their victories were driven by the nation's urban centers in the Northeast and West, concentrations of voters that countered the Republican strongholds in the Midwest and South.

Tellingly, given the pervasive mix of image with reality and flash over substance in the 1980s, Cartwright's analysis speaks to the era and pulls a thread tight between the 1980s and the 1920s. He says:

> To whatever degree Gatsby has won Nick over, he has won him not by
> an appeal to evidence but by an appeal to imagination. Because of his
> impressionability, Nick grasps an image and decks it out with his own
> bright feathers. But through this submersion, Nick's belief has in some
> measure grown. Fascination breeds credulity. Indeed, Gatsby is such a
> cliché that on the flimsiest of bona fides he becomes a miracle. [18]

The idea that a person can win the day with flash and meager proof encapsulates the 1980s. The era seemed to be another in a seemingly long string of American time frames that could be labeled the "me" decade.

According to Cartwright, Fitzgerald portrays Nick getting duped by the "great" Gatsby, yet the sinews of believability compel him to accept the man's tales. "Nick's confusions, then, become values in the reader's portrait of Gatsby," Cartwright explains, "making him powerful even as he is remote; plausible yet strange; possible. Thanks, curiously, to the distance Fitzgerald establishes between Nick and his reader, even Gatsby can happen here, without any particular wonder."[19] So, Gatsby can be borne on half-truths and a pretty gloss, just like an actor/cowboy could become president of the United States or the son of wealth and privilege who is able to transform himself into a man of the people.

In *The Great Gatsby*, Nick's fawning narration—despite our disbelief in an awful lot of what he says—ensures that Gatsby will remain great. Just as he served as Gatsby's surrogate and friend after the murder, he will immortalize the man in the novel he is writing. In an era that thrived on public relations and glitzy marketing campaigns, Nick turns into Gatsby's main publicist and historian, writing the book about him, even though he claims to want no more of the East or its wildness after that year in West Egg.

The point here must be that the victors (or possibly survivors) are the ones permitted to write a land's history. We might not trust Nick, nor even like him based on his wispy mannerisms and willingness to watch as all these different threads unraveled, yet there is something there that compels us to root for him and his mysterious friend. We believe the hype.

THE LEGACY OF THE 1980S

The end of each decade leads to a sometimes insightful, sometimes ponderous probing of what the last ten years connoted and what might be forming at the dawn of the next ten. As the 1980s swept out to sea, commentators noted the dichotomy in the way Americans thought of themselves versus the way they acted.

For example, Charles Bremner, a correspondent for the *Times* of London, told readers that while Americans congratulated themselves for jailing Wall Street manipulators, mainstream consumers "shopped on, flocking to the air-conditioned suburban malls where for a few hundred dollars you can enter Ralph Lauren's world of polo-playing old WASP-dom, or buy into Laura Ashley's dream of English pastoral serenity."[20] As soon as the economic chaos of Black Monday slipped into memory and consumers regained their buying power, they hit the stores in search for the goodies and gadgets they denied themselves in the wake of the Wall Street downturn.

Alas, according to Bremner, in the postcrash nation, conspicuous consumption went out of fashion. Instead, buyers looked for "plush frugality," which he explains as a way of downplaying one's wealth. Here Bremner's thinking predates that of writer and newspaper columnist David Brooks, who would shoot to best-sellerdom with *Bobos in Paradise: The New Upper Class and How They Got There* (2000), a snappy sociological examination of the baby boomers' ideological mix of 1960s bohemian idealism and the consumerism rampant in the 1980s. Bremner satirized this new breed as those who were "cruising Park Avenue in a four-wheel-drive Jeep while attired as a backwoodsman or woman" or "in favor of the pseudo-worker look, as embodied in Soviet chic."[21]

Bremner, Brooks, and other commentators sensed a change in the air, but virtually no one thought that America would curb its excessive spending spree unless forced. The *Times* foreign correspondent reported the results of a national poll examining heroic traits people coveted, which revealed that they yearned for a nostalgic 1950s-era father figure. Not surprisingly, though, the new hero had to make enough money to live comfortably in late 1980s and 1990s America. The idea of getting by modestly had essentially vanished at the hands of the decade's excesses. Like Pandora's box, the consumer demons unleashed in the 1980s would continue to haunt the country unabated.

Humorist Russell Baker caught the air of indignation the public let out after reading about the multimillion-dollar birthday bashes thrown for tycoons Malcolm Forbes and Saul Steinberg, which featured jet-setting guests, celebrities, and more excess than even Gatsby could have imagined. With heavy satire, Baker has a typical American wife wondering about such events and why she had to throw a backyard party for her own husband: "A sensible woman, she knew that despite its inanity the rich-and-famous crowd performed a vital public service. They provided people with daydreams and poisonous envy and entertained them in TV bromides and supermarket headlines."[22] Next, the female character (via Baker's sharp wit) rails against trophy wives, old age, and the disparity between the ultrarich and regular people.

Famed journalist Tom Wolfe turned a kind of Gatsby for the 1980s into a literary best-seller in 1985 with *The Bonfire of the Vanities*, a thick social history of the decade filling some nine hundred pages. In the novel, Wolfe chronicles the interlocked worlds of Wall Street finance, Brooklyn politics, and Harlem's disadvantaged African Americans. The main character is Sherman McCoy, a Wall Street broker who sees himself as a "Master of the Universe." McCoy's limited perspective from his $10 million Park Avenue apartment and his office suite downtown prevents him from objectivity. He allows his spoiled wife and child to pamper themselves while he conducts an affair with Maria Ruskin, a trash-talking Southern belle married to Arthur Ruskin, a corporate mogul who made his money offering discount trips to the Holy Land for Jewish families.

Picking Maria up at the airport one night, Sherman makes a wrong turn toward the Bronx, where he mistakes two black youths for gang members. In escaping the scene, Maria, driving the car, hits Henry Lamb, one of the teens, knocking him into a coma. Suddenly, the "Master of the Universe" finds himself embroiled in a scandal when Maria refuses to take responsibility. Wolfe uses this centerpiece to craft a story around greed, corruption, the changing state of journalism, and race relations.

One of the novel's most brilliant moments follows Sherman through a socialite party, peopled with "Lemon Tarts" (the youthful, vapid, very blonde female dates of elderly men) and "Social X-rays" (the wives of the other elderly men, so thin one could see the light through their skin). Wolfe's keen eye and sharp pen assist the reader in understanding this outrageous world of excess as Sherman watches his wife interact within "the hive" of this social order. Wolfe shows that Sherman comprehends

the superficiality of the culture, but he realizes that this is what he deserves, as he will not extract himself from it. A savage indictment of
Reagan's America, *The Bonfire of the Vanities* is a powerful novel that
exposes corruption in an effort to prove that very little separates the
"haves" and the "have-nots."

Perhaps for a brief slice in time, the great Jay Gatsby would have been
ridiculed and jeered, just as Fitzgerald found himself in the 1930s, too old
and broken to relive youth's wildness and unable to mentally break from
the glamorous days of yore. Those who bought books not only overlooked the exquisite *Tender Is the Night*, but they basically forgot about
the author as a symbol of the heady past that was no more. For the first
time since the Fitzgerald revival hit its stride in the mid-1940s, the end of
the 1980s may have squelched its significance if people actually bought
into the notion that the 1990s would signal a return to simpler ideas about
living a good life.

GATSBY IN THE 1990S

On the large landscape of American culture, the 1990s launched with the
economic baggage of the 1980s. For most observers, it seemed the gaudy,
money-is-no-object aura of the previous decade ended. Commentators
cautioned the public to expect more conservative times ahead. In this
transitional phase—prior to the economic fireworks set off in the Clinton
administration—the term *Gatsby*-esque equated to one's dream of having
an endless amount of goods and money.[23]

This idea would fizzle for a while during Clinton's early years but
would later come roaring back to life as the technology age took over the
nation. Suddenly, twenty-year-olds creating Internet companies turned
into paper millionaires, followed closely by a trail of venture capitalists,
the Svengali figures whispering in their ears about going public and doing
deals. Everyone was a celebrity and magazines reportedly about business
started catering to the rumored *Gatsby*-like parties raging deep into the
night on the nation's coasts.

The Great Gatsby is filled with popular culture, not just real-life characters, but also caricatures of invented celebrities, which Fitzgerald employed to provide historical context. As a result, the tale glimmered with
snapshots of Broadway actresses, gossip rags, wild parties, and slick cars.

It is no surprise, then, that the focus on culture links *Gatsby* with the celebrity obsession that came to its full fruition in the 1990s, then carried on at an even faster pace in the 2000s. The decade earned this distinction based on the introduction and promulgation of the Internet. The web provided the public with an additional screen filled with all the tabloid-like minutiae it desired, both replicating and expanding on the star-filled world of the 1980s.

By the late twentieth century and early twenty-first century, popular culture transformed from a part of the overall cultural scene to its foundation—an omnipresent part of the typical American's day-to-day life. While readers saw the earliest inklings of this change in *Gatsby* and the silent films of the era (the first film version of *Gatsby* appeared in 1926, starring Hollywood icon Warner Baxter), its full appropriation took place as technology brought more entertainment into people's lives. In Fitzgerald's day and for many decades after, one could choose to disconnect from popular culture. With the spread of the web—like the faux machine-created reality of *The Matrix*—no one could escape.

Using *Gatsby* as a kind of benchmark, careful observers can recognize the way popular culture infiltrated modern society in the 1920s and the similarities to the 1990s and 2000s. The fundamental transformation led to complete totality. Not only are people in today's world unable to stop the pop culture noise; increasingly they are taught to believe that an "always on" mind-set is typical. Rather than criticize people who carry on a variety of simultaneous conversations and odd jobs at once, "multitasking" is applauded. This situation echoes the feelings of chaos and despair that course through *Gatsby*. Syndicated columnist George Will captured this notion, explaining:

> Fitzgerald was born with ragtime, movies and airplanes, amidst an expansive sense of possibility. Production soared; speculation soared more. Producing goods lost stature next to marketing, advertising, salesmanship. The new virtues were poise, self-assurance, personality. . . . Gorgeous, if you overlook the fact he was a gangster.[24]

In the novel, the latest technologies that were widely adopted—automobiles and telephones—are constant presences. The shrill sound of the telephone causes a jolt for characters already on the edge, particularly Daisy, who sees the calls as a nail Tom drives through their marriage. Gatsby seems to be on the telephone more often than not, the persistent interruptions by some butler telling him that some distant caller awaits provide a kind of cover that camouflages the man, allowing him to hide from both the people at his parties and the reader going through the text. Remarkably to today's readers, so many of the characters in *Gatsby* simply cannot drive well. Sometimes, accidents are the result of too much alcohol consumed, but others take place when the power and speed of the mighty automobiles are too much for the driver to control. This occurs when Jordan clips the button off a workman's jacket and in the harrowing scene when Daisy accidently kills Myrtle Wilson.

In contemporary times, the pervasiveness of technology has had a similar consequence, basically numbing people to everything outside technology's grasp. For example, children barely able to reach the mouse are urged to learn computer skills and do K–3 lessons on an iPad. For many preschoolers, going online to Nickelodeon or Disney and interacting virtually with the characters they watch on television is a natural act.

At its essence, however, popular culture is about context. Studying the actions of political or corporate leaders provides the framework for understanding shifts in popular culture over time. It is impossible, for example, to quantify Bill Clinton's or George W. Bush's impact on the cultural developments of the 1990s and 2000s, but understanding them as leaders working within the mass communication structure enables one to grasp the broader meaning of culture during their time as president.

The ability to examine the actions of the government or a particular leader or group of leaders is arguably the most positive aspect of popular culture. Rooted in free speech, the rise of mass media enabled Americans to criticize their leaders and institutions, thus opening new opportunities for collective education and information. At the same time, free speech allows for humor. As a result, Jon Stewart can openly mock the president on *The Daily Show* and *Saturday Night Live*'s Darrell Hammond could impersonate Clinton weekly on the hit show without concern over his personal safety.

The Great Gatsby also seemed big game for would-be aspirants to literary greatness. They stalked Fitzgerald's turf, presenting Nick-like unreliable narrators and quasi-heroes in the *Gatsby* vein. In 1996, for example, Carter Coleman ripped Jay McInerney's novel *The Last of the Savages* for attempting *Gatsby* heights but ultimately falling short. Even if the novel is good, as Coleman claims McInerney's is, the book "suffers by comparison, as almost any novel would."[25] Ultimately, Fitzgerald set the bar so high that anything similar seems at least derivative and slightly off.

A SCANDALOUS AGE

As millions of Americans interacted with mass media, whether watching the same movies or listening to radio programs, a common language developed that opened lines of communication between disparate groups. The downside to this unintended focus on mass communication, some argued, was that a growing fascination with pop culture actually diverted attention from important challenges the nation faced, ultimately serving as a kind of placebo. Therefore, popular culture enabled people to feel good about the world around them without really forcing them to directly confront critical issues.

Arguably, no president in history blurred the line between the office and popular culture more than Bill Clinton. He served as a kind of walking symbol of how society changed over the last several decades. After Clinton, for example, any vestiges of regality or luster the office held virtually disappeared. However, he was an incredibly popular president, routinely receiving high approval ratings.

Clinton was still "Mr. President," but for most people and the media, he was "Bubba" or "Slick Willy," a down-home, good ol' country boy from Arkansas—the kind of guy you would want to drink a beer with, listen to tell jokes and stories, but never leave alone with your sister—wink, wink. Clinton's homespun image emerged despite ties to Washington, D.C., and education at Georgetown University, Yale Law School, and a Rhodes scholarship to University College, Oxford. Acknowledged as a masterful politician, both critics and admirers wondered which was the real Clinton. In hindsight, however, Clinton seemed simply too complex to put in a tidy box. He embodied traits of both and used them strategically to achieve his goals.

U.S. history is filled with stories of political, financial, and sexual misconduct. The general public has always had a curious fascination with the lives of those in power, including politicians, entertainers, and business leaders, particularly when these people fall from grace. Before Watergate, the mainstream media did not rush to expose the shortcomings of influential people. Presidents and entertainers were often protected from national scandal by a media that looked the other way. Beginning in the 1970s and intensifying with the advent of the information age, the national media has stopped covering for public figures. Instead, under the guise of dishonesty or hypocrisy, the media has focused on sensational, scandal-ridden stories, ultimately making misconduct and public scandal a part of everyday life.

The dual-headed media monster of Vietnam and Watergate changed journalism forever. The combination of an unpopular war and criminal behavior in the president's office expanded the scope of what broadcasters chose to expose about their leaders—the floodgates were opened. The Internet has fueled the sensationalist aspects of society, since people now have almost instantaneous access to news and opinion. People no longer expect movie stars, politicians, athletes, chief executive officers, or even the president of the United States to remain scandal-free. The idea that everyone has skeletons in their closet waiting to be exposed is pretty much universal.

Political scandal remains a constant reminder of human frailty. After Watergate forced President Richard M. Nixon to resign from office, investigations into political misconduct expanded. The Iran-Contra scandal of the 1980s not only destroyed the careers of several high-ranking officials in the Ronald Reagan administration, it caused a national crisis of confidence in the democratic system.

A variety of scandals during the presidency of Bill Clinton, from the Whitewater real estate scheme to the president's affair with White House intern Monica Lewinsky revealed the way public opinion about misconduct changed. Initially, scandal focused primarily on criminal or financial wrongdoing. During the Clinton years, however, presidential scandal turned more intimate as the press reported on the president's numerous sexual liaisons, including blunt discussions of oral sex and semen-stained dresses. Many pop culture experts agreed that salacious television programs, such as *The Jerry Springer Show*, which featured crude behavior, incest, fistfights, and the glorification of the lowest common denominator, fueled the public craving for this kind of intimate detail.

As a result of ever-intensifying media coverage and instantaneous access to information, the United States now thrives on a culture of scandal. As a matter of fact, many individuals ride to great heights of fame based on disgrace. Infamy now seems part of an overall scheme to increase the "buzz" around a given entertainer, politician, or public figure as part of a campaign to make the person even more famous. Depending on the severity of the scandal, many infamous people are eventually welcomed back into the limelight.

The outcome of the scandal culture is an increase in public distrust and cynicism. As a result, there are fewer heroes in the world for people to look to in times of crisis. In an increasingly competitive media landscape and twenty-four-hour information age, however, it seems a culture of scandal is here to stay.

THE CENTURY BEATS ON: A NEW FILM

After the decadence of Wall Street greed in the 1980s and the superficial laid-back corruption of the dot-com boom, *Gatsby*'s popular culture influence seemed to reach a new zenith. As discussed above, there were novels that aped its themes and films that presented new versions of Nick and Gatsby as the movie and fictional industries presented audiences with mirrors on their own worlds. The terms associated with the novel even entered the political lexicon, let alone the ubiquity of such taxonomy in the business and entertainment press.

Given the times, it is no wonder that the 2000s began with a high-profile version of *Gatsby*, starring Toby Stephens as the title character, Mira Sorvino as Daisy, and Paul Rudd as Nick. The fourth attempt at filming Fitzgerald's novel, this one was a television movie coproduced by the A&E cable network.

Several changes from the novel are readily apparent, beginning with the opening scene of a seagull flying over water and a barren shoreline. Setting the tone for the film, this shot establishes that what follows will be pastoral. The Long Island setting seems more remote. As music plays in the background, Nick narrates over it, emphasizing the words "criticize" and "advantages" from the infamous opening monologues. The mention of Gatsby is changed from a book Nick is writing in the novel to "story" that he will retell.

The A&E version moves the murder/suicide to the beginning of the action. First, Gatsby appears from an overhead perspective, so the viewer is looking down on him in the pool. He seems agitated or upset, examining cuff links he holds tightly in his hand. In the next frame, shot from underwater looking upward and out of the pool, the shooter appears, his image bouncing on the shimmering water's surface. He draws the gun up from his side and fires. Two shots ring out.

Given that the television film could not compete with the resources allocated to a Hollywood film, the 2000 adaptation (debuting in January 2001) is scaled down considerably. The Buchanan mansion, for example, is not as ostentatious as one would imagine. Director Robert Markowitz also shoots the film in a tighter frame while the actors are speaking. As a result, the actors' facial features are more noticeable. Tom is more oafish, slurping his soup like a commoner at the initial dinner with Nick. Later, he swigs from a flask outside Wilson's garage, playing to the Prohibition era.

The valley of ashes, a key aspect of the story, is done well in the Markowitz version. It is appropriately desolate, industrial, and decrepit. Myrtle is a rougher character than in the novel. For example, the minimal decorum Fitzgerald had them exhibit is completely gone in the film. Tom and Myrtle are more overt and sexually aggressive.

When Gatsby finally appears, the character is revealed to be a huckster or salesman type. Nick even makes fun of him when he uses "old sport," then openly chuckles while Gatsby recreates the story of his life. Central, however, is the romance between Jay and Daisy.

In the film, the core of their romance centers on their love and mutual longing for one another in their younger years. They act as coconspirators before he goes off to war. She knows that he is poor yet attempts to conceal this from her family and attempts to fool them into believing he is in the same social class. In a flashback, Daisy thinks about her first encounter with the young army officer, one where she mistakenly calls him "Gatsby." He then adopts the name.

After they reconnect, Daisy swoons at the size of his house. They stop to dance in the orchestra room and he is shown overcome with emotion. Yet, later, in the confrontation between Tom and Jay at the hotel in New York City, the actors play the scene with little feeling.

Accenting Gatsby's criminal behavior, a detective searches the mansion for missing bonds and questions Nick, since he is a bond salesman. When Nick answers the telephone call from Slagle (which in the novel provides a glimpse at Gatsby's illegal activities), the man is sinister and tells Nick that the cops are onto them about the missing bonds. After the police have turned the mansion upside down, Nick then finds the missing bonds Gatsby forged in a secret compartment in a trunk—direct evidence of Gatsby's underhandedness. Before leaving West Egg for the last time, Nick burns the bonds down at the shoreline, as well as Gatsby's clippings of Daisy. Then, he throws the monogrammed cuff links out into the water toward Daisy's.

Given the timeliness of *Gatsby* at the dawn of the new millennium, one would have expected more from this version, but the cast simply seemed unable to rise to the occasion, like a soggy sandwich left out after a midafternoon summer rain. Writing for *Variety*, Steven Oxman says that the A&E adaptation "demonstrates once again how this breezily told tale can be transformed into a languorous affair, replete with visual attractiveness and yet somehow dull to its core." Rather than focus on the layered storytelling, the film turns the narrative into a "whodunit," which Oxman calls "a bizarre, and clearly poor, choice which robs the story of a truly dramatic twist."[26] In the end, however, the weight of the summer setting and expectations surrounding the novel weighed the movie down, essentially turning a Jazz Age barnburner into a Model T with a flat tire.

In an interview, director Markowitz seemed to understand the novel and its themes, explaining that from the film, the viewer should "better understand the nature of the country we live in in regards to the pursuit of the American Dream and the price we have to pay for it—sometimes to lose your own soul. . . . It's about all of our lives as we pursue a dream defined by other people."[27] Markowitz realized the place of meta-*Gatsby* as a cultural touchstone for Americans, but he could not find a way to adequately bring that to life on film.

* * *

In 1998, an esteemed group of novelists, historians, and publishing insiders who served as the editorial board for publisher Modern Library compiled a list of the one hundred best novels of the twentieth century. *Gatsby* came in second to James Joyce's *Ulysses*, after a reshuffling took place when five different novels tied for first. While many panelists and other commentators argued for or against works in the top five or ten, *Ulysses* and *Gatsby* were virtually unanimous at the top.[28]

Ironically, the life of these two novels is full of hullabaloo, chaos, esteem, and ultimate redemption. Although Joyce is considered one of the greatest writers of all time, *Ulysses* was banned in the United States and deemed obscene. The book could not be purchased legally until a judge interceded in 1933. *Gatsby*, though not judged indecent or banned, nevertheless hit critics and book buyers with a resounding thud, not living up to the publisher's or Fitzgerald's expectations of its potential.

Fast-forward to the end of the century, though, and the two stellar works stood at the top of the literary mountain, demonstrating that sales at publication and critical perspectives that go along with it do not necessarily establish long-term importance. (As an aside, one wonders how Hemingway would have reacted to the Modern Library list given his long-standing competiveness with Fitzgerald. His great book *The Sun Also Rises* placed at a distant forty-five.)

Gatsby's effectiveness as a tool to assess the American Dream is critical in the novel's long-term utility. A tangential equation here that is less frequently discussed is how this notion relates to trust, because if the populace does not trust that the American Dream is still possible, then the whole idea implodes. What the 1981 to 2000 era revealed is that trust served as a kind of token, gambled back and forth in high-stakes games across global, socioeconomic, and cultural lines. One could certainly argue, for example, that each presidential election in the United States in this period hinged on trust, whether contemplating one's feelings about patriotism or the current economic status. Or, one could simply look at television shows, like *The Cosby Show* in the 1980s or *Frasier* in the 1990s to see how the idea of trust disseminated.

Meta-*Gatsby* offers readers and viewers, whether actively engaged in critical thinking or just passively listening to a lecture or watching a film, the opportunity to contemplate trust as a cornerstone of our world, since the entire novel is built on conviction and disbelief existing simultaneously. I contend that meta-*Gatsby* took on an increasingly important role in our national discourse in this era since the boom and bust economic picture melded with the increasing obsession regarding entertainment and celebrity culture. The result seemed to be a kind of *Gatsby*-on-steroids world that needed all the tools at its disposal to make sense.

6

GATSBY TODAY, 2001–PRESENT

I never blame failure—there are too many complicated situations in life—but I am absolutely merciless toward lack of effort.—F. Scott Fitzgerald, letter to his daughter, 1940

Bewildering questions about *The Great Gatsby* remain, even as the novel approaches its one hundredth anniversary and eclipses sales figures in the tens of millions, not to mention readership reaching into the hundreds of millions. Primarily, one must wonder, despite Fitzgerald's profound hopes (and keen internal knowledge of the book's significance), how did *Gatsby* transform from mixed reviews and lackluster sales to become one of the most important novels ever written? Why are audiences and readers still transfixed by this slim volume that on publication seemed to most people as little more than a time capsule of the Roaring Twenties by a writer of great promise, but one who had still not completely realized his skills?

In an attempt to answer this question, I contend that *Gatsby* is not only the most important novel in our literary history, it is the "Great American Novel." Exhibit A in supporting these pronouncements is today's world. Fitzgerald's book—by exploring the timeless elements of love and romance, personal transformation, wealth, and the pursuit of the unattainable—achieves the coveted title, and, more importantly, explains to students, scholars, and fans alike what makes *Gatsby* so great.

Are there more than a handful of novels that could even be considered the "Great American Novel"? Yes, there are many phenomenal literary works that go a long way toward understanding the nation at various times in its history or even illuminate a topic in new and innovative ways. Yet none of them are employed to address the concerns of contemporary times like Fitzgerald's masterpiece. In this regard, *Gatsby* is like a race car with an extra gear that enables it to remain applicable well past the limitations on significant competitors. Here and throughout this book, I dub this extension of the novel as a cultural touchstone meta-*Gatsby*.

Why do we still care about this novel? More importantly, how does *Gatsby* help us make sense of our own lives and times? Think for a moment, do great works like *Lolita*, *The Sun Also Rises*, *The Grapes of Wrath*, *The Naked and the Dead*, *Rabbit Run*, *White Noise*, *Beloved*, *The Amazing Adventures of Kavalier & Clay*, or *American Pastoral* even get similar consideration or any of the dozen or so others one could list as possible contenders for Great American Novel?

Outside the academic world of scholars highly attuned to critical analysis, very few people are attempting to interpret the contemporary world via the important books mentioned above. Despite the power and critical acclaim these novels rightly deserve, each serves to capture a moment in time or an important foundational topic, yet there is no lasting power as a tool to maneuver modern times. Thinking about these works in light of Fitzgerald's quickly validates the significance of *Gatsby*.

Try to make a similar list yourself. See if you can find anything that compares—not *Huck Finn*, *The Scarlet Letter*, nor anything written in the middle or late twentieth century. Nothing . . . just *The Great Gatsby*.

While many of his friends and colleagues sold more books and seemed to have more secured literary reputations, Fitzgerald wrote a book that is essentially timeless. Part of this immutability centers on the themes and ideas at the heart of the book. Much of its endurance is also based on the author's technique, in other words, crafting a tale within a tale that enables the reader to both advocate and question the themes and issues fundamental to life as an American in the modern world. It is this basic freedom that Fitzgerald champions in *Gatsby* that makes the novel a persuasive device for understanding essential aspects of our national character. *Gatsby* asks—no, demands—that we interrogate the ideas at the heart of our sociocultural world. Meta-*Gatsby* abides.

***

Contemporary society is propelled by the always-on demand of the Internet and its trappings, from headlines filled with celebrity intrigue and corporate greed to the human tragedy at the heart of the roller-coaster economy. An unsettling aspect of the developing cyber crutch is that the web is changing the way people think, analyze, and interpret their environments. The speed and supposed efficiency of finding information by searching Google, combined with the tiny packets of information delivered on web pages, Twitter feeds, and Facebook status updates, is turning people into self-selecting consumers of small snippets of data that can be quickly digested, especially versus the relentless churn of information constantly available via the Internet. Under the spell of technology, one might think that classic literature has little bearing, particularly in a world obsessed with the bells and whistles offered by the web.

What we lose in this trade-off over time, however, is the ability to think critically and contextually. The long-term consequence of ignoring critical-thinking skills is that people rely on "facts" and equate that with knowledge. Rather than carefully thinking through challenges, people then fall back on emotion or what most people deem their "gut reaction." Sadly, this kind of thinking is rewarded in today's society. The political parties, for example, play off people's emotional response to hot-button issues, such as the continuing divisiveness of the pro-choice versus pro-life argument, jobs, and gun control.

When "facts," represented by Google and search engine results, become the dominant structure of knowledge, then more important concepts, such as critical thinking and wisdom, fall by the wayside. This phenomenon is in direct contrast to what is considered higher-level learning. Instead, I advocate that wisdom or context be elevated for the betterment of society, particularly as personal technological gadgets enable people to access "facts" anywhere, almost instantly.

Yet, given the dominance of the web and its consequences, *Gatsby* has developed into part of the fiber of the American ethos and an important tool in helping readers to better comprehend their lives and the broader world around them. The novel and films, particularly with the release of the Luhrmann version in May 2013, help people explore a variety of topics essential to their emotional and intellectual well-being.

This chapter explores how and why *Gatsby* remains relevant, particularly given the extremes of the contemporary world, which one might imagine would create a progressive society that has moved beyond the novel. What we find, however, is that the ideas central to the intellectual core of the book still reverberate across today's landscape.

Most intriguing, perhaps, is the way *Gatsby* addresses wealth and the consequences of living within a society that makes one's economic status seem flexible, yet simultaneously erects barriers that allow few to make significant climbs through social class. Richard Brody, writing in the *New Yorker*, contemplates why *Gatsby* endures in this area. He determines that the novel's current popularity is, in part, its arrival "in another glittering age of incommensurable inequality." What Fitzgerald delivered, after all, is "a novel of conspicuous consumption—not even of appetite but of the ineluctable connection between wealth and spectacle."[1] It is in this area, principally as it helps the reader comprehend the American Dream, that Fitzgerald's book resonates with contemporary readers who struggle with similar uncertainties today.

Journalist Philip Hensher sees Fitzgerald's novel as a barometer for other works that followed, particularly when addressing social class. This aspect of *Gatsby* serves as a bridge between the author's time and ours. Hensher says, "There's something permanent about it, but also something rather current, too."[2] The book is valuable today, he explains, because "the novel, with its clear sense that money comes and goes, and that detachment from opulence is as empty a gesture as indulgence in it, seems to come to mind whenever we aren't doing so well ourselves."[3] Reading *Gatsby* forces us to think about our own place in the economic caste system and then bounce that notion off what we establish as our own dreams and aspirations.

GATSBY IN A NEW AMERICA

The list of national and global crises in the first couple of decades of the twenty-first century could nearly drive a person mad. Undoubtedly, the chaos of these years might leave one questioning just exactly how far humanity has come in its life span. Perhaps an argument could be made that progress is no longer possible, especially in a world where mankind seems hell-bent on destroying itself via direct confrontation or through the gradual destruction of the planet and its ability to sustain life. From this perspective, one hopes that the themes and ideas at the core of meta-

Gatsby might help people, particularly young, educated audiences, to find a coping mechanism for these kinds of global ills.

In the United States, the new millennium has witnessed years of explosions and upheavals that have both influenced and transformed American life, including the September 11, 2001, terrorist attacks and the ensuing wars in Iraq and Afghanistan; the nation's governmental response to natural and human-made phenomena, such as the devastation of Hurricane Katrina; and Wall Street's implosion resulting from the real estate mess driven by the arrogance and ineptitude of the nation's banking industry. More recently, the ties to 9/11 and global terrorism were revisited when two terrorists planted homemade bombs at the finish line of the 2013 Boston Marathon, causing death and mayhem at one of the nation's most revered sporting events. The subsequent manhunt shut down most of the city and captivated the nation, both reopening and still tending to the wounds of the initial attacks some dozen years earlier.

The range of challenges and serious issues forced the public into a situation in which it is constantly facing action, reaction, and interpretation. The tools for such contemplation include aspects of popular culture, the federal government's maneuvers, and personal contemplation. For example, technology, economics, and innovation combine to produce culture-shifting products, such as the iPod, Wi-Fi hubs, and smartphones. These goods then set in motion a shift in popular culture as these products influence people far beyond their intended functions. In turn, users come to define themselves by them—the kinds of music they download, the movies they watch, and television shows they record via TiVo.

A key aspect of *Gatsby* that links the 1925 novel with the early decades of the twenty-first century is that Fitzgerald's masterwork provides readers with a peek behind the curtain into a world that most people will never actually experience. Yet in making this forthright statement, the corollary is that while people may never comprehend the wealth depicted in *Gatsby* or understand what it means to exist in that echelon, life in contemporary America is built on offering audiences pseudoevents and faux incidents that seem authentic.

In today's cultural landscape, reality television is part of this cycle. The genre allows curious audiences privileged access to other people's lives, essentially peeking inside their medicine cabinets and poking around their daily being. Yet reality television is not as frivolous as many critics like to argue. Scholar Leigh Edwards explains, "Rather than mere sensationalism, the genre is making substantive arguments at the heart of contemporary social issues, whether that is how media shapes people's everyday lives or how the family unit is still central to American social life."[4] These kinds of critical issues are at the core of television programming and have been across the medium's history.

One may view the link between *Gatsby* and reality TV as a stretch, but consider another outcome of the latter—creating a new social class of pseudocelebrities. This was an important undercurrent in Fitzgerald's work and is imperative in understanding how money and consumer culture merge. The outcome that Fitzgerald examined created an expanded gene pool of celebrities and faux fame, like Myrtle's sister Catherine, a young woman who is not wealthy but is able to travel to Europe and find her way to Gatsby's parties once a month.

As if Fitzgerald possessed a crystal ball, he nailed the look and feel of celebrity, particularly when a person could achieve it without actually doing anything expressly noteworthy. In the novel, Nick lists a number of "names" that came to Gatsby's parties, all celebrated people by the fact that he is cataloging them, but many would certainly be regarded as infamous or notorious. There are also the numerous "young Englishmen" who attend in search of wealthy American heiresses, "all talking in low earnest voices to solid and prosperous Americans . . . agonizingly aware of the easy money in the vicinity and convinced that it was theirs for a few words in the right key."[5] There are two important things taking place in this section: first, Fitzgerald is commenting on wealth and celebrity in his era; second, Nick, as author of the book about Gatsby, provides a portrait of the rich that is both informative and scattered, demonstrating the senselessness of how these people are emulated and placed on society's pedestal.

From his experiences living in Great Neck, Long Island, and among many wealthy friends and acquaintances, Fitzgerald had all the background information he needed to absolutely skewer the rich. But he did so with such a deft stroke that generations of misinformed readers regard the author as a sycophant to that class. Like us, the glance into their lives intrigued him, but he did not hold them up on a pedestal. Literary critic Clive James notes Fitzgerald's ability to get this picture right, saying that *Gatsby* "is a cautionary tale, but the tale is about us more than about him."[6] His portrait of Tom Buchanan is an obvious example of his feelings about America's moneyed aristocracy.

WHEN THE GREEN LIGHT IS MONEY

Writing in late 2002, *New York Times* columnist and Princeton professor Paul Krugman railed against the vast income gap that existed between the rich and everyone else in early twenty-first-century America. One might have expected that the dot-com meltdown that threw the nation's coasts into a panic would have leveled this phenomenon a bit, but instead Krugman focuses directly on the disparity.

First, he took a jab at Jack Welch, the then-newly divorced former General Electric chief executive. Welch's divorce proceedings bared to the world the golden parachute the corporation gave its old leader (in the 1980s nicknamed "Neutron Jack" for his propensity for mass firings). Welch's perks included lifetime use of a Manhattan apartment, use of corporate jets, and other luxuries. As Krugman correctly pointed out, though, these benefits amounted to chump change for Welch, whose final year at the top resulted in a $123 million payday.[7]

More or less providing the intellectual rationale for the Occupy Wall Street movement that would erupt a decade later, Krugman cited Congressional Budget Office (CBO) studies that revealed that the after-tax incomes of the top 1 percent of the wealth ladder experienced a 157 percent gain between 1979 and 1997. These figures contrast to about a 10 percent increase in the average annual salary (adjusted for inflation) over approximately the same time frame. While Bill Gates and the few at the very top got more Bill Gates-y, the rest of the nation wallowed. According to Krugman, the nation returned to *Gatsby* days: "After 30 years in which the income shares of the top 10 percent of taxpayers, the top 1 percent and so on were far below their levels in the 1920s, all are very nearly back where they were."[8]

The challenge in drawing comparisons between the characters in Fitzgerald's novel and the exorbitant pay drawn by CEOs is that Jay Gatsby benefited from overt criminal activities and Tom's wealth came from inheritance. Although it is implied that the latter carries on some business activities, the reader can only infer the depth of his knowledge (for example, he knows the bond business well enough to know that Nick's firm is not one of the main players). A swindler or a megarich squire, however, could appreciate the scam modern-day corporate bosses orchestrated, which Krugman outlined as filling the board of trustees with toadies, friends, and lackeys who ultimately determined salary, perks, and how stock options were divvied.

Rather than the "invisible hand of the market," Krugman explains, these CEOs gained their largesse via "the invisible handshake in the boardroom." After decades of forcing the idea that executives somehow deserved these gargantuan salaries, the notion finally stuck in the public's mind. The little guy—also buying into the sanctity of the market—needed to believe that a corporate demigod could push their investments through the roof.[9]

Even the global recession initiated by the seedy mixture of real estate loan arbitrage and big-bank malfeasance seems to have not slowed down the vicious capitalism that rocks the nation. In these times, *Gatsby* stands as a beacon for understanding what price we pay for ruthless power grabs and the economic devastation of a winner-takes-all mentality.

Ironically, I write this on a day in which one of the two biggest news stories is a devastating tornado 1.3 miles wide with two-hundred-mile-per-hour winds that ripped through Moore, Oklahoma, a suburb of Oklahoma City. The rampage leveled the entire town, killing dozens and causing an estimated $2 billion in damages. At the same time, the media is having a field day covering Apple chief executive Tim Cook's appearance before a U.S. Senate subcommittee to discuss the methods the company employed to divert funds offshore to avoid paying U.S. taxes. What the subcommittee revealed is that from 2009 to 2012, Apple used tax loopholes to circumvent taxes on $44 billion, including three subsidiaries in Ireland that have no official residency anywhere.[10]

While *Gatsby* can do nothing to explain away a natural disaster like the killer tornado in Oklahoma or the countless calamities that take place, Fitzgerald's novel can provide a guiding light as we mull over the lengths corporations and individuals will go to bilk and deceive in their own interests. From this perspective, there is value in the generic ways that the term "Gatsby" has been deployed and transformed within a meta-*Gatsby* culture. One might hope that in an increasingly corrupt environment that using "Gatsby" terminology could serve as a rallying point. The ubiquity of these terms, then, might energize activists and other parties to rise up against this kind of corporate misconduct.

GATSBY IN A FLAT WORLD

Globalization is not a new term. Over many decades, various economic powers have emerged at different times to rival the United States. However, the interconnectedness of twenty-first-century society shows a cohesion among global trading partners that is unprecedented. While one might assume that the interdependence would strengthen the entire structure, there is a competing notion that any small fissure could cause the whole thing to fall apart. The simple fact that frequent national and regional crises call the system into question demonstrates its strength and fragility simultaneously.

Scholars Krishnamurthy Sriramesh and Dejan Verič refer to this new era as a "multipolar world" in which "different countries and different cultures have begun to compete more or less peacefully on the global stage." While the Cold War superpowers still have enormous power based on the existence of nuclear weaponry, others are exerting economic might. The entire world has marveled at China's rise to dominance, which is well documented and seemingly unprecedented, yet other nations also seem poised to develop into economic powerhouses. [11]

America remains the center of world finance, but its dependence on foreign nations to finance its growing national debt, Middle Eastern oil reserves, and Chinese imports reveals the shaky nature of that position. *New York Times* columnist Thomas L. Friedman coined the phrase "the world is flat" to describe the consequences of globalization on the United States in his 2005 best-seller The *World Is Flat: A Brief History of the Twenty-First Century.*

After visiting India, Friedman astutely realized that globalization provided global nations a level playing field economically and removed many barriers to foreign trade that previously existed. For example, one of Friedman's examples is the outsourcing trend occurring in corporate America. Companies sent jobs to overseas knowledge centers, which saved them money, instead of offering the same services using American employees. Companies like Dell, Microsoft, Citigroup, and many others outsourced IT and customer service functions to India, China, and other Far Eastern nations.

Despite the backlash against such practices, outsourcing provided a greater return on investment. The International Association of Outsourcing Professionals estimated that American companies spent $4.2 trillion on outsourcing in 2006, up from $3.1 trillion just three years earlier. Obviously, with trillions of dollars being put into outsourcing the trend is not going to stop. Rather, the question for U.S. corporations is how to best use it strategically. For example, some organizations are moving away from India, the traditional power base in the field, to places such as Russia, the Philippines, and Mexico. Any nation with a workforce strong in software and engineering and English-language skills is a potential hotbed for outsourcing. [12]

While the business world flattens the distance between nations economically, American culture virtually obliterates any gap. For instance, one of the interesting tangential side effects of the 2013 *Gatsby* film is that it serves as a kind of new introduction of the novel and its time to the rest of the world. The global intrigue regarding 1920s America, for example, found a home in fashion-crazed China, where the novel is known as *The Amazing Gai-Ci-Bi*. Writing for the *New Yorker*, Evan Osnos quotes a men's dress shirt advertisement for the Chinese label Masa Maso that speaks to the power of the character's shirts, reading, "It's true: Put on a flower-print shirt, and it will show you the door to a whole new world." [13]

Jing Daily, which bills itself as the outlet for "the business of luxury & culture in China," reports on the Chinese version of *Vogue* magazine, which spotlights a *Gatsby*-like photo spread featuring Prada, Tiffany, and the Wangfujing luxury shopping district. The shoot stars Chinese supermodels Du Juan and Sui He "in *Gatsby*-inspired 1920s attire as they pose in decidedly modern locations of Beijing." While the response to the American Jazz Age fashions was limited because the film had not yet opened in mainland China or made its way there via the black market, many Chinese fashion bloggers and commentators gushed over the style. [14]

The infusion of *Gatsby*-themed fashion and other cultural inroads expands the idea of meta-*Gatsby* globally. For example, Osnos claims that the novel/movie's themes of "self-invention and stupendous wealth, of hidden pasts and imagined futures—could hardly find a more fitting audience than in China in the opening years of the twenty-first century." Moreover, he reports, many people in China have read *Gatsby* and are tracking its themes, basically comparing and contrasting the ideas Fitzgerald concentrates on and what these notions mean for them in modern China. [15] The mind boggles at what an inroad into China might portend for that nation, which is the economic engine of the world. The idea that meta-*Gatsby* could become an analytical tool across the globe is a stunning acknowledgment of the timelessness of the novel and a case study in cultural diplomacy.

GATSBY AND POPULAR CULTURE

The Great Gatsby is an important piece of Americana. Over the last six decades it has moved from forgotten time stamp to legendary status. Since teachers in high schools and colleges use the book so frequently, and it stands as one of the few works of literature that nearly everyone is at least acquainted with in text or film form, its influence is broad and important as a part of popular culture. The myriad of interpretations and ideas *Gatsby* represents shows its utility. For example, novelist Jennifer Egan explains that the novel "tells a story of a reinvention and a transformation. It captures a strong part of what I think of as American identity: You can be anyone that you want here, though it doesn't always work out."[16]

Ideas about identity and the myriad of topics related to it comprise much of American popular culture. The significance of culture on the nation is in the way it connects people. The ubiquity of the web and around-the-clock access via handheld devices makes this an era of hyper-popular culture in which people not only expect, but demand, continual entrée to mass communications. People also need tools to help them codify and comprehend all the streaming blips and beeps blasting through their lives.

Technological innovation and our enslavement to it transforms the way we think about culture, not as a kind of thing, as most definitions attempt to explain, like the antithesis of high art or culture, but as the link that exists in the impulses that draw members of the global community to a person, thing, topic, or issue that arises out of the juncture of mass communications, technology, political systems, and economic institutions. In other words, I am proposing that we view popular culture not as an object, say, Andy Warhol's famous Campbell's Soup can painting, but as the interface itself that draws viewers to or repels them from that artwork.

Examining Warhol's piece, it is not that a person says, "Wow, that is popular culture." Instead, it is the confluence of seeing the image; interacting with it based on one's own life experiences; adding context, history, experience, and personality; and then creating a new meaning of it personally that defines popular culture. In other words, popular culture is more than what people like or enjoy in the large scheme of entertainment. Popular culture is our national dialogue via cultural engagement.

Scholar Ray B. Browne once defined popular culture, saying, "It is the everyday world around us: the mass media, entertainments, diversions, heroes, icons, rituals, psychology, religion—our total life picture."[17] My redefinition asks that we acknowledge that it is more than just the world around us; it also includes the exchange between a popular culture object and a person's assimilation of the thing—all the thoughts, emotions, and manners in which one consumes it. This meaning of popular culture exists in absorption and consumption rather than in attempting to define a tangible object as low-, high-, or middlebrow on a fabricated scale of hierarchies. In this respect, "popular culture" should be seen as a verb, not a noun, the total interaction with a topic and the new synthesis or creation that occurs as a result of that fusion.

Returning to the notion of popular culture as a connector between people, it is no wonder then that film and television play a central role. These mass communications channels define and encompass our national dialogue. Television and film are the great equalizers—essentially providing Americans with basic talking points across race, political ties, gender differences, or any other demographic features that usually separate them. The narratives, regardless of the reason they attract or repel us, give context and a way of interpreting society and culture. As millions of Americans interact with mass media, whether watching the same movies and television shows or listening to radio programs, a common language develops that opens new lines of communication.

The downside, however, is that the fascination with popular culture diverts attention from important challenges the nation confronts. In this light, popular culture serves as a kind of placebo. The obsessive, loving nature of cult objects, for example, intensifies this diversion critique of popular culture because the focus on a specific cult influence distracts people and, at the same time, enables them to feel good about the world without really forcing them to directly confront critical issues.

The beauty and value of popular culture is its ability to let people explore the ideas, topics, people, and influences that matter to them most. This exercise actually forces people to engage in higher-order critical-thinking skills involved in the formation of new ideas and impulses. As we wrestle with our own thoughts, dreams, and aspirations through popular culture exploration, we obtain, strengthen, and evolve our personal worldviews or core guiding ideologies.

I believe that popular culture scholars have a critical impact by helping the public better understand the necessity of humanities-based education and the broader education system, particularly K–12 battles over standardized testing, such as the ravages of No Child Left Behind. Scholar Brendan Riley addresses how academics might play a more critical role in helping the public engage in the education system. He explains:

> The conversation about education has become very vocational in the last twenty years, with students and the public seeing college as job-training rather than person-training. But the modern economy requires flexible workers; people who can problem solve, work with others in complex ways, and engage difficult questions creatively. All of these things arise from the work we do in the Humanities, we just need to remind people of that—and public scholarship is just the way to do it. As the scholars most directly poised to bridge the town/gown divide (because we write about things people care about), we should be on the front lines of the battle over education in the twenty first century. [18]

Scholar Brian Cogan looks at the big picture, saying, "We study the 'meaning making' process, how people use popular culture artifacts to give themselves hopes, dreams, aspirations and ethical systems, but people don't get this easily, or the importance of Elvis, as an example, in people's lives." Cogan, however, points to the power of popular culture studies, concluding, "I like to think of us as cultural barometers, we are trying a very difficult type of analysis, looking at mostly the current mediated ecosystem and asking questions about it, not as cheerleaders or naysayers, but asking objective questions about the ideas, stories, and artifacts that define not just individuals, but culture as well." [19]

The many manifestations of *Gatsby* across popular culture demonstrate what Cogan emphasizes as the central narratives that audiences use to make sense of the world around them and that scholars employ in analyzing culture as a whole. An example of *Gatsby*'s influence is witnessed on the hit Showtime cable television series *Californication*, created by Tom Kapinos, which centers on Hank Moody (played by David Duchovny), a self-absorbed writer who attempts to drink and bed his way through contemporary Los Angeles while still hanging on to the love of his former wife and teen daughter.

When the then-new television series *Californication* debuted on August 13, 2007, Duchovny had just turned forty-seven years old. In comparison, novelist Fitzgerald never made it to that age. In 1940 he succumbed to heart failure at just forty-four years old in the Hollywood apartment of his girlfriend, gossip columnist Sheilah Graham. By all accounts, after decades of alcohol abuse and stress brought on by family and financial problems, Fitzgerald's body gave out.

In season two of *Californication*, the entire premise of the run is a loose adaptation of *Gatsby*. Hank plays the role of a debauched and drunken Nick Carraway, while famous record producer Lew Ashby is a modern-day Jay Gatsby (played by the wonderful character actor Callum Keith Rennie). Unlike Fitzgerald, the boozing, drug-taking, womanizing Moody does not worry about the consequences of his actions on his body. Fictional characters in viable series seem to never die or even fade away.

The protagonists initially meet in a stunning Laurel Canyon mansion with so many rooms that one could get lost inside, but Hank does not know who Ashby is. Hank, half-naked and completely loaded, bumps into him without knowing that it is Ashby's party or mansion, just like Nick's first meeting with Gatsby. Other aspects of the mansion and the circumstances are similar to *Gatsby*.

Ashby, a record mogul, later hires Hank to write his biography. Hank initially turns down the offer because he does not want to put out a hack job about Ashby's wealth. Hank agrees only after the producer opens up to him about his first, lost love. After listing his many successes, Ashby quietly reflects, "All I want is her." As a result, Hank claims that Ashby's biography has "a theme" and accepts the job. I do not want to spoil the plot, but the rest of the season continued in its *Gatsby*-like mode, so its ending should not surprise anyone.

Importantly, the use of *Gatsby* had consequences for the executives in charge of the series. In only its second season, *Californication* needed to connect to an audience to secure its place in Showtime's lineup. Therefore, employing the *Gatsby* trope served as a way to connect the show to the classic novel, more or less equating Hank to Fitzgerald and the show to an updated version of the Great American Novel. Its creators attempted to link the public's general understanding of global celebrity across generations, as well as connect to the notion of lost love that *Gatsby* centered on.

While *Californication*'s detractors cannot move past the drinking, nudity, and general debauchery of the show, Hank's role as a kind of fallen Nick Carraway was little more salacious than Fitzgerald's novel was for its age. For example, in the TV series the two main characters have their first real conversation in a jail cell: Hank arrested for assaulting a police officer and Lew for accusations of domestic abuse. We often forget, though, that in Fitzgerald's day, the mayhem and orgy-like festivities in the love nest Tom and Myrtle rent seemed just as lewd and sensational.

Californication creator/writer Tom Kapinos claims that he attempted to make Hank Moody "the perfect romantic antihero."[20] Jay Gatsby, too, is one of popular culture's most infamous antiheroes. In this sense, Hank falls in line with the current crop of television antiheroes, ranging from loveable serial killer Dexter Morgan on Showtime's *Dexter* to *Mad Men*'s Don Draper. The small screen is filled with characters audiences love to hate, particularly when one adds in the infinite number of antiheroes on reality television programming. One might go so far as to call this the age of the antihero.

Hank fits the mold. His list of illegal, immoral, and decadent behaviors sends critics of *Californication* into a rage. One doubts if there is a sexual position or situation that has not been attempted or discussed over its run. Certainly, part of Hank's charm is boosted by the intelligence, wit, and charisma of Duchovny. His wry smile keeps the audience on Hank's side. Furthermore, in an odd twist, Duchovny himself went into treatment for sex addiction one month prior to the second-season debut, which caused him to split with his wife, actress Tea Leoni. Yet, despite the similarities between the on-screen Hank and the offscreen Duchovny, audiences did not turn on him or stop watching the show. Similarly, readers of Fitzgerald's novel and the millions who have seen one of the several film adaptations forgive Jay Gatsby, despite his illegal and immoral actions.

Strangely, Hank revels in being principled in an odd, twenty-first-century definition of the word, despite his own often immoral or just plain stupid behavior. Hank speaks the truth as he sees it without the filter that most real people possess, a kind of go-for-broke mentality that audiences enjoy. One television critic explains, "He may be sexually loose, but

Hank is not unprincipled, which helps keep the character from becoming reprehensible."[21]

In this way, Moody has quite a bit in common with Jon Hamm's character Don Draper on *Mad Men*. Audiences enjoy the voyeuristic peek into the life of a character that acts with little or no reproach, except the agony that they sometimes exude based on their own actions. In the second season, *Californication* is direct in equating Hank as a kind of mix between Nick as storyteller and Fitzgerald as artist—two lives audiences have a great deal of insider information about—with Ashby saying to Hank about the latter's first, famous novel: "*God Hates Us All*, that was your *Gatsby*."

While Hank Moody is patterned after Fitzgerald, he is not a stand-in for him. Some sources claim that the famed poet Charles Bukowski served as the model (Bukowski's nickname was Hank), but one could speculate that Kapinos had a stylized version of Fitzgerald in mind, perhaps the young, iconic Fitzgerald who got drunk and was the life of the party who is transported to Los Angeles at the height of his fame, not at the end of a gin-soaked life.

Hank is definitely in line with the kind of lifestyle Fitzgerald once lived. Duchovny told a reporter, "A friend said this is the guy you don't want in your house, but you're going to invite [him] to the party and you know something is going to happen." He explained, "That's really the magic trick of the show. . . . Somehow he gets punished just enough in life, but we don't want to punish him too much."[22] Reading through Fitzgerald's letters and reminisces by people who knew him at the height of his fame, both he and wife Zelda had that "life of the party" mentality—mercurial, spontaneous, and unpredictable.

The major difference is that Hank's hard-core partying does not seem to take any real toll on his body, whereas the lifestyle of the 1920s and 1930s turned Fitzgerald old beyond his years. Fitzgerald's poor health from 1935 to 1937 had dire consequences. He could not physically write, which compounded his writer's block and put him further behind financially. Nearly destitute and living under the umbrella of constant pain, Fitzgerald snapped, declaring in early 1937 to his agent, Harold Ober, "My biggest loss is confidence."[23] So far, after six seasons of decadence, Hank has yet to pay for his sins. I guess that's the benefit of being a fictional character and not a fiction writer.

***

Literary critic Clive James represents many commentators when he calls *Gatsby* "one of the prophetic books of the twentieth century."[24] Fitzgerald's little gem fulfills many needs for today's readers, from those who encounter it as a part of the high school or college curriculum or others who want to understand many of the thematic issues at the heart of American culture. The success of the 2013 film (eclipsing the magical $100 million mark in its second week in broad release) adds to the overall notion that *Gatsby* is and will remain essential.

Fitzgerald hemmed and hawed over the title of the book. He never really settled on it, and then later blamed the title in part for the book's mediocre sales. However, the title *The Great Gatsby* speaks to the book's enduring importance, even in the twenty-first century. Frankly, labeling the title character "great," then having him murdered at the end, obliges the reader to ponder Fitzgerald's account of his greatness and its broader implication. The engagement between the author, reader, and the ideas in the text sets up a kind of forced critical thinking. The reader cannot answer questions about the legitimacy of the "great" label without taking into account many disparate themes at the novel's core.

The title also contains a kind of hope that attracts readers and stimulates their curiosity, even in an era like ours of dark economic scenes and global uncertainty about the future. An aura of mystery exists in the gap between Jay Gatsby's rise from nothing to vast wealth, the vision he hopes to fulfill, and his ultimate death that enables one to continue believing in the American Dream, even though Gatsby paid the price for his conviction.

In this sense, one can read the novel as support for the rags-to-riches story and the American Dream, particularly if the emphasis is on the title character's rise to wealth and the lavish parties thrown as a lure to capture Daisy's heart. One could argue that reading *Gatsby* as a support for these ideas misinterprets Fitzgerald's intentions, thus making the novel similar to Hollywood's attempts at commoditizing both the American Dream and optimism, despite the difficulties audiences face in any given era. Yet there is a "get mine" attitude at the heart of the American Dream that is essential in understanding its modern meaning. Many people would gladly trade health or long life for a shot at fame and riches. Writer Philip Norman explains, "Gatsby is also a very modern figment of the consumer society and its tawdry values, with his vast, yellow, open-topped limousine and the gorgeous shirts he pulls out of his wardrobe in his attempts to impress Daisy. He was into 'bling,' too, 80 years ahead of the pack."[25] The old adage "He who dies with the most toys wins" is perfect in conceptualizing the consumerism that Fitzgerald critiqued and which is rampant today.

Fitzgerald's ending sermon about continually working against the past, full of hope for a better future is a kind of call for a different vision of America, and more optimistic. One could read this as Fitzgerald championing morality, ethics, and hard work as traits that set people apart. These qualities then define our national dreams and lead to a more truly democratic vision. It is hope—in Fitzgerald's 1920s and our own twenty-first century—that drives us to reach further and trek faster toward our dreams, the goal just tickling against our feverish fingers as we push on, believing that one day our goals will be achieved.

Part III

Gatsby and the Shifting American Dream

7

THE AMERICAN DREAM

*I look out at it—and I think it is the most beautiful history in the world.
. . . It is the history of all aspiration—not just the American dream but
the human dream and if I came at the end of it that too is a place in the
line of pioneers.*—F. Scott Fitzgerald, *Notebooks*, n.d.

Rather than "old sport," Alabama congressman Frank W. Boykin
(1885–1969) called nearly everyone he met "cousin" or "pardner" in a
thick, Southern drawl. He became famous around the country, though, by
singing, repeating, and more or less branding the phrase "Everything's
Made for Love," the title of a hit song by 1920s crooner Gene Austin, at
one time the best-selling recording artist in history. Boykin, however,
used it as a greeting, a way to draw attention to himself—a short, hulking
(upward of 250 pounds), flamboyant, and boisterous character—the kind
of insider that used to haunt the nation's capital. Reportedly, when President Franklin D. Roosevelt first met Boykin in the Oval Office, he
shouted the catchphrase out to him, bringing a round of laughter from
everyone who witnessed the scene.

By all accounts, Boykin was no statesman during his twenty-eight-
year career in Washington, but he pulled extensive press coverage for the
lavish parties he threw for the nation's elite on his hundred-thousand-acre
hunting compound in Choctaw County in his home state. Like the most
famous boys club at the time, Washington insiders were shuttled in and
out of southwestern Alabama to hunt deer, wild boar, and other game on
the preserve. His fame grew so extensive that in 1965 *Time* magazine
labeled him a "Dixie Gatsby" for his high-priced, yet down-home, galas. [1]

49, for example, Boykin threw a party for powerhouse Speaker ouse Sam Rayburn from the larger-than-life state of Texas at a Washington. More than nine hundred guests showed up for the fete, which featured a menu of exotic game ranging from Montana elk to bear meat and antelope. Boykin, who made millions of dollars by gobbling up land, timber, and mineral rights in Alabama, picked up the tab, estimated at $16,000 (about $150,000 in 2012 dollars).[2]

Closer to home, on his expansive hunting preserve, Boykin's ostentatious courting of the nation's power elite took place to store up and gather favors that he might need later, whether these were for his Mobile, Alabama, congressional district or one of his business deals. While most of his constituents seemed to look the other way regarding Boykin's mixture of personal business with congressional work, critics blasted him for supposed illegalities. Late in his career, Boykin finally got pinched for using his power as a legislator to lobby for a business partner. The 1963 trial ended in Boykin's conviction, along with his colleague, but the judge basically slapped him on the wrist, fining the multimillionaire a paltry $40,000 and sparing him prison time based on his age and health concerns. Interviewed after the jury sealed his fate, Boykin kept to his old mantra: everything's made for love.[3]

In the late 1950s, still at the peak of his influence, Boykin furnished his office suite with exotic memorabilia, ranging from mounted deer heads to pistols owned by famed outlaw Jesse James. Another piece, however, always drew a crooked eyebrow—a mummified whale penis. For Boykin, these curiosities gave visitors and him something to talk about, perfect for a congressman who ran his office from the front door, like some kind of exalted Walmart greeter of today, ever ready with a wink and big smile.[4]

On the surface, Boykin shared almost nothing with Jay Gatsby, particularly in how the Southern legislator used his charisma and gregariousness to his own advantage, particularly when his clout as a national legislator helped line his own pocket. Labeling Boykin the "Dixie Gatsby" and using the notion of *Gatsby* as explanation, however, commentators and journalists demonstrated how the idea of *Gatsby* permeated the national discourse. Ironically, though, their conception of Jay Gatsby boiled down to little more than a stand-in for someone who throws lavish parties, as if the term "Gatsby" merely equates to the notion of extravagance.

From examining the tens of thousands of pages of similar uses across the global mass media from the 1940s to the early 2010s, one sees that this kind of misdirection is more common than not. Unfortunately, what it also reveals is that either people using it in this manner do not understand the novel and its characters well or that it is just an easy example to pull out of one's writing bag of tricks, regardless of its meaning. In other words, *The Great Gatsby* is reduced to a generic group of synonyms to describe just about any person, scheme, or character. Over and over again, one sees "Gatsby" as a substitute for ideas such as "wealthy," "lavish," or "rags to riches." The important question here is what it means for a novel to enter the cultural mind-set of a nation, particularly if that appearance opens the book up to wild, speculative, or even incorrect uses. Time and again, "Gatsby" is used in ways that reduce the novel to some basic dictum or idea that usually oversimplifies what Fitzgerald actually wrote to the point of trivializing his intentions.

For example, the fact that Boykin threw extravagant, expensive parties is hardly the most interesting relation he had to the mythical Gatsby. Looking back even further into his career shows that Boykin's rise from nothing to immense wealth through some highly nefarious methods mirror Gatsby's, though Boykin did not have an aristocratic beauty as his motivating force. Like so many people in American history who achieve rags-to-riches fame, the congressman simply wanted the riches that often accompany such journeys. From my perspective, an examination of Boykin's early life exhibits the way the American Dream may unfold in reality, thus providing Fitzgerald's vision with a real-world case study.

More directly concurrent with Gatsby or a Gatsby-esque rise to power, a Prohibition raid in Mobile in late 1923 found Boykin (then a young, budding entrepreneur) and many of the city's most prominent leaders arrested, including the county sheriff, city police chief, and many top business leaders. Boykin, though not a leader among the city's throngs of alcohol racketeers, used his access to powerbrokers in Washington, D.C., to ensure that local whiskey sellers would not get busted. [5]

Although Boykin got off on a technicality in one trial, another was lined up to go after him directly for outright bootlegging. When the jury acquitted Boykin and his codefendants, another trial began the very next day, accusing him of bribing a federal agent. The third time turned out to be a charm for Prohibition officials when the jury found him guilty. The initial sentence gave Boykin two years in the state penitentiary, but the judge let him post bond. A year later, Boykin's attorneys finagled the indictment, which got overturned. Boykin claimed that he had been framed, but in the end he never spent a night in prison.[6]

Perhaps journalists writing in the pre-Internet days did not have access to information about Boykin's racketeering past; he certainly did not talk about it as he rose in both wealth and fame. However, that link to Gatsby would have made for a much more interesting story and connection to the novel character. Returning to Boykin's motto—everything's made for love—maybe he himself would have found the similarity ironic based on a stanza Gene Austin sang:

> What do men slave for
> What do they save for
> And when cupid calls
> Why do we go and spend all of our dough
> To see Niagra Falls . . .

Austin seemed to get the reason why Gatsby would hold out for the green light at the distant shore. For Gatsby, everything was made of love. A more appropriate motto for Boykin might have been "everything's done for money." Using Gatsby as a term in describing Boykin served, therefore, as a bastardization of the ideas contained in Fitzgerald's work. Even here, though, it is a slippery slope. Should we appreciate the attempt or condemn the swing and miss?

***

As the American Dream unfolds in the twenty-first century, one might simply wonder: Is the idea an illusion or a reality?

Can you touch it, roll it around in your hands, and feel its weight? Is the American Dream the car you drive or the feeling of the cold brick on your palm when you open the front door of your house? Is it you, your job, or where your children go to college? Maybe it is all the tangible objects around you . . . maybe it is none.

Often, perspective depends on where one believes one sits in the food chain. But even more revealing, a person's belief in the American Dream is probably hitched closer to what one *thinks* one can achieve or what the future holds for oneself and one's family. Adding weight to this understanding is that one's own individual interpretation of the idea is more or less sacrosanct. In other words, *my* American Dream is mine and by its very definition as mine is appropriate. In exchange for you acknowledging my notion of my American Dream, I will in turn accept yours.

Thinking about all this for a moment, it becomes clear that the American Dream remains a moving target and represents many different visions of what makes for an ideal life. Writer and consultant Lawrence R. Samuel bluntly proclaims that the American Dream "is the guiding mythology of the most powerful civilization in history."[7] The simple fact of the matter, he explains, is that it is a mythology, tightly wrapped up with the many other beliefs and principles that serve to create American culture. The mutability of the idea provides its power, because it can be almost anything to anyone who chooses to employ it as a driving narrative in his or her life.

Advertisers and marketing agencies use the shifting ideas at the heart of the American Dream to sell goods and services by appealing to the cultural tenets of consumers. For instance, Southwest Airlines dumped its quirky low-fare image in March 2013 and moved upscale with messages equating the American Dream with hard work. Its new TV commercials featured images of a baby crawling down a hallway, a young ballerina, a woman walking into a boardroom, and other nontraditional airline imagery mixed in with more typical shots of planes, ground crew, and cabins to underscore the tag: "The American Dream just doesn't happen. It's something you have to work for." Rather than tout its heritage as one of the world's great discount fare carriers, the corporation changed tactics to emphasize its new status as the nation's largest domestic airline.[8] While some critics of the new focus may be left shaking their heads at such a dramatic move, marketers know that the broader appeal to the American Dream carries predetermined messages and symbols that can elevate a brand almost immediately.

Arthur Mizener, one of the nation's greatest literary critics, sees Fitzgerald's conception of the American Dream clearly illustrated in the novel, concluding:

> Americans are no doubt proud of their wealth. . . . But they are seldom content with a merely material life; that kind of life seems to them, as Gatsby's life seemed to him after he lost faith in Daisy, material without being real. Only when it is animated by an ideal purpose does it seem real to them . . . that dream is something possessed by each of us individually.[9]

)oints to the challenge of writing about the concept because of
...ent duality. Yet Gatsby's tragic commitment to his American
Dream is so wrapped in how it is fulfilled via Daisy's that he cannot see
her for what she has become. He hints that it is as base as it seems when
he talks of her voice being filled with money, but even then, he longs to
relive the past, essentially starting over again with her or picking up from
years earlier. As such, his desire to marry Daisy on the steps of her
parents' home in Louisville after she leaves Tom is ludicrous and almost
laughable. Though money is the key in keeping Daisy and Tom together,
their standing among the nation's moneyed aristocracy is the real glue.
No matter how much money Gatsby makes, he cannot buy into the peer-
age.

This chapter examines how Fitzgerald's novel has helped us (and
continues to assist us) as we assess the American Dream. Evaluating the
Boykin example above, the label "Dixie Gatsby" does little to really
elucidate the novel, yet the term has meaning, even if it is misguided. In
other eras, *Gatsby* is linked with different ideas that interrogate the meaning of the American Dream, particularly when it is linked to notions of a
person's rags-to-riches march up the economic ladder.

Again, however, we should think about how these shortcut uses of the
book help or hinder us as reflective individuals exhibiting our critical-
thinking skills. Could these generic applications of *Gatsby* just be a way
to outsource our thinking, a kind of mental white noise or filler to get us
from point A to point B in an article or essay? There is no doubt that
Gatsby and the American Dream are deeply connected, yet we must
consider how the two converge to help us understand this critical concept.

THE DREAM LIVES ON

The American Dream is a unifying national belief (some might even
argue that it is now a global ideal), yet at the same time it is both highly
individualized and extremely difficult to define. While many people today equate the concept with a singular achievement, goal reached, or
acquisition, others view it as a more encompassing idea of what it is to
live a good, prosperous, or worthy life. As a result, achieving the
American Dream can be as broad as getting into medical school or owning a new home. Over time, the idea developed into a central tenet of

what it means to be an American, thus establishing its place in the collective popular culture as both a thing to be achieved and model for living one's life.

What seems nearly universal when considering the American Dream is that the pursuit is about freedom—the belief that individuals have the right to chase it, particularly if the primary obstacles are based on gender, race, religious views, or other cultural differences. Yet, in modern society, it seems that some dreams are privileged above others, especially if the result vaults the pursuer into the realm of celebrity. As such, young people are applauded for spending hundreds or thousands of hours playing basketball, kicking around on the soccer field, or working out physically in hopes of achieving a one-in-a-million chance at athletic stardom.

In Fitzgerald's time and ever since, the American Dream has been a critical component of our cultural heritage. As the American Dream became more deeply entwined within popular culture, the idea fostered a sense of hope and renewal that enabled people to keep moving forward during the dark days of warfare, economic collapse, and personal challenges. This idea itself is wholly American—we continually analyze the past to derive lessons, while at the same time yearning to see into the future for glimpses of what is blurrily developing on the next horizon.

Employing the notion of the American Dream, the nation's citizens found a way to interpret themselves, those around them, and the world as a whole. We trumpeted our national vision, even when we did not live up to its ideals. Sometimes, this willingness toward self-delusion meant that people turned away from difficult societal challenges, instead finding solace in the latest film, radio program, or four-color advertisement for a flashy car. People used popular culture and the American Dream to serve their needs, whether to ignore problems or unify us in a common battle against such evils. Either way, the American Dream served as a force for reinterpreting the nation from within. Each person, it seemed, had the choice to use it as a way to assess society or mask reality in favor of a Hollywood dream version of life that ended with sunshine and rainbows. Regardless, the American Dream enabled these choices on a moment-by-moment scale.

The Great Gatsby resides amid this fog of ambiguity, because Fitzgerald wrapped the novel in so many ideas that almost any way a person might define the American Dream, he or she could uncover a means of examining it through the book. Scholar Anthony Larson sees fiction "as a vealing the truth about a world around us; the relationship ction and reality is reversed so that it is fiction which serves to erstand and read reality." From this perspective, he says, "*Gats-by* is read as a moral lesson on the excesses and failures of a certain America and—perhaps—the American dream itself."[10] It is not in the excesses of Gatsby or Tom Buchanan that Fitzgerald fixes the failure of the American Dream in Larson's view. Rather, it is in the vast wasteland of George Wilson and the valley of ashes. Here, "the reader is quick to recognize the emptiness holding all of this up, the moral price paid by America for its capitalist excess."[11]

CELEBRITY AS AN ELIXIR

The American Dream also resides within complicated ideas about celebrity, which Fitzgerald certainly understood. He used the book as a pointed commentary on the celebrity status afforded the movie stars, Broadway singers and dancers, and film executives that populated Gatsby's parties. These newly rich partygoers, whether from West Egg or on a jaunt in from the city, were different from the well-heeled East Eggers; the latter might be famous based on a family name, but not for being celebrities, like their counterparts who had to work for their wealth. Capitalism allowed for some small percentage of people to rise in economic rank, but the system had little influence on social and cultural standards.

Today, certainly on a grander scale than in Fitzgerald's era because of the rise of reality television and its offshoots, the nation fixates on celebrity and its relation to the American Dream. The rise from nowhere to icon is a central narrative across mass media. For example, few would find fault with a would-be teen beauty leaving her family and small town behind and heading to Hollywood or Broadway. This is a well-worn path for potential film and television stars. The idea of the rural farm girl heading to Los Angeles or New York City to find success has developed into a central trope in popular culture narratives.

People view the chance to become the next big thing as alluring and worth the risk. Later, if one overcomes the odds and achieves stardom, the struggle reinforces the idea that this kind of American Dream is possible. In this respect, the American Dream is a fantasy built on fame and the wealth that accompanies such a life. Moreover, it is a version of the dream that millions of people buy into, perhaps thinking that with the right guidance their son or daughter can become the next big thing on an international scale. And, if the trials and tribulations of celebrity-as-celebrity fame-mongers like the Kardashians or the casts on any of the dozens of popular reality TV shows demonstrate, then perhaps the pursuit is attainable.

Historian Jim Cullen discusses the impact Hollywood has had on the American Dream, showing the tight connection between illusion and appeal. People today, he contends, understand that the allure of Hollywood and its extravagant lifestyle is a canard, yet the draw is so strong that many simply cannot fight its magnetism. Cullen sees that the entertainment industry has created a "democracy of desire" that we all realize is false and meant to separate us from our money, but nonetheless holds a "tattered validity."[12]

In other words, consumers are not the dupes that some advertisers and marketers believe. They participate in the exchange because the transaction and its results hold meaning. Cullen explains this duality, saying, "I know the fable of abundance depicted on the page of a magazine is a marketing ploy, but the magic it appropriates has a life that cannot be wholly contained by a slogan, an image, a bill of goods . . . [and] preys on my worst impulses—greed, lust, gluttony." However, he concludes, "Every once in a while there is good to be seized among the goods," which he equates with the works of art that come from production.[13]

Without the link between the American Dream, consumerism, and celebrity there is no Bruce Springsteen, Tom Hanks, or Frank Lloyd Wright. Furthermore, there would be no need for *Gatsby*. Yet since this tie exists and centers ideas at the core of the national psyche, the need for Fitzgerald's masterpiece increases geometrically, particularly as the consumer/celebrity world tightens its grip on everyday life.

MY MANSION IS BIGGER THAN YOURS

On a cloudy, late April day in 2011, massive yellow bulldozers some forty or fifty feet high massed outside the decaying hulk of a once-brilliant mansion. These great beasts would soon chortle and puff, ultimately tearing apart the twenty-thousand-square-foot manor, ripping through its rotting wood, delicate fixtures, and ornate hand-painted wallpaper. In short order the Stanford White–designed 1902 masterpiece, once a grand dame overlooking the Long Island Sound in Sands Point, New York, was gone, leaving only its great dual chimneys standing in the wake.

As sad as it is to destroy outdated or overly expensive homes in the name of progress, the mansions of yesteryear are increasingly rare as developers have learned that they can make more money by breaking up grand estates and selling them off piecemeal. Yet this particular demolition drew global interest. According to local lore and general knowledge, this estate served as Fitzgerald's model for Daisy and Tom Buchanan's place in East Egg, with its enduring green light and manifestation of Tom's old-money heritage that would ultimately lead to Gatsby's demise.

Even Fitzgerald's influence and a longing for history could not save the place, which cost its owner $30 million and some $4,500 a day to maintain. The sagging fortress, with a peeling roof, broken-out windows, and paint ravaged by the sea air simply could not be saved. Instead, after demolition, the lot would be broken up into five individual homesites, each in the $10 million range. Perhaps a bit less *Gatsby*-esque than the original, but certainly still reaching epic proportions, even for that section of tony Long Island.[14]

The passionate outrage over tearing down such a historically significant site paired with the general inability to do much more than mourn the loss of Fitzgerald's muse combined to show how important a building can be in the national psyche. Just as Gatsby's mansion symbolized the fact that he had made it in the fictionalized West Egg, this real-life estate took on a life of its own in its prime, owned by journalist Herbert Bayard Swope, who held the grand parties that included young Fitzgerald and his stunning wife, Zelda. When news spread of the home's demise, news outlets and television stations appeared on the scene to put its history into perspective. The resulting ire revealed the tight bond between the ideas of success and owning a home.[15]

The American Dream is most concrete and most illusory when it comes to the notion of homeownership as its central facet. Fitzgerald sensed this in his own life as he moved in and around wealthy friends and families. He then turned the Gatsby and Buchanan mansions into star characters in *Gatsby*. The houses do more than provide setting; they reflect the era, its people, and, in effect, all ages, since the desperate desire to own a home is central to how we see ourselves and others. Even in the midst of the Great Recession plaguing the world in the late 2000s with millions of homes at or near foreclosure, owning a home remained a central theme.

One needs look no further than what writer Terry Castle calls the "house porn" industry, which runs the gamut from the cable television channel HGTV (Home and Garden Television) to the dozens of "shelter" magazines, such as *dwell*, *House Beautiful*, or *Architectural Digest* to observe how the house and the idea of the home serves as the sun in the universe of the mind for those hoping to achieve the American Dream. [16] At any given time in a twenty-four-hour period, one can turn to HGTV for shows dedicated to buying a first home, buying and flipping a home for profit, redecorating or remodeling the kitchen, or purchasing internationally. Yet, despite the industry that has sprung up to fortify and accentuate homeownership, the tie to that notion and the American Dream is driven by capitalism and corporate forces that gain in the merger of dream and reality.

Given that *Gatsby* is set on Long Island amid the real mansions of the nation's elite in the early decades of the twentieth century, one of the most constant uses of terms associated with the novel comes from the *New York Times* as its reporters keep an eye on the real estate market on the famed Gold Coast. Writing articles on that region and its real estate fortunes allows the *Times* to appeal to local tastes, link to *Gatsby* via the pithy use of quotations from the book, and entice readers across economic classes with glimpses of longed-for mansions and estates.

In early 2010 in an article titled "Gatsby Would Feel at Home," for example, reporter Marcelle S. Fischler takes readers into the pristine, exclusive Kings Point village, where a remarkable twenty-two new homes were under construction, despite the widespread recession and market downturn felt by most of the nation. According to one designer, each of the eight-thousand-square-foot homes built on one acre of land would cost about $4 million to $6 million, while larger homes with more land could run $6 million to $10 million or more. The typical exchange began with a buyer purchasing a lot and home (in the 3,500-square-foot range) that they then planned to have demolished. The new home would then be beefed up to its full potential and thus a mansion was born. Many of the new homes were not only extravagant, but they aped the design of the early decades of the last century, featuring enormous columns, hand-crafted moldings, and limestone facades. [17]

The idea that the Gold Coast existed—then and now—as a playground for the nation's elite serves as an elixir for *New York Times* readers bent on both reveling in the region's past glories and gaining a peek inside the medicine cabinets of the rich. As a result, the uses of terms related to Fitzgerald's novel when referring to real estate and houses has spread around the country. Whether one is on Long Island or in ritzy sections of major American cities, one almost always sees references to "*Gatsby*-style" or "*Gatsby*-esque," particularly when dealing with upscale real estate. Given the over-the-top mansion at the heart of the 2013 film version of *Gatsby*, one can only imagine that the influence on real estate jargon will continue into the foreseeable future.

SELLING THE DREAM

Capitalism necessitates producers and buyers of goods and services. The relatively young United States excelled at creating both sellers and customers: the former via an entrepreneurial culture that rewarded innovation and creation, and the latter through population growth, immigration, and geographic expansion. Based on these broad trends, America quickly developed into a laboratory for consumer culture.

The vicious cycle of production and consumption ensued, propelled by cultural ideas that tied them together. An example is the notion of how acquisition and the American Dream are linked. Status and accumulation grow hand in hand as one marches "up" toward some heady definition of success. Yet, with no real goal in sight, the earnest consumer is urged to acquire more and more. The idea came to roost: one can never have enough. There is always another rung to climb once one buys into the idea that having more than the person next door or down the street equals winning.

Companies, whether small-town grocers or burgeoning corporate entities, yearned for consumers. As a result, business leaders developed innovative methods to encourage wide-scale shopping. Advertising, long in use in European markets, emerged as the most pervasive technique for promoting the budding consumer culture. More importantly, advertising provided a means for conveying information about products and services, as well as establishing a consumer culture that accentuated the good life associated with accumulation.

According to advertising historian Stuart Ewen, business leaders and advertisers worked together to create ads designed to "turn consumption into an inner compulsion."[18] The burgeoning advertising industry, quickly becoming a profession alongside the corporate behemoth, worked to match business thinkers in terms of innovative and clever ways to get people to buy goods. The manufacturers developed new products and the advertisers came up with ways to sell them, a perfect circle that fed off capitalist prowess. Retailers, such as Macy's and Wanamaker's, for example, used scientific methods for tracking sales by department in the early 1900s, which also enabled grading the efficiency of individual salespeople. This effort at quantifying retailing mirrored the kind of efficiency studies being conducted by Frederick Taylor on the assembly lines at Ford and other heavy manufacturing plants.[19]

Certainly, advertisements did not become ubiquitous overnight. From the earliest days of colonial America through the Civil War, most advertising meant placing announcements in newspapers and magazines, or simply handing out ad sheets. As the demand for goods took hold, advertisers devised methods for selling products, and America soon found itself awash in advertising. Photographs from many early twentieth-century cities reveal a culture saturated by ads. Signs peddling goods and services appeared everywhere— on billboards, in store windows, on the outside of buildings, and almost any surface that could be found. Magazine ads and billboards urged consumers to validate their self-worth via the products they purchased. Thus, since a person could never acquire everything, "more" became the psychological crutch that advertisers exploited.

As advertising created consumers hell-bent on accumulation, the idea grew embedded in people's daily consciousness. As a result, class and social status even more clearly marked the difference between society's "haves" and "have-nots" in American culture. While the demarcation between rich and poor solidified in terms of actual wealth, corporate America's real victory centered on persuading people that they could climb the ladder of wealth, as long as they bought the right things and worked hard. Under the spell of advertising, people kept reaching for goals just beyond their grasp. Consumerism enabled people to feel good about their purchases (and lives), because they could own the same kinds of things they saw peddled across mass communication channels all around them.

Another of advertising's goals centered on creating relationships between consumers and products, which today we call "branding." Certainly, a great deal of branding served to create a social construct, as described above, that kept people constantly yearning for more or better products. What one discovers when reading through Fitzgerald's correspondence with his editor Max Perkins and his agent Harold Ober is a writer who understood that his personal brand and product could be used to sell books. Unlike many writers who stay removed from branding efforts, Fitzgerald often discussed marketing ideas, such as how endorsements (blurbs) should be used in ads for his work and how his novels and story collections should be priced.

Another aspect of building the brand relationship meant explaining how consumers should use certain products in their daily lives. As such, corporations created cans, bottles, and other packages designed for practicality and aesthetic appeal. These innovations, such as wax-sealed cartons, kept foods fresh, while also providing advertisers with space to create a brand image. Advertisers realized that appealing to customers visually would enable certain products to stand out on store shelves. Brand identification and loyalty, in turn, drove sales, especially as shoppers (primarily females) looked to the familiar logos of trusted products.

A nation of consumers needs to have places to buy goods. Mass merchandisers realized the importance of creating marketplaces for shoppers to buy consumer items, so they lured people into cities by creating department stores. Gradually, these stores grew into otherworldly emporiums, designed to not only meet every shopper's wishes, but also to provide those with disposable income and free time a place to spend leisure time.

The shopping experience itself changed people's lives. Michael Schudson explains, "People thought of the stores as social centers and dressed up to go shopping."[20] In 1902, for example, both Marshall Field's and Macy's built cavernous new stores with more than one million square feet of floor space. These grand palaces offered almost any product purchasable and gave shoppers a new experience on each visit. In the created world of the department store, anyone could encounter a bit of glamour.

Advertisers realized that ads did not have to discuss the potential strengths of a certain product or service, but instead could sell a lifestyle that consumers coveted. "What advertising does, among other things, is manufacture desire and shape it, and thus create people who are insatiable and who have been conditioned to continually lust for more things," says scholar Arthur Asa Berger. "And the more we have the more we want."[21] Advertisers interpreted the dreams and aspirations of consumers, presented them back to the public with bright-colored bows, and equated these ideas with specific products and services to ensure that buyers understood the link.

HOPE AND FULFILLMENT

Jay Gatsby yearns to relive the past. Beyond all else, he hopes that the power of his romantic visions will convince Daisy to return to him. The lethal scent of this dream is so overpowering that Gatsby even believes that they can return to Daisy's parents' house in faraway Louisville to marry on the front steps where they first kissed and fell in love. This vision of hope and possible fulfillment despite all the odds stacked against him is the essence of the character's greatness. The reader either agrees or disagrees based in large part on whether or not the reader accepts this idea.

There is a duality at the heart of *Gatsby* that its titular character represents, which also symbolizes the American Dream. Writing in the early 1950s, scholar Marius Bewley identifies this two-headed notion, explaining, "Gatsby never succeeds in seeing through the sham of his world . . . very clearly. It is of the essence of his romantic American vision that it should lack the seasoned powers of discrimination. But it invests those illusions with its own faith, and thus it discovers its projected goodness in the frauds of its crippled world." The battle between idea, hope, and illusion, therefore, "becomes the acting out of the tragedy of the American vision."[22]

Gatsby's conception of the American Dream resided in the hope he held for its inevitability. Yet, as his plan materialized, he could not see the fragility at its foundation, nor could he envisage Tom's desire to rise up against him, in the latter's mind impeding the demise of the American family. According to scholar David F. Trask:

> Gatz plainly imagined himself a Christ—one of the anointed—born of earthly parents but actually a son of God. This is what Fitzgerald sought to convey in establishing that "Jay Gatsby of West Egg, Long Island, sprang from his Platonic conception of himself." That concep-

tion moved him to seek out goodness and beauty—certainly a prosti-
tuted goodness and beauty, but goodness and beauty nevertheless.[23]

What ultimately leads to Gatsby's death, though, is that all his hopes
and aspirations are wrapped up in a woman that cannot live up to his
dreams. Despite her outward charm and the pleasure she seems to feel in
her fling with her long-lost lover, Daisy is too settled—even in the midst
of an unfulfilled life—to risk her future on Gatsby. Writer Brian Sutton
calls Daisy "corrupt" and "thus perfectly suited for marriage with Tom,
with whom she shares membership in an exclusive society from which
Gatsby is barred."[24] What strikes the contemporary reader, steeped in
soap-operatic narratives and a lifetime full of dramatic story lines, is that
Gatsby thought it would all be easy. This self-delusion indicates the
depths of his romanticism and inability to assess the situation realistically.

Daisy, on the other hand, is a realist, even as she plays along with her
lover's fantasies of them together. When challenged in front of Tom in
the scene at the Plaza Hotel, Daisy counters, "You want too much."[25]
With that, Tom's victory is complete, as is Gatsby's inescapable demise.
Gatsby's idea of the perfect life together with his soul mate cannot hold
up to the pressure of Daisy's materiality, including her rich lifestyle,
status in the upper class, and family ties to wealth.

Gatsby could never achieve his all-consuming goal, even though people around him may have contended that his wealth and power were the
final aspiration. Most people would trade those symbols of success over
getting the girl ninety-nine out of a hundred times. Certainly, Fitzgerald
demonstrated keen insight into Gatsby's real desire by making all the
traditional signs of success (flashy cars, mansion, extravagant clothes,
giant parties) inconsequential. For Gatsby, these trinkets only mattered if
they impressed Daisy, like the rain of new, beautiful shirts that he tosses
around the room when showing her and Nick his bedroom. The only time
he ever seems impressed with his acquisitions is when Nick first sees his
sporty automobile, but even that moment of pride is fleeting.

Only winning Daisy's heart and erasing Tom's place in her mind and
memory could satisfy Gatsby. The character's weakness, according to
scholar John F. Callahan, is that he cannot meet Fitzgerald's dictum
postulated in "The Crack-Up" essay from the February 1936 issue of
Esquire regarding "first rate intelligence," which hinges on holding "two

opposed ideas in the mind at the same time and still retain[ing] the ability to function."[26] Both Gatsby and Dick Diver of *Tender Is the Night* suffer, Callahan relates, because they "could live in the world only with a single, consuming mission."[27] Neither held the first-rate intelligence that may have granted them the ability to overcome their fixations.

As the narrator of the story and Gatsby's champion, Nick also yearns for fulfillment, though the events of that summer in 1922 make it impossible for him to not undergo a transformation. After that tragic period, he exclaims, "I felt that I wanted the world to be in uniform and at a sort of moral attention forever." Even though he brags about being "privy to the secret griefs of wild, unknown men," he later realizes "I wanted no more riotous excursions with privileged glimpses into the human heart."[28]

Nick is changed by Gatsby's death and what the finality of his murder says about his own future. He cannot stay in the East, because New York City and the bond business cater to the wealthy, particularly the old-money rich represented by Tom and Daisy. Nick cannot stay because his hope is tied with Gatsby's and when the latter is murdered, both their dreams die. His fulfillment will not take place in the East, which is associated with evil. Nick must return to his home, the homeland of his father and their ancestors. The tie to the place and the land is his salvation. His post-East American Dream must play out in the Midwest.

Nick tries to hold on to Gatsby for as long as possible. He watches over the mansion after its owner's murder and records who comes and goes, including one car that Nick speculates "was some final guest who had been away at the ends of the earth and didn't know that the party was over."[29] As the author of the book about Gatsby, Nick, however, ensures that the summer will not be forgotten, though as readers we never really know what he will or won't say about the saga. Is it a work of fiction that Nick mentions will be titled *Gatsby* or a nonfiction account of those months? More importantly, is writing the book the only way Nick can put a close on the tragedy and find his own sense of fulfillment, even though he is forced to rehash Gatsby's dashed dreams?

On the final page of the novel, Nick explains how close Gatsby was to his dream, "so close that he could hardly fail to grasp it," yet as readers we now know that he paid for that vision with his life. By choosing to romanticize Gatsby at the expense of Tom and Daisy, Nick determines what it is we trust in his version of the tragedy. Nick equates that dream with the sense of wonder that the first Dutch sailors held on seeing the

New World, "the last time in history with something commensurate to his capacity for wonder." By doing so, he privileges the notion that after stripping away everything else, like the teeming lands of the primitive island, having a dream is the most important thing one can hold. This is what forces us to "run faster, stretch out our arms farther," and force the boat forward, despite the impeding current.[30]

***

In the early decades of the twenty-first century, America seems angry. There is a sense—beginning with the terrorist attacks on 9/11, the subsequent wars in Afghanistan and Iraq, and then carrying on through the economic hardships of high unemployment and the ongoing real estate bust—that the United States has fallen from its pedestal. Moreover, it feels like the American Dream is under assault from internal and external forces that make its achievement seem more and more remote. What, for example, is the point of attaining a great job or dream home when the global environment is being choked to death by toxic levels of carbon emissions? The media is filled with dire reports of global warming, disease, tainted or poisonous food outbreaks, and violence.

The evidence demonstrating rage within the nation is pervasive, often to the point of becoming stifling. The anger is reflected in the hateful rhetoric of America's political leaders and media pundits, who seem more interested in stoking ideological fires than attempting to eradicate the challenges the country faces. We see the fury represented in grassroots movements against the status quo, such as the Tea Party uprising in the 2010 congressional elections and 2012 presidential campaign, as well as in the political workers' rights demonstrations in Wisconsin and Ohio.

Most often, the struggle is depicted as class warfare with winner-take-all stakes with nothing less than the nation's future hanging in the balance. Listen, for example, to Richard L. Trumka, president of the AFL-CIO, declare, "Mass unemployment and growing inequality threaten our democracy. We need to act—and act boldly—to strike at the roots of working people's anger and shut down the forces of hatred and racism."[31] The call for addressing the needs of the working class as an antidote to what Trumka views as the hatemongering of the conservatives reveals the depths of the blue-collar struggle in contemporary America.

More damaging over the long term, though, is that perhaps this ire and its consequences hint at the end of the "American Dream." The political rhetoric essentially pitting classes against one another is a viable means of illuminating the differences in economic status, which politicians and commentators wanted to deny in the past. Certainly, one senses the clarion call of national aspiration dwindling under the weight of the around-the-clock news cycle and its hunger for sensationalism.

Perhaps the larger question is whether or not the American Dream can exist in a country that no longer considers itself exceptional. If Americans do not see a way to climb upward through the class system, or feel that they can have better lives than their ancestors, then a significant facet of what it means to be an American disappears as well.

Surprisingly, given the widespread anger, basic optimism remains, particularly among working-class whites. According to scholars Alan Abramowitz and Ruy Teixeira, it is almost as if this demographic has a split personality. On one hand, nearly two-thirds see "increasing uncertainty as coming closer to their views." But, on the other side of the coin, "an amazing 60 percent nevertheless thought that they themselves would achieve the [American] 'dream.'"[32] The intersection between potential and actual is where *The Great Gatsby* continues as a tool in helping people, particularly students, come to an understanding of the topic and its consequences.

Each year countless thousands of students in high schools and college courses skim, read, study, grapple with, and get exasperated by *The Great Gatsby*. Some fall in love with the novel, while others throw it across the room in disgust. Either way, they are forced to grapple with the ideas at the heart of the American Dream. Literary critic Gail McDonald explains: "Often mentioned as a contender for the Great American Novel, Fitzgerald's book owes its esteem partly to its having captured so memorably the contradictory nature of American aspiration—both the idealistic and the most debased quests of the nation."[33]

Fitzgerald's ability to confront the idea of the American Dream in such a tricky manner—allowing the reader to interpret its positives and negatives—ensures that the novel remains relevant, even as its era becomes more and more removed from the world of today's readers. By laying out various blueprints and consequences from one's interaction with the American Dream, Fitzgerald provides a path toward comprehension and contemplation. If *Gatsby* is either a tool for understanding or potentially an antidote against the draw of rampant consumerism, then its application will continue to guide readers as they explore their daily lives.

8

WEALTH AND POWER

I have never been able to forgive the rich for being rich, and it has colored my entire life and works.—F. Scott Fitzgerald, in a letter to Anne Ober, March 4, 1938

Donald Trump is no Jay Gatsby—neither is Bill Gates, John DeLorean, Mark Zuckerberg, Jay-Z, or the countless other (real-life) people all over the world who have been compared and contrasted to the literary figure. Yet, for nearly a century, media wags and other commentators have made the association, particularly when assessing wealthy men who have a predilection for ostentation.

The simple explanation for why this comparison does not work is that the vast fortune Gatsby accumulated meant almost nothing to him as mere riches. His willingness to accumulate wealth quickly and by any means necessary centered on getting Daisy back, which he knew necessitated the kind of money that could support the lifestyle she demanded. In contrast, the real-life individuals mentioned in the same breath as the literary character pursued wealth for money's sake, often purely to become rich and/or famous. Gatsby possessed higher aspirations; according to William Voegeli, "Rather, he got rich quick out of a sense of urgency and desperation and crazy hopefulness, out of refusing to get over a broken heart and give up the love of his life."[1]

The items Gatsby collected were to create an environment where he could win Daisy's hand, thus fulfilling his dreams. In my reading, there are only two times that Gatsby seems showy regarding his wealth: when he asks Nick if his house looks good and then when he takes pride in his

first time he takes Nick into the city. Contrast this to the overin-
:e and extreme displays of wealth showcased in contemporary
society.

One needs look no further than HGTV's series of real estate shows
where a typically upper-middle-class or wealthy family is searching for a
dream home or vacation residence vastly more expensive than the average person could afford, but still usually below the $1 million range,
which is the demarcation that delineates between wealth and flamboy-
ance. These shows and others that overpopulate cable television are
meant to portray the bounty of the wealthy, but in a way that its viewers
(directed at middle-aged women) do not find overly ostentatious.

Ironically, when journalists and commentators use the comparison between *Gatsby* and actual people, the analogy possesses meaning for their
readers. Audiences have been conditioned by numerous uses across mass
communications channels to equate *Gatsby* with the kind of rich, excessive lifestyles led by people like Trump and others. Research, though,
reveals that the understanding of *Gatsby* as a taxonomy has changed over
time.

In the 1980s, when writers employed generic *Gatsby* terms to contextualize real individuals, the usage occurred most often to symbolize a
Horatio Alger–like rise and subsequent downfall. These examples include
Colorado senator Gary Hart, who seemed a likely candidate for president
until a series of gaffes and an extramarital affair derailed him. Another
often-cited "Gatsby-esque" character from the era was John DeLorean,
the erstwhile car executive. His rise and fall ended with an arrest for drug
trafficking, though he was found not guilty due to government entrap-
ment.

In the 1990s and 2000s, the generic terms related to *Gatsby* shifted to
be used mainly to indicate grandiose entertainment. For example, the
numerous corporate party excesses that came to light in the last handful
of years are almost always called "*Gatsby*-esque," despite the intent of
the event or its hosts. Individuals associated with these kinds of bacchanalia include former Tyco chief executive Dennis Kozlowski, who used
company funds to pay for half of the $2 million birthday party he orga-
nized for his wife. Revealing that CEOs rarely learn from the past, in June
2012, Yammer boss David Sacks threw himself a $1.4 million party.
Probably the only thing that saved Sacks from the *Gatsby* label—which
was thrown around a bit—was that the party already had a theme, harking

back to eighteenth-century France and the Marie Antoinette era. The portrait Fitzgerald achieved in his description of the lavishness of the wealthy created a vivid image that has lived on past the normal expiration date a distinguished novel would usually generate.

The fact that terms, symbols, and imagery from *Gatsby* can be used in these generic ways demonstrates the novel's contemporary appeal. In contrast, we do not often hear people referencing or equating an item from contemporary culture with almost any other novel, if the typical American could even name more than one or two literary characters. Occasionally, one might hear some coquettish, young pop music singer compared to Nabokov's *Lolita*. Perhaps a bit more frequently, a writer will refer to something ominous or heavy-handed as being like "Big Brother" from George Orwell's *1984*.

***

This chapter reveals the abundant ways that the novel and film versions of *The Great Gatsby* have influenced people's thinking about wealth and power. Particularly significant is how Fitzgerald uses Nick to elevate Gatsby's use of wealth in pursuit of a misbegotten dream versus Tom Buchanan's inherited wealth and its inherent evil if threatened. The battle of old money and new money that plays out in the book has morphed into a more "us versus them" usage in contemporary America that is closely linked to our current unease at the disparity between the rich and everyone else.

As with so many aspects of Fitzgerald's novel, Jay Gatsby represents a duality that can lead the reader to a multitude of differing views, some quite divergent. When considering wealth and power, Gatsby's rise demonstrates that the rags-to-riches myth can be a reality. He attains both via illegal maneuverings, but perhaps in no more corrupt ways than others around him. Throughout the book, for example, Tom Buchanan drinks illegal liquor, but it is only with Gatsby that he launches into the role of moral arbiter, lashing out at the man for being a "big bootlegger."[2] As such, a reader could examine Gatsby's life and view it as a model for getting wealth.

On the other hand, Gatsby's demise—from war hero to crook to being murdered—could also be read as a censure. According to writer Alexander Nazaryan, the essential point also centers on destruction. He explains,

"Destruction fuels the novel's plot, a sort of primal American myth in its own right. A pauper from the Midwest, Jimmy Gatz scraps his commonplace identity. . . . Through the violence of World War I and the profiteering of Prohibition, Gatsby becomes the Long Island bon vivant that Nick encounters."[3] In other words, the quest for riches and power for the wrong reasons is doomed. Furthermore, by calling this point to question via the novel, Fitzgerald is asking the reader to rethink the American Dream itself.

From a societal viewpoint, Fitzgerald reveals that the barriers to entering the enclave of the wealthy are beyond most people, even if they seem to have made it. According to scholar David Minter, "His world, which pretends to be receptive to dreamers, in fact protects those who have been born to riches and power."[4] Tom and Daisy, for example, escape that fateful summer unscathed.

Yet, even here, we live in a world where some small percentage of individuals do find their way into wealth. As Tom looked down at Gatsby's new wealth and scoffed, we find today's media playing a similar role when a Hollywood celebrity or famous music personality enters into grotesque displays of wealth. Simultaneously, we want to know about fabulous, elite parties and are repelled by the conspicuous vulgarity.

THE TRIUMPH OF CONSUMERISM

The popular imagination regarding *The Great Gatsby* is a fantasy of life filled with all-night parties, overflowing champagne glasses tinkling deep into the night, and the gaudy spectacle of it all leading to some kind of boozy mysterious nirvana. The depiction of these parties served as a central element of the 1974 film version of the novel starring Robert Redford and Mia Farrow. The elegant portrayal featured lots of partygoers dancing in full, shimmering eveningwear, which provided the movie an added layer of glitz that captivated filmgoers and the era's fashionistas.

Baz Luhrmann's 2013 production starring Leonardo DiCaprio, in comparison, takes the parties and the mansion to an even more spectacular level. The house itself fills the nighttime horizon in a carnivalesque fashion—klieg lights filling the sky. The parties explode on the screen, nearly bigger than one could comprehend, and using 3-D technology to make it seem as if the galas burst into the theater. There are not doze even hundreds of partiers like in earlier film versions of the novel, seemingly thousands that pulsate into the night. Finally, the recent film captures the dazzling enormity one finds in the novel. Under Luhrmann's watchful eye, the excursions transform into spectacles worthy of Fitzgerald's vision of Gatsby's grandiosity.

When considering the novel, however, the pageantry of Gatsby's parties almost blinds the reader to the deft criticism Fitzgerald lays at the feet of family wealth, the new rich, and strivers who hoped to pull themselves up into these ranks. The challenge is to not conflate the spectacle with supposed support or celebration of elite lifestyles. A lifelong observer of the relations between wealthy and those not in the same class, Fitzgerald understood both groups intuitively.

In a 1938 letter to Anne Ober, for example, he compared his life among the wealthy with his daughter Scottie's, explaining that he stood "a poor boy in a rich town; a poor boy in a rich boy's school; a poor boy in a rich man's club at Princeton." Fitzgerald assessed the consequences of these experiences, saying, "I have never been able to forgive the rich for being rich, and it has colored my entire life and works."[5] This insight enabled him to convincingly develop both Tom Buchanan and Myrtle Wilson, arguably the strongest characters in the novel. Although from opposite ends of the socioeconomic scale, the merger of Tom and Myrtle demonstrates how consumer culture has become the dominant ideology in American history.

What links the rich patriarch and the poor gas station attendant's wife even closer than their status as adulterous lovers is their representation of their respective economic classes. Tom, as an old-money aristocrat, exhibits his vast wealth through lifestyle choices that befit one at the top of the economic strata. Fitzgerald makes a case for how out of touch the inherited rich are by describing the string of polo horses Tom brings from Chicago and the $350,000 pearl necklace he gives Daisy as an engagement present. These consumer choices, as lavish as they are, provide the reader with proof of the illegitimacy of that lifestyle and the flippancy of the ultrawealthy.

Myrtle, as a member of the working poor, is essential to the book in exposing how quickly a person can be changed by money physically and spiritually. Myrtle's New York City love nest apartment, for example, is filled with expensive tapestries and decorations that flaunt her newfound wealth to both outsiders and those within her newfound social circle. Without acknowledging the illicit nature of how she comes into wealth, Myrtle's self-worth is wrapped up in accumulating consumer goods that will show off her rank to her neighbors and acquaintances. As a result, Myrtle can pump gas in the afternoon in the beaten-down garage in the middle of the valley of ashes but later that evening transform herself into a lady of the manor. For example, when in the apartment with Tom, Myrtle looks down her nose at the hotel staff and others now beneath her on a self-created economic scale. Her snobbery demonstrates her complete transformation. Money allows Myrtle to erect a false barrier between these two halves of her life. Exploiting the differences between Tom and his lower-class lover, Fitzgerald critiques consumer culture from the perspective of inherited wealth and the countless individuals scratching and clawing in an attempt to get rich.

As a stand-in for American consumerism, Myrtle's posturing shows how quickly money corrupts those yearning for a better life based on nothing more tangible than naked opulence. Her demise, therefore, warns against pinning one's dreams to materialism. Yet, in Fitzgerald's day and our own, consumerism is a powerful force that organizes people's everyday lives. According to historian Gary Cross, "Maintaining a reciprocal relationship between consumption and work keeps the economic system running and orders daily life." Consumerism cannot simply be laid at the feet of producers or merchandisers, he contends, "It is a choice, never consciously made, to define self and community through the ownership of goods."[6] For Fitzgerald, then, as well as his contemporary readers, Myrtle's fate is intricately tied to culture's commitment to materialism and accumulation. We see the outcome of a blind desire for more, particularly when one's fate is lashed to those higher up on the economic food chain. Even though Tom tells Nick that he was broken up by Myrtle's death, he pays no price for her death, just as he escapes recrimination in Gatsby's death. Wealth trumps all.

Furthermore, when one examines the array of guests at Gatsby's parties, the critique again comes to life. Many of the celebrities who drink the host's bootlegged alcohol and partake in the endless revelries attain wealth and status via the era's fascination with fame, not traditional American values, such as hard work or through prudent lifestyle choices.

Instead, in the midst of the Roaring Twenties, certain people are hoisted up on a pedestal, essentially turning into commodities that can be bought and sold. Simultaneously, the rags-to-riches narrative used to solidify the star's brand enabled those around them to believe that the same could happen, if in the right place at the right time. In brief snippets, Fitzgerald reveals a great deal about the newly rich and famous people that attend Gatsby's festivities, often revealing these people to be callow and mean spirited.

What Fitzgerald caught extremely well regarding the burgeoning consumer culture is the freedoms and carefree attitudes that the merger of technology and goods symbolized. Gary Cross estimates that discretionary spending as a percentage of total expenditures nearly doubled in the first three decades of the twentieth century, which accentuated the nation's status as an economic and military superpower. In other words, a country awash in newfound wealth could afford the gaudy spending spree Fitzgerald lived through and wrote about. Moreover, consumption as a chief facet of American culture expanded. Cross explains, "American prosperity gave quite ordinary citizens cars, electric gadgets, telephones, and ready-to-wear fashions for which European masses would have to wait until mid-century."[7] Fitzgerald is able to capture this transition via simply reproducing guest lists from the extravaganzas and mention how these people acquired their wealth. The presumption of wealth enabled poor guests like Myrtle's sister Catherine to attend, as well as the poor British aristocrats searching for well-heeled rich wives.

The entire culture centralized around spending, which Fitzgerald understood would continue as class distinctions blurred, therefore giving so-called "regular" people a taste of upper-class life and the idea that they too could have more. People could make themselves feel like a part of the elite culture by hobnobbing with the wealthy or mimicking their lifestyles via consumer goods, but the actual entry into that privileged class could not be attained. Gatsby and Myrtle demonstrate how the upper reaches of the moneyed class consorted to keep the wannabes from entering. Although class distinctions did not disappear with the broad acceptance of consumerism, its arrival signaled a safe way to blur class lines enough to keep people contented. The faux fluidity of the American class system based on the false god of consumerism is a trend that has influenced people ever since.

Fitzgerald's decision to reveal the inanities of the rich and those who strive to enter that class drives much of *Gatsby*'s continuing influence in contemporary society. Early in the Fitzgerald revival, for example, the novel helped readers comprehend how consumerism and expendable income had consequences, particularly as these factors changed the nation after World War II, from suburbanization and the creation of a car-based culture to increased education opportunities and a wide array of shopping outlets.

According to historian Joshua B. Freeman, those promoting consumerism "reached greater sophistication and unmatched pervasiveness after World War II . . . the national culture had largely repudiated the virtue of thrift."[8] While some might argue that *Gatsby* presents such an idyllic vision of parties that some young readers might aspire to that lifestyle, certainly readers who grasp the book realized the potential outcomes if money is one's primary objective. Educators, in attempting to instill an ethical and moral code in their students, clearly found *Gatsby* a useful tool in that endeavor in the postwar years, which also remains important today.

GET RICH QUICK—1920S-STYLE

In the late 1910s, a Cincinnati attorney named George Remus did so well as a lawyer that he made $50,000 a year (or about $650,000 in 2012 dollars). Yet he realized that some of his clients made more than he did selling bootlegged liquor during Prohibition. Always entrepreneurial, Remus decided to jump to the other side of the law, despite the fact that he did not even drink. The taste of money served as Remus's elixir. He yearned for the drippings of wealth, including fine food, wine, art, and expensive homes. The lure of money proved all the intoxication Remus needed.

Ironically, Remus had been a pharmacist before turning to the law, so the opportunity to shift into bootlegging seemed natural. He used the drug training to set up an illegal booze empire. One reporter estimated that at his height of power, Remus operated "10 distilleries [and] employed 3,000 people" on a fifty-acre section on the city's West Side.[9] While it is amazing to think of this vast network, what is surprising is that three thousand people also looked the other way as they broke the law.

Remus lived a lavish lifestyle, not only buying into the rich enclave of Newport, Rhode Island, but also filling his Cincinnati mansion with rare art and books. Writer Steve Kemme estimates that Remus amassed a

fortune in the "hundreds of millions of dollars." Some have also speculated that Remus, who many considered "the king of the bootleggers,"
served as Fitzgerald's model for Jay Gatsby. There seem to be some
similarities, such as Remus's not drinking and affinity for swimming,
spending $100,000 to build a pool and pool house in 1921. [10]

Unlike Gatsby, however, Remus did not end up murdered in that pool.
His extravagant lifestyle soon ended, though. Remus's downfall began
with a three-year jail stint after a Prohibition violation, which his wife
Imogene Holmes unwittingly contributed to by starting an affair with an
undercover FBI agent. Later, just weeks after his release, he murdered his
wife in a rage after she stole everything from his mansion while he sat in
jail. The murder trial gained national coverage, accentuated by Remus
representing himself at the proceedings. Judged insane, the bootlegger
spent six months in a mental hospital, and then lived quietly and modestly
outside Cincinnati until he died in 1952. [11]

When examining the topics of wealth and power as each relates to
Gatsby, one realizes that these ideas play an important role in the novel's
lasting popularity. When one explores wealth and power, violence and
immorality are usually nearby. Readers and other audiences have always
found these extreme traits fascinating, which provides the novel with
much of its cinematic vibe.

The 1949 film version of *The Great Gatsby* presented the main character as a crime boss, willing to take out his competitors with machine
guns during high-speed chases through the streets of New York City.
While some commentators blanched at this alteration of the novel, making Gatsby a gangster not only reflected the popular image of the 1920s
but also addressed the nation's fear of unlawfulness in the late 1940s. The
two eras shared a fear of the massive upheaval that occurs during periods
rife with excessive wealth and the sociocultural transformations that concurrently take place.

So much drinking takes place in *Gatsby* that one almost forgets that
the novel is set during Prohibition. Yet much of the mystery about Jay
Gatsby's wealth and outward projection to the world centers on alcohol.
Obviously, one sees this notion represented in the way the main charac-
ters constantly drink or talk about drinking, as well in the whispers about
Gatsby's bootlegging activities.

In January 1919, the Eighteenth Amendment became law, banning the
manufacture, transportation, importation, and sale of intoxicating liquors

in the United States the next year. Commonly known as Prohibition, the amendment stood as the culmination of more than a century of attempts to remove alcohol from society by various temperance organizations. Many large cities and states actually went dry in 1918. Americans could no longer legally drink or buy alcohol. The people who illegally made, imported, or sold alcohol during this time—like Gatsby reportedly did— were called bootleggers. Even to this day, there are still bootleggers in operation in the southern United States, those people who own and operate illegal stills to manufacture and sell alcohol.

In contrast to its original intent, Prohibition actually caused a permanent change in the way the nation viewed authority, the court system, and wealth and class. Particularly damning was the lack of enforcement, which led to the rise of the mob and notorious criminals such as Al Capone. Congress attempted to enforce Prohibition by passing the "Volstead Act" in late 1919, which created the Prohibition Bureau, but never provided the agency with the resources necessary to really back the amendment. As a result, bootlegging became big business, often as immigrants took hold of power in urban centers. Meyer Wolfsheim, Gatsby's confidant and mentor, represents a figure similar to Remus. However, there are hints of a more sinister, Capone-like aura, particularly when the older man recounts his friend being gunned down outside the restaurant and his unwillingness to sit in a room with his back to the door.

What *Gatsby* depicts perfectly is that despite enforcement efforts by federal, state, and local officers, Prohibition actually instigated a national drinking spree that persisted until the law was repealed thirteen years later. One sees examples of the ways ordinary citizens got around the laws against drinking across popular culture, such as the films *The Untouchables* (1987) and *A River Runs Through It* (1992). Many cities proudly proclaimed that they were the nation's wettest, directly challenging the authority of the federal law and its enforcers.

In the early 1920s, for example, Chicago had more than seven thousand drinking parlors, or speakeasies. On a person-to-person level, physicians around the nation dispensed prescriptions for medicinal alcohol, while pharmacies applied for liquor licenses. Alcohol was available for a price and delivered with a wink and wry smile. In *Gatsby*, despite the pervasiveness of drinking and its deleterious effects on many of the partygoers at Gatsby's shindigs, no one seems to question or worry too much about the law.

The effects on the American national psyche were long lasting, ushering in a general cynicism and distrust. Given the pervasive lawlessness during Prohibition, bootlegging seemed omnipresent. The operations varied in size, but much of it came alive in the nation's cities through an intricate network of smugglers, middlemen, and local suppliers. To escape prosecution, men like Remus used bribery, heavily armed guards, and medicinal licenses to circumvent the law. More ruthless gangsters, such as Capone, did not stop in their relentless pursuit of controlling crime syndicates. Capone and his gang resorted to intimidation and murder. Under these conditions, the nation's cities were ripe for crime, and many immigrants, barred from respectable positions, acted to fill the void. In cities like Pittsburgh and Cleveland, numerous ethnic gangs fought to control the local bootlegging activities. In Chicago, eight hundred gangsters were killed in gang warfare during Prohibition, primarily due to the fight over alcohol sales.

Bootleggers counterfeited prescriptions and liquor licenses to gain access to alcohol. The most common practice was to import liquor from other countries aboard ships. The Detroit River, dividing the United States and Canada, thrived as an entry point, as did the overland method on the long border between the two countries. Bootleggers also evaded authorities by building secret breweries with intricate security systems and lookouts. In addition to eluding the police, bootleggers had to fend off other bootleggers who would steal the precious cargo for their own sale. Bootleggers began a national controversy by selling adulterated liquor, which resulted in countless fatalities and poisonings.

Bootlegging grew into a vast illegal empire, in part, because of widespread bribery. Many enforcement agents received monthly retainers (some up to $300,000 a month) to look the other way. Critics said that Prohibition Bureau agents had a license to make money through bribes from bootleggers. The corruption among agents was so prevalent that President Warren G. Harding commented on it in his State of the Union address in 1922.

Prohibition and the era of illegal bootlegging remains an interesting topic across contemporary American popular culture, not just in Fitzgerald's masterpiece. Part of the attraction is the glamour of the Jazz Age and the national prosperity that accompanied it (and Fitzgerald marketed in his work). People also look back on that era and wonder how such a law could ever be passed, particularly given that issues so much more important have languished for decades or longer or are never brought to vote at all. What one cannot discount, though, is that Prohibition is a part of the American mythos. *Gatsby* alone ensures that visions of gangsters, glittering revelries, and the clinking of glasses spilling over with illegal alcohol will stay on the cultural radar.

GET RICH QUICK—2000S-STYLE

Characterizing the early years of the new millennium from an economic perspective might quickly turn sinister. The era began with the dot-com crash, which caused massive downsizing and economic peril, not only knocking down the paper millionaires in Silicon Valley, but also reverberating to workers far removed from the tech bubble. The wars in the Middle East after 9/11 led to more uncertainty as many corporations hoarded cash and resources to buffet against the chaos. Critics of the wars saw the multibillion-dollar contracts awarded and resulting shabby work as a blatant attempt by corporations to pillage the federal defense budget. By the mid to late 2000s, the housing bubble burst, throwing the world into the Great Recession, which (arguably) is over by early 2013 but is still being felt by people all over the country in the form of joblessness, housing woes, and living paycheck to paycheck.

It is no wonder that the buzzwords of the 2012 presidential election between Democrat Barack Obama and Republican challenger Mitt Romney centered on "jobs," and the mythical idea that all the economic misfortunes could be fixed via one party's plan to increase job opportunities. Pandering to voters this way could be construed as a typical political ploy in an election year, but the emphasis on jobs and who might create better employment returns reveals the deep turmoil the nation faces in the twenty-first century.

While an analysis of the news coverage and chatter over the web might lead one to believe that the corporate world is more corrupt today than ever before, the counterargument might be that with more mass media channels and eyes focused on business, the stories that went unnoticed previously now take center stage. Overall, the general population is more attuned to the stock market and daily corporate maneuverings, particularly in light of the financial data one can find on just about any company or executive via the Internet. For example, three clicks on a corporate profile at Yahoo! Finance provides more information than most investors could access for hundreds of years. As a result, there is little kept behind the curtains in today's investing world. At the same time, however, those who wish to game the system also have more weapons at their disposal.

In light of the way wealth and power occupy a central narrative in today's culture, one could imagine that *Gatsby* would be marginalized—acknowledging the complexities of contemporary challenges—or alternatively, that the novel would become more handy, since it helps in grasping deep societal issues at the core of class and wealth. Examining the tens of thousands of pages of "Gatsby" references in the popular media in the 2000s and 2010s, one finds that the term is still used as a generic fill-in for numerous themes, some of them only marginally associated with what Fitzgerald intended.

For example, in late 2002, health care financier Lance Poulsen, the founder and chief executive officer of National Century Financial Enterprises, faced criminal charges and lawsuits accusing him of fraud, embezzlement, and tampering with evidence. Given the tycoon's lavish lifestyle—including a $2 million yacht (the *Enterprise*) and three-story mansion in tony Port Charlotte, Florida—and connections to major Republican politicians, including Florida governor Jeb Bush (the president's brother), the media dug into coverage.[12]

Journalists, investigators, attorneys, and others uncovered a far-flung Ponzi scheme that enabled Poulsen to embezzle upward of $2 billion by bilking health care facilities out of Medicare payments and other criminal doings that eventually landed the former executive a thirty-year jail sentence. Poulsen's misdeeds were so intricate and difficult to unravel that bond rating company Moody's Investor Service and Fitch Ratings were fooled into backing its bonds, which did not change until an anonymous whistle-blower exposed the company's wrongdoing.[13]

Given the intrigue surrounding Poulsen's posh lifestyle and political ties, which contrasted with his overtly criminal behavior, his rise and fall from grace captured headlines. The way *USA Today* reporter Edward Iwata compared Poulsen with Jay Gatsby, however, demonstrated how Fitzgerald's novel is both central to the way people use it to interpret culture and society and how *Gatsby* is misunderstood. Iwata, like so many other writers using the novel as a hook for his article, gets the analogy about one-third right. "He was a modern-day Gatsby," the reporter explains, "a smooth talker and sharp dresser who floated across the room to greet the moneyed crowd." In this instance, Iwata gets the most insignificant point correct: Gatsby did dress stylishly, though too flashy for the old-money types who lived across the bay in East Egg. The other details—about the way Gatsby spoke and greeted guests—are way off. As a matter of fact, Gatsby rarely speaks in the novel and when he does, it is carefully considered and in hesitating patterns. Nor does Gatsby reach out to the rich hordes that fill his mansion in a sycophantic manner as Iwata suggests. His interactions with guests are minimal at best, by his own admission. He later confesses to Nick that he is not a very good host. The simple fact that no one at the parties seems to know him or ever even see him while there demonstrates the weakness of this comparison.[14]

In the early decades of the twenty-first century, perhaps a truly "Gatsby-esque" figure could not exist. In this era, the desire for fame or wealth seems to be enough in and of itself to warrant whatever steps are necessary to achieve these twin goals. Given the preoccupation on attaining wealth and fame across modern culture, there does not seem to be a higher calling beyond self-aggrandizement. Readers do know, however, that the misuse of "Gatsby" as a substitute for "slick" or "money hungry" does not capture the essence of the character or his aspirations.

The task of assigning the moniker to someone who attained great riches without necessarily having wealth as a major objective is problematic. For example, the two great Harvard dropouts Bill Gates and Mark Zuckerberg were entrepreneurial at a young age and interested in technology. Those characteristics, though, did not necessarily mean that they wanted to be phenomenally wealthy. Each later built an empire and became a billionaire, but it would be difficult to attach some greater goal to their efforts. Subsequently, Gates's philanthropic work may eclipse his role as the founder of Microsoft (if one could be divorced from the other), but this higher calling came after the wealth, just as Zuckerberg's next move might be.

Interestingly, while applying the labels "Gatsby" or "Gatsby-esque" to success stories like Gates and Zuckerberg might be misleading, there is value in knowing how the novel might help us comprehend individuals who achieve great riches, or in the case of Tom Buchanan, inherit wealth and then go about building a life around their fortune. In these instances, if readers can use *Gatsby* as a tool for clarifying their own worldviews, then the power of the novel at nearly ninety years old becomes palpable.

***

The quest for wealth and power is a central narrative in American culture. It stands alone as a goal and is linked to the vision of achieving the American Dream. Some might even argue that it is the most important facet of the American Dream. People want riches so they can purchase their way to happiness. They want to win the lottery so they can tell their bosses where to go and buy the mansion with a pool and a fast car that allows them to insulate themselves from the traditional challenges that encumber daily life.

The fascination with wealth and power drives television shows like *Celebrity Apprentice*, hosted by the gonzo-Gatsby Donald Trump, who has turned his name and brand into a marketable product. We see it in the journey played out in competitive reality TV shows, like *Survivor* and *The Amazing Race*, where people who seem like regular people all of a sudden transform into cutthroat strategists willing to sell their mothers' soul to win financial reward. The obsession with wealth and power and the constant yearning for more drove otherwise intelligent rich people to believe in a charlatan and con artist like Bernie Madoff, who fleeced his Palm Beach, Florida, neighbors and others to the tune of somewhere between $12 to $20 billion. According to financial journalist Daniel Gross, Madoff worked off the idea of exclusivity and "fiendishly exploiting the unique, clubby culture of [the city] and of the global jet set that congregates there."[15]

Fitzgerald indicts the wealthy in *Gatsby*. His stunning depiction provides readers with a tool to assess the class structure and its imbalances in today's society. Yet it is hard to determine whether wealth has won and now it is Fitzgerald's ideas that are beating on against the current of celebrity and wealth culture that is at the center of our national idea.

The forces of power, greed, and hubris are central elements of contemporary life, ingrained so deeply in our fiber that it is difficult to imagine a different way. Maybe the bad guys won. In the end, though, I see great literature as a way to another path. I agree with writer Eric Olsen when he concludes, "I suspect that if there was ever a time we needed a new Great American Novel, or at least someone to take a stab at one, it's now," even though he does not think *Gatsby* is it.[16]

Life today is trying and difficult for the multitude of reasons presented in this chapter and plenty of others, not least of which is the always-on mentality that has gripped us in the Internet or Google age. People are now asked to fit more stuff from a broader array of channels into the same twenty-four-hour day. Olsen is right in asking that we find tools to help in this journey. I contend that meta-*Gatsby* offers this pathway toward possible new ways of approaching life in contemporary America.

9

CELEBRITY . . . AN OBSESSION

She narrowed her eyes and shivered. . . . We all turned and looked around for Gatsby. It was testimony to the romantic speculation he inspired that there were whispers about him from those who had found little that it was necessary to whisper about in this world.—Nick, *The Great Gatsby*

Icon. The word is flippantly tossed around in contemporary America. The latest one-hit wonder pop star gets tagged with the label as quickly as a legitimately splendid artist, athlete, or architect. The subjectivity of the term enables it to be used ubiquitously, whether it is in advertising taglines or marketing copy for goods and services being sold or in labeling historic eras or time frames.

People fixate on terms like "icon" because popular culture drives American culture. As scholar Larry Z. Leslie explains, "Contemporary culture is, for all practical purposes, popular culture . . . what we are most interested in and pay the most attention to. Celebrities are one of popular culture's most important products."[1] What Fitzgerald possessed, perhaps unlike any other writer of his era, was deep insight into the role of the burgeoning celebrity industry in the United States. His own five years of intense global stardom between 1920 and 1925 certainly intensified his comprehension of celebrity and its genesis. Even after his fall from the A-list of American celebrities, Fitzgerald filled notebooks and scrapbooks with mentions of his name, reviews, and other clippings that demonstrated his fixation with fame. He then used these pieces to gauge his place in the celebrity industry and literary history, thus equating the two, when there is no real value in linking them.

The obsession with celebrity—both the famous and infamous—and what it illuminates is a primary catalyst of the story line in *The Great Gatsby*. Fitzgerald understood the way people were obliged to fame and wealth and built the novel around those ideas and impulses. "Because celebrities are important to many of us," Leslie says, "understanding what celebrity is all about can be useful in helping us understand ourselves."[2] This deep comprehension served as one of Fitzgerald's most insightful gifts. Therefore, by analyzing *Gatsby*, contemporary readers may learn to more fully engage with the role of celebrity in their own lives.

Indeed, Fitzgerald's fame skyrocketed on the back of a unique era. In the 1920s, more people across class divisions enjoyed greater leisure time than ever before. Members of the middle and working classes, for example, witnessed a steep drop in working hours—from about sixty hours per week to forty-five—while simultaneously enjoying higher wages. Quite naturally, with additional free time and more money, people searched for different outlets. These included sporting events, movies, and vacations, among others.

The addiction to celebrity culture had always existed in the United States, but the 1920s thrust it into a new stratosphere. The entertainment industry boomed in the decade. Between 1919 and 1929, American spending on recreation almost doubled to $4 billion annually, a figure that would not be eclipsed until after World War II. Successive waves of celebrity-influenced fads and trends took hold that kept the mania at the forefront, whether it was the flapper, the 1920s "new woman" who emphasized a carefree attitude and style that embodied the era, or the rise of tabloids following in the wake of the burgeoning film industry and bright lights of Broadway.

Fame and celebrity served as much more than mere distractions or tools for getting consumers' money out of their pockets and into the hands of those dominating the entertainment industry. The language of popular culture effectively created a cultural space for people to populate with items meaningful to them. Furthermore, as millions of Americans interacted with the burgeoning mass media, whether watching the same films or listening to radio programs, a common language developed that opened lines of communication between disparate groups that might otherwise never connect.

While there were benefits that grew from this new common language based on mass culture, some critics argued that the downside led to an unhealthy devotion to popular culture. From this perspective, the commitment to entertainments and other novelties seemed to divert attention from the serious challenges the nation faced. In other words, popular culture and mass media might function like a kind of placebo, numbing people to critical issues that otherwise demanded their attention. One might wrap oneself in a bubble of mass media imagery and sounds without ever really being forced to confront critical social issues.

Fitzgerald seems to have recognized both sides in this argument. Myrtle's preoccupation with fashion and tabloid magazines represents the potential problem in using mass media as a distraction. Myrtle fills her secret life and city apartment with fluff, which demonstrates how a person in the Roaring Twenties could keep reality at bay via the entertainment industry. She does not have to confront her grubby apartment alongside the train tracks because her illusory life in the city is filled with thoughts of Broadway stars and buying knickknacks that litter her world with faux majesty and deliver a kind of barrier to reality via consumerism.

***

Given Fitzgerald's broad comprehension of celebrity culture, which he lived firsthand and wrote about in *Gatsby*, this chapter examines how the novel not only helped define the topic but continues to provide insight for contemporary readers. As a matter of fact, gossip (arguably the beating heart of the celebrity industry) is one of the most important topics in the book, one that Nick Carraway discusses at its very outset. Although he claims his desire is to reserve judgment, he immediately begins assessing everyone and everything around him. The entire novel, then, from one vantage could be viewed as a man's interaction with the celebrity culture of the early twentieth century.

Interestingly, Nick is playing the role of ultimate Gatsby fan by foisting his dead celebrity up in a book that he is narrating. As a matter of fact, for all the discussion of Jay Gatsby as a proponent of the American Dream, in some ways Nick is both more romantic, nostalgic, and obsessed with the ideas at the heart of the dream theme. For example, when he finally decides to return home at the end of the narrative, Nick's mind races back to the train rides and Wisconsin snow, which he calls "real snow, our snow." There is a sense of longing that he never relinquishes, even as he is bastardized by the East, Yale, and the Great War in that long, hot summer with Gatsby.[3] Nick juxtaposes this wonderful memory of a joyful past with the description of an El Greco painting featuring a woman drunk and out cold being carried away from the bacchanalia on a stretcher. No one knows who she is and no one cares, which to Nick reveals the ultimate hollowness of the East.

The cold, brutal reality that Nick comes to comprehend as Gatsby lives and dies is that people do not matter, but celebrity persists. An individual's fame is fleeting and can be destroyed, just as after Gatsby is killed. The parties, though, they continue, simply moving on to another momentary locale where fireworks will fill the nighttime sky and music will roar through the din.

What makes this chapter so compelling is the combined effect of Fitzgerald's personal interaction with fame and the way it is presented in the book. He is not only presenting his living experiences with the topic, but in doing so, providing readers with a tool for understanding how fame works in modern society. Fitzgerald's audience in the 1920s certainly comprehended the growing importance of fame in their time, but that fascination has only increased across the twentieth and twenty-first centuries.

As a result, Fitzgerald and *Gatsby* have fused into Americana. According to cultural scholar Marshall Fishwick, "Icons are symbols and mindmarks. They tie in with myth, legend, values, idols, aspirations . . . icons, like everything else, adapt accordingly. Objects are the building-blocks; ideas the cement holding them together. Modern man is starved for ideas and objects that give coherence to electric-age culture."[4] What we find over and over again is that *Gatsby* grants readers the ability to discern what its themes mean in their own times. Given the polemic that passes for discourse in contemporary America, it is a gift to have literature that enables a broader, more intellectual manner of thinking through life's challenges.

YOUNG, GLAMOROUS, AND CAREFREE

In the late 1990s and early 2000s, the opulence of newly rich young professionals in Silicon Valley and New York City begat images of Gatsby's immaculate parties for journalists and magazine writers who needed a way to demonstrate the link between the new crop of tech millionaires and those from the industrial past. In these instances, using "Gatsby" as a way of inferring luxury or opulence meant more to the curious reading public than the real-life characters from the 1920s, such as J. P. Morgan or John D. Rockefeller. These great industrial titans certainly lived in splendor but were essentially stodgy old men in the national consciousness—images of Morgan's bulbous nose and Rockefeller's hollow, ghostly presence would not sell magazines or newspapers at the end of the twentieth century.

Jay Gatsby, however, a figure self-created and who had arisen from nothing, now this was a character who not only embodied what people wanted to believe possible via the American Dream, but also possessed glamour and good looks (with the young Robert Redford providing an example of the character based on the 1974 film). For the would-be titans of the 1980s and 1990s, who flourished in a blossoming celebrity age driven by increased access first through technology and later the web and other booming mass media channels, the idea of *Gatsby* served as a kind of role model. The newly minted Internet millionaire, for example, had little or no training in how to act once rich, but he or she might certainly remember reading of the high times embodied in Fitzgerald's novel or seeing a clip of the affluence represented in the film.

In early 1998, *New York Times* writer Michael Specter called those celebrities/icons who possessed the largest egos "giga-egos." The group, including Bill Gates, Martha Stewart, Ted Turner, and others, according to Specter, "somehow managed to convince themselves, and millions around them, that the American Dream rises and falls with every breath they take."[5] Although this notion centered on the unmatched arrogance of America's ultrawealthy class, Specter duly notes that without an audience that agrees, this level of self-importance cannot be easily reached. Just as Gatsby needed the throngs of partygoers to question his background and raise his profile, the megalomaniacs of the 1990s, whether Turner and Stewart or some twenty-something Internet whiz, had to have onlookers willing to buy the hype. While Gates and the others were not necessarily "young" giga-egos in the late 1990s, they were considerably younger than other business tycoons who found themselves writ large across the national consciousness.

Similarly, at the height of the Jazz Age, the synergy created when technology intersected with celebrity enabled Fitzgerald and others to become central figures in the public's conception of fame. For a time, Scott and Zelda stood as two of the most talked about celebrities of the era. In comparison, they were as big or bigger than Brad Pitt and Angelina Jolie or similar famous couples whose dual place in the spotlight both magnifies and intensifies the glare. Audiences in the 1920s simply had fewer mass culture distractions, which made the attention that much more concentrated.

What is so easy to forget today is exactly how young the Fitzgeralds were when they stormed New York City in 1920. They were a stunning couple in an age that recognized the growing power of the youth market. The success of Scott's first novel, *This Side of Paradise*, at the time a revelation and tribute to the young people of the post–World War I generation, pushed them onto the front pages of magazines everywhere. Even writer Dorothy Parker, hardened to the shimmer and shine of celebrity, realized their allure, saying, "They did both look as though they had just stepped out of the sun; their youth was striking. *Everyone* wanted to meet him."[6]

What took place in Silicon Valley during the dot-com boom seemed—in retrospect—eerily similar to what happened during the early 1920s. As a matter of fact, both eras were a kind of speculative ruse, allowing the truly wealthy to move in and out of the game at will with little at stake, but then leaving the masses to pay the price when the scheme came tumbling to earth. The gold rush centered on the high-tech industry created paper millionaires who rode that notoriety to instant fame in numerous publications that existed to hype the Internet, such as *Red Herring*, *eCompany Now*, *Upside*, *Business 2.0*, and *Fast Company*.

At the height of both the Roaring Twenties and the dot-com "revolution" a kind of national euphoria swept the country, capturing Wall Street, corporate America, the general public, and the media. In the later period, the Internet and the use of innovative technology genuinely exhilarated people. Yet, as the mania took hold, the financial picture grew shakier, fueled by an "Internet bubble" of market speculation and frenzied investment, primarily small investors who could use web-based trading sites to easily buy and sell stocks online.

The ensuing stock market boom revolutionized the way businesses operated by providing the capital to invest in new technology. Perhaps more important, the dot-com revolution fundamentally changed the way people communicated through Internet-based technologies, such as e-mail, message boards, chat rooms, and others. Thus despite the failure of most dot-com companies, the transformation continued through the use of technology and the Internet for business purposes.

In its broadest sense, the dot-com revolution served as a massive growth engine for the American economy. For the first time in recent history, the power and mystique of small, entrepreneurial companies began to dwarf that of established corporations. Given the public's willingness to invest in Internet-based startups, their valuations soared.

Finally given the chance at riches gained from stock options and participation in initial public offerings (IPOs), workers flocked to dot-coms, despite the risk involved. Added to the possibility for quick riches, the quirky, decentralized culture of web companies drew generation X workers (born 1965 to 1980) in droves. The media added fuel to the mass exodus from the Fortune 500 by reveling in stories of office foosball tournaments and game rooms, company-sponsored espresso machines, and a constant state of "business casual" clothing.

Tech entrepreneurs also promoted work as a way of achieving a more spiritual or fulfilling state, which appealed to the sullen masses of workers awash in endless rows of drab, gray cubicles in the nation's large companies. Startups were seen as antiauthoritarian and laid back, mirroring the lifestyle exuded in Northern California since the 1960s. Some of the early companies included PayPal, pets.com, eToys.com, dot-com "incubator" Internet Capital Group, and a slew of service firms to publicize and advertise these entities, such as Organic Online, Scient, and USWeb/CKS. The list of now-defunct dot-coms reads like a comedy sketch, ranging from fashion site Boo.com, which "burned" through its $135 million investment before declaring bankruptcy, to online toy retailer eToys, online newspaper LocalBusiness.com, and the self-descriptive FurnitureAndBedding.com. Online grocer Webvan may be the biggest failure in Internet history, churning through an estimated $1 billion before shutting down.

The companies that flamed out at the tail end of the New Economy bubble were like kindling for the recession wildfire that gripped the United States at the dawn of the new century. Over the course of one month (March 10, 2000, to April 6, 2000), the NASDAQ stock market lost $1 trillion in value; the figure then jumped to nearly $1.8 trillion by the end of the year.[7] The tsunami destroyed the dreams of many dot-coms in its wake and startled tech investors back to reality. For employees at start-ups, from the CEO on down, stock options ended up "underwater," worthless scraps of paper that would never regain their luster.

Even after NASDAQ crashed in spring 2000, investors rushed in to buy shares of depressed stocks, many of which would rebound slightly before falling for good. The media (fueled by business cable stations, like CNBC, which turned Internet CEOs into celebrities, and the plump ad-soaked tech magazines) made folk heroes out of people like Amazon.com's Jeff Bezos and Yahoo!'s Jerry Yang. So many Internet legends were tales of rags-to-riches glory or college students coming up with an idea in their dorm rooms that by focusing on them, the media made it seem easy.

By the end of 2001, thousands of dot-com companies went bankrupt and countless tens of thousands of employees lost their jobs. The massive failure of the New Economy and the subsequent trickle of new investments in technology companies, combined with corporate governance scandals and the September 11 terrorist attacks, sparked a recession that plagued businesses in the early years of the twentieth century. High-tech centers, such as Silicon Valley, San Francisco, Washington, D.C., New York, and Austin, Texas, were especially hard hit by the demise of the dot-com revolution.

Despite the meltdown, the high-tech revolution continued, though on a more modest scale, as traditional businesses used e-commerce and the Internet to meld online and physical storefronts. Companies used web-based services and technologies to become more efficient and profitable. It is nearly impossible to find an industry that has not been improved through Internet-based technology, whether it is in education and non-profits or financial services and manufacturing.

The dot-com revolution ended in early 2000, but innovation continued to propel companies into novel areas that mix business and the Internet. Figures released by the United Nations revealed that there were 655 million registered Internet users worldwide in 2002 and that global e-commerce topped $2.3 billion, doubling the figure from 2001.[8]

Linking the earlier period with the end of the twentieth century, a mix of venture capitalists and company leaders served as the era's new Scott and Zelda. The tech and business media filled countless posts and pages of stories hyping these individuals, fitting many of their narratives into either rags-to-riches journeys from humble beginnings to dot-com paper millionaire status or profiling the shenanigans of these young people as they got their first taste of wealth and fame. A great deal of the news coming out of Silicon Valley, New York City (dubbed "Silicon Alley"), and other tech hot spots seemed like a mixture of Jay Gatsby and Scott Fitzgerald tales updated for the late 1990s and early 2000s.

FITZGERALD AND FAME THAT ROARED THROUGH THE TWENTIES

The challenge with celebrity is drawing a line between it and everything else. In the case of the Fitzgeralds, fame grew exponentially and engulfed their fragile psyches beyond what they were capable of handling. The alcohol-fueled antics and reckless way they spent money are two obvious examples of their inability to deal with the chaos that flies alongside celebrity.

Ever since the rejuvenation of *Gatsby* and its incredible subsequent life as an important novel, public perception of Scott and Zelda is inextricably tied to the way people view the novel. Interestingly, what surely links the lives of the couple and the novel is the centrality of celebrity in their lives and those of the characters in the novel. We now know that the young couple attended opulent parties on Long Island that set the tone for the book. And, like so much of Fitzgerald's work, the intensity of the desire Gatsby feels for Daisy is a composite of Zelda and several other early loves in the author's life.

Regarding Fitzgerald, however, the common and historical view of him as a celebrity rather than an artist detracts from accepting his brilliance. This backlash has not gathered enough steam to be considered a revisionist movement, but there has been a more concerted effort at portraying Fitzgerald more fully as a serious writer and artist. As literary scholar Ruth Prigozy explains, "The evolving popularization of the Fitzgerald icon was shallowly concerned with sensationalism and fleeting celebrity, much more so than with the reality of Fitzgerald's art."[9] Prigozy's distinction between Fitzgerald the icon and the author as artist is spot on and demonstrates the balance and care one should take in examining the contrasting viewpoints of the author's persona and life.

Perhaps more challenging is differentiating between Fitzgerald's fame, his work, and the way he and Zelda were engaged by the mass media to essentially sell the Jazz Age. For example, the recklessness, self-indulgence, and faux-celebrity antics of the flapper transformed the women who lived by this code into one of the era's most lauded symbols. As such, it is easy to understand why the glamorous Zelda Fitzgerald is often considered the first great flapper.

Although her dashing young husband fueled her fame, the couple grew notorious as they caught the eye of the nation's tabloids, newspapers, and gossip hounds, a veritable industry that sprouted up to cash in on the thirst for such chatter. American corporations and advertising agencies pushed forth in this area as well, featuring slick, artistic ads that sold glamour along with products. By the late 1920s, for example, Hollywood stars such as Gloria Swanson, Joan Crawford, and Clara Bow appeared in fashion ads that peddled the latest designs to middle-class buyers. As a matter of fact, Scott and Zelda looked like they could have emerged from the pages of a print ad, both exemplars of the age in grace and appeal.

Advertising agencies and marketing firms also facilitated the development of America's consumer culture both in Fitzgerald's day and in contemporary society. Thus, with each leap, whether based on some new innovation or tick upward in standard of living, corporations and advertisers benefited by linking efforts in both the physical accumulation of goods and the metaphysical feeling that acquisition instilled.

In other words, advertising and business prospered as the idea of the American Dream melded with the desire to consume. Actually, advertising created and then molded people's basic yearning for accumulation and consumption. Much of this effort required celebrity and fame as conduits for making the system work effectively. A consumer might need a new pair of shoes, but actually desire the same shoes worn by Swanson or Bow. Expanding the idea of a need into a deep longing effectively transformed the way people thought about consumer goods.

The resulting mix between selling, celebrity, and instilling culture formed a foundational tenet of modern capitalist America. Historian Jackson Lears explains, "Advertisements did more than stir up desire; they also sought to manage it—to stabilize the sorcery of the marketplace by containing dreams of personal transformation within a broader rhetoric of control."[10] The inside-outside control ultimately came to reside within corporate management initiatives, according to Lears. In other words, there is a structure underneath the vision of life advertising promotes based on the value system of the business world.[11] Advertising helped the nation define its consumerist dreams, while the industrial world worked diligently to ensure that such products were readily available.

Historian Stuart Ewen viewed the 1920s, in particular, as an era driven by the marriage of mass consumption and advertising, which resulted from the need for an ever-expanding consumer base in a mass-production-centered economic system. On its own, however, mass production did not present a compelling narrative that would capture the public's imagination. In response, by glamorizing industrialization and its products via advertising and celebrity endorsement, corporations and their agencies gained a foothold in creating culture.[12] The vision of what consumer goods a person or family needed to be living "the good life" fell to the advertisers who worked in concert with corporations to present that ideal image to American shoppers.

Whitman's Chocolates, for example, ran the first four-color ads in the *Saturday Evening Post*, capitalizing on the magic of chocolate, not the assembly lines that produced the product. A 1925 ad featured a golfer on the putting green in a bucolic rural setting and a group of flappers and their male chaperones divvying a box of chocolates while standing next to a beautiful, shiny blue automobile. Although the ad hopes to actually sell boxes of chocolates, it is clear that aspirations are on sale, too, since there is nothing inherently stylish, modern, or cool about eating chocolate or buying Whitman's. Eating "fresh" chocolates, according to the copy, however, provides the "pep" one demands within a busy schedule of summer play.[13]

Whitman's advertising announced to consumers that it stood as a hip product, reflecting the hot styles of the day with an aura of prestige: flappers with the customary low-slung hats and young men in natty suits or golf attire. Consumers who purchased the product, in essence, bought into a lifestyle the chocolate company created for itself via advertising.

The demographic Whitman's targeted is specific. These are society's elites, as evidenced by their summer filled with frivolity, not those hapless souls toiling away at low-paying factory jobs or working as clerks. The Whitman's Chocolates ads did not feature a celebrity directly but rather played off the hottest fashion styles of the day to create composite characters consumers might emulate.

Rather than portray the era via illustrations or paintings, a 1930 ad for Sunkist California lemons designed by legendary firm Foote, Cone & Belding used real Hollywood actresses in an attempt to get women to rinse their hair with lemon juice. Each star had her picture in the ad, along with a short quote plugging the product. Starlet Constance Bennett, for example, tells female consumers, "If I were making a list of beauty suggestions, I would place the lemon rinse right up close to the top." One might notice that the voice attributed to Bennett is folksy and nonthreatening, appealing to the reader hoping to replicate the fashion sense of a Hollywood actress. Other stars who appeared in the ad included Betty Compson, Marian Nixon, and the ill-fated Mary Nolan, whose career exploded and then quickly fizzled due to relationship and drug challenges.[14]

One of the most interesting tidbits regarding Fitzgerald's past is that he attempted to launch a career in the advertising business in New York City just after his stint in the army ended. Although he failed, as he would in Hollywood much later, because he simply could not write to other people's dictums, he obviously gained some insight into marketing and branding that he later put to use for himself. His letters to Perkins over the decades showed a keen interest in marketing and branding, though neither writer nor editor used the terms as we do today. Nevertheless, Fitzgerald, even at the early points of his career, comprehended how his personal brand could be used to boost his career.

For example, Fitzgerald walked both sides of the fence when accused of writing autobiography and passing it off as fiction. Scholar Kirk Curnutt contends: "Despite Fitzgerald's claims that he was chronicling generational uncertainties, it remain inarguable that he capitalized upon his early success to fashion a personal mythology that the media eagerly promulgated." These efforts included writing his own ad copy, "puff pieces about himself" for newspapers, and appearances in gossip columns. Later, as his fame intensified, Curnutt explains, Fitzgerald also wrote sarcastic nonfiction essays lampooning the celebrity status he and Zelda attained, including the popular "How to Live on $36,000 a Year."[15]

What Fitzgerald's efforts in personal branding reveal is an astute comprehension of celebrity and the burgeoning mass media industry. Although the popular image in today's mind is one of him on a decade-long bender, the young author could be quite shrewd. Often, for example, he would attach his name to essays Zelda wrote to force the editors to pay his freelance rates, rather than hers, since he stood as one of the highest-paid writers in the country. While the term "calculating" might be too judgmental to affix to Fitzgerald's marketing efforts, he clearly realized that this work had meaning in a world increasingly looking to the stars on Broadway and in Hollywood.

GATSBY-ESQUE CELEBRITY CULTURE

Drawing on his own experience with meteoric fame, Fitzgerald anticipated how intricately wound the vision of success is with celebrity in America. As a result, readers are about a third of the way through the novel before they encounter Gatsby in any meaningful way. Even here, though, it is indirect, taking place in a conversation among strangers at one of his extravagant parties. The anonymous guests, a handful of the hundreds or more on hand, speculate about their host's past because that is what people do at such events. They gossip and react to gossip, which merely fuels the desire for more information.

After one woman confesses that she heard he "killed a man," the tone of the conversation shifts to both wonder and awe. In some respects, the nameless guest, merely referred to as "the first girl," is a pseudocelebrity for the moment, playing the valued role as keeper of information, another vital cog in a society obsessed with celebrity. "A thrill passed over all of us," Nick explains. "The three Mr. Mumbles bent forward and listened eagerly."[16] Fitzgerald realized that keeping the novel's namesake cloaked in secrecy would reveal deeper meanings about the quest for celebrity and the disparity between the growing importance of the surface sheen and inner person.

Fitzgerald's sophisticated awareness of fame also enabled him to portray what it is like for people to be near celebrity, to essentially be in the presence of wealth and myth and the thrill it delivers, even among those who are also rich and otherwise successful. The many partygoers do not really care that they do not know Gatsby. Instead, they accept, or perhaps even ingest, his aura by attending the parties. Whether or not he is a murderer, German spy, or war hero does not really matter to the throngs at the party. Representative of America in the 1920s, they just want to be where the action is and bask in the glory of Gatsby's largesse.

Being rich affords the wealthy with an opportunity to basically rent celebrity or buy into its trappings, which automatically excludes anyone who cannot pay the fee. Gatsby imports gaudy representations of wealth, ranging from inanimate items like crates of lemons and oranges and exotic liquors to people themselves, whether famous orchestra leaders or Broadway cast members. Money grants access and confers fame.

In the real world, supermarket checkout lanes and magazine racks are filled with homages to the nation's celebrity obsession: bursting with full-color exposés and intrigue enveloping Hollywood's elite. Myrtle Wilson's copies of *Town Tattle* strewn around the New York City love nest bejeweled with Tom Buchanan's money were replaced by the real thing: *People* magazine, the *National Enquirer*, and dozens of similar glossies. The thirst for celebrity news surged when the television program *Entertainment Tonight* launched in September 1981. Melding the focus of the tabloid with a news format ushered in a new desire for all things celebrity.

The culture industry alive in the twenty-first century did not just spring to life with the advent of the grocery store tabloids, entertainment news shows, or the Internet. The fascination with celebrity took hold at the dawn of the last century, when the great rivers of technology, media, and spending power melded to form a powerful American popular culture stronger than it had been before people were inextricably linked by these forces. The huge, transformational cultural waves were fortified by the nation's burgeoning strength as an economic, military, and political force globally.

People used popular culture as a guidepost in these early days, essentially navigating among one another using its signs, symbols, representations, and ideas to makes sense of the changes taking place around them and the larger world that seemed nearer than ever before. Popular culture, then, proved to be a kind of common language that crossed many of the socioeconomic and race-related barriers that often divided people. American music, literature, style, consumer products, and technology—

certainly unique from its European counterparts and roots—gave people new means of engaging with one another and the ideals altering the nation.

Contemporary culture bursts with similar examples of the ultrarich mingling with celebrities, each side hoping some of the other's magic dust will rub off. The rock band Kings of Leon, for example, performed at a 2012 New Year's Eve party hosted by Russian billionaire Roman Abramovich. The party, held on a yacht off the resort island St. Barts, included numerous additional celebrities, from actor Jake Gyllenhaal to *Star Wars* creator George Lucas. [17] Even those less fantastically wealthy can mingle with actors, athletes, and other celebrities by playing golf at charity pro-am and celebrity tournaments. These events typically carry entry fees for noncelebrities in the $5,000 to $10,000 range, though the fabled AT&T Pebble Beach National Pro-Am, part of the PGA Tour and televised globally, costs in excess of $25,000. [18] Expectedly, most of the people who enter these tournaments are high-powered corporate CEOs, local business leaders, and other pseudocelebrities.

What these kinds of pay-for-play events demonstrate is that everything is for sale in a capitalist economic system. With enough money, one can get an audience with a U.S. senator or hire a pop star to play at a child's sixteenth birthday celebration. Fitzgerald anticipated the inauthentic moment that enabled people to live vicariously through celebrity and wealth, which sullied the romance of the moment.

The parties in the novel are all external, intended to demonstrate Gatsby's wealth, while he himself hides away, purposely removed from the scene. Yet, in hiding from the guests, Gatsby intensifies his exclusivity and position above them. He represents the ultimate VIP section, roped off spiritually by the labyrinth mansion and physically by bodyguards and lackeys who do his bidding.

***

In 1935 Fitzgerald was at a low point financially and spiritually. *Esquire* editor Arnold Gingrich suggested that he write something—anything—that would justify an advance from the magazine, which at the time was essential in keeping the writer from eviction or starving. The result was three essays published in *Esquire* for February, March, and April 1936: "The Crack-Up," "Pasting It Together," and "Handle with Care." In this series, Fitzgerald develops a key theme: his concept of emotional bank-ruptcy, the idea that it is possible to use up one's capacity for emotion and be left with nothing.

In Fitzgerald's era, many people (perhaps led by his ultramacho, sometime friend Ernest Hemingway) found such confessional writing a sign of weakness. Literary greats—most thought—should not position themselves as fragile or possessing insecurities. In retrospect, however, one might reinterpret Fitzgerald's memoir/essays in *Esquire* as an early indicator of what currently fuels much of the contemporary publishing industry. Today's readers want to see into the minutiae of those deemed famous, even if the celebrity industry has created them.

Much of the modern obsession with celebrities and their lives is driven by obtrusive investigation into their daily habits. In the twentieth and twenty-first centuries, the outlets for the tidal wave of celebrity clutter grew as technology enabled television to expand from a handful to thou-sands of stations, then grew exponentially as the Internet provided count-less new vehicles for disseminating celebrity-focused images and infor-mation.

Interestingly, Fitzgerald had an eye on this possible future, at least the aspect of investigation and its consequences. In the novel, what started as gossip among partygoers about their host's riches, for example, later led to Tom leading an investigation into Gatsby's past. In addition, a news-paper reporter shows up at Nick's door, snooping around after rumors of the mysterious Gatsby filtered to him.

The cycle at work in Fitzgerald's book: from seemingly innocent gos-sip to more pointed rumors to real investigation, both private and media driven, is one at work in modern celebrity culture. Today, though, the media wolves are always ready to pounce, even if rumors cannot be substantiated. Sensationalism sells, while the potential for retraction gets buried to the degree that it is not a concern among those on the chase for dirt. The challenge has become more disconcerting as the formal media increasingly gives way to citizen journalists and others with little or no training in journalistic ethics. Given the number of outlets the web presents, anyone with a cell phone camera and the ability to type can self-identify as a journalist.

The real media firestorm activates, however, if rumors turn into real-ity. Stampede mode occurs, like when Tiger Woods knocked over a fire hydrant with his SUV in the middle of the night near his home. The oddness of the incident subsequently set off a string of investigations into the golf star's private life that turned his seemingly charmed existence on its ear. Jordan Baker is portrayed as one of the nation's top female golfers, appearing on the front of the sports page enough that Nick thinks he recognizes her when they meet. Although Nick seems a casual fan, he has heard rumors of her cheating. In today's age, there are good odds that someone would have caught the indiscretion on tape—maybe a video recorder on an iPhone—and the resulting story would lead on countless thousands of websites, video sites, news programs, and ESPN.

Across popular culture mediums, ironically, early death is another avenue for celebrities to become iconic. Fitzgerald as the angelic star of the 1920s fits this bill similarly to the Doors lead singer Jim Morrison or Nirvana front man Kurt Cobain. Fitzgerald's resurrection at the hands of readers and the academic community is another link to celebrities who die but are kept in the public eye by fans who will not let them fade completely from the spotlight.

Gatsby also slides into this category. Nick's book with him at the center will ensure that the legend will live on as the narrator sees it, not necessarily tied to reality. Fitzgerald saw the dark side, too: according to critic Clive James, the author had special foresight when it came to fame, explaining, "Fitzgerald guessed where celebrity, if pursued for itself, was bound to end up: as a dead body in the swimming pool."[19] What he could not have foreseen is that early death might serve as a boost, potentially transforming a celebrity into something larger and more important than he ever achieved in life.

Gatsby is in some senses fueled by celebrity the famous and infamous individuals that flock to his West Egg mansion in search of fleeting fun and bootlegged whiskey. Scholar Stephen Gundle explains that Jay Gatsby "is not just an ambitious individual but a man who has a dream, a dream that can be seen as the American dream of success and personal happiness." In an era of illusion like the one Fitzgerald unraveled into its essential bits, one sees the clear ties between celebrity and publicity. Or, as Gundle proclaims: "He is a New Man who represents his age."[20] The old-moneyed elites balked at such base efforts, but as Fitzgerald demonstrates, image and celebrity are quintessential American traits.

Weaving all these connected threads together, one realizes that there is an unbreakable tie between Fitzgerald as celebrity author and his work, particularly *Gatsby*, since it deals so explicitly with fame and wealth.

Whether avid readers and we scholars agree with the link or not, it is bigger than our individual concerns, emerging as part of Americana. Writer John Updike, whose alternative career as a literary critic stands alongside Edmund Wilson's as one of the most brilliant in history, summarizes, "The life of F. Scott Fitzgerald, in the half-century since it ended, has become more celebrated and paradigmatic than any of the lives found in his fiction."[21] Given his keen comprehension of life as a celebrated author and literary standout and its marketing component, Updike sees the mixture of legend and reality as it pertains to the whole as Fitzgeraldian folklore. As a result of Fitzgerald's literary output and ever-evolving fame, Updike concludes, he joins Hemingway and Faulkner as "the third of a sacred trinity."[22]

What I exert, though, in adding to Updike's thought is that the popular image of Fitzgerald and his place in popular culture makes him the dominant member of this trinity, even though Hemingway also graces culture across various channels. In a culture always concentrated on celebrity and fame, Fitzgerald has risen to the summit of the nation's literary greats. The elevation above his rivals and colleagues, however, has been on this mix of quality and celebrity. No one could have imagined at the time of Fitzgerald's death that this nearly forgotten author would transform into a national icon. In true American fashion, Fitzgerald attained this station via talent and stardom.

Part IV

Gatsby Lives: The Enduring Legacy of the Great American Novel

10

IS ROMANCE TIMELESS?

Then he kissed her. At his lips' touch she blossomed for him like a flower and the incarnation was complete.—The Great Gatsby

The "2012 Harlequin Romance Report" surveyed single women across the United States to find out how they felt about romance in the twenty-first century. The report also delineated what these women thought the future might hold for romance as both an idea and a practical aspect of their daily lives. The results of the survey clearly indicate that romance is an important part of women's lives, particularly their mental selves. More than half (55 percent) admitted that romance is "very important" to their overall happiness, which ranked the topic right alongside personal health as the top item.

Despite the importance single women place on romance as a factor in determining their personal happiness, a huge disconnect exists when they assess their current love lives. As a whole, the survey revealed that satisfaction with the amount of romance in one's life decreases with age. Only 36 percent of eighteen- to twenty-year-olds said that they are "very satisfied" versus just 20 percent of thirty-six- to forty-year-old respondents. Moreover, just 39 percent of the latter group claims that they experience romance when they are seriously dating someone. [1]

Sadly, although single women yearn for romance, these results indicate that most never really attain it at a satisfactory level whether young or old. If popular culture representations of married life carry any truth at all, then one can only imagine the complete deprivation of romance married women experience in their lives. From this rather harrowing news about how women feel about romance and the utter lack of it in their relationships one can only conclude that there is something terribly amiss between the two sexes in contemporary America.

There may be a silver lining, though. Despite the Harlequin findings, single females remain optimistic. Some 84 percent of them believe that romance is out there waiting for them and that they will find it. Wake up, guys! The path to your dream girl's heart is obvious: in one word— romance. [2]

While it would be impossible to quantify the numerous factors that lead to a person's feelings about romance, *Gatsby*'s ubiquity—the meta-*Gatsby* that exists within our culture—certainly makes it a candidate for a strong impulse in this area. Many people are first exposed to the book at a formative age, as young as thirteen or fourteen years old as high school freshmen, while others read and study it in the subsequent high school years. Then, the ideas and themes are revisited in college, another seminal period when the novel's premises are studied in a more mature way. Furthermore, the fact that the two most recent film adaptations center on the romance between Jay and Daisy provides additional evidence not only of romance's centrality in popular culture, but how *Gatsby* plays a role in dispersing those ideas.

In examining Jay Gatsby, one must assess the character as one filled with romance, both in a loving nature and as an obsessive force. Scholar Ronald Berman discusses the notion of romantic love and how understanding the Jazz Age from a contextual viewpoint helps the reader comprehend the title character better. "Gatsby has many flaws," Berman says, "but they do not include the conception of sacred love. What is 'too much' to be demanded? Not the idea that Daisy is worth devotion nor the idea that life changes profoundly, in its very identity, through love." [3] And doesn't this sound like a plausible definition of romance?

Fitzgerald produced a stunningly romantic novel that is at its core completely unromantic. As readers and viewers, we applaud or root for Gatsby's ideal vision of romance, yet in the real world, it would probably get him a restraining order or at least labeled a "creeper," which in today's technology world is the slang term for someone who cyberstalks or acts creepy online.

The notion of granting hope to Gatsby in his quest is also made plausible by the fact that Tom Buchanan is a certifiable scoundrel and an outright hypocrite. In addition, we long for Gatsby's dream because it is the eternal story of lost love, which I contend is a much more important theme in today's world, because it has been completely woven throughout culture. In other words, we have more experience with the idea of lost and/or secret love than audiences did in Fitzgerald's day.

***

This chapter examines the romantic aspects of *The Great Gatsby* and addresses the notion of romance in the contemporary world. I argue that the two are linked, with *Gatsby* serving as classic literature's version of a modern-day romance novel. Over time, the novel has served as a showcase or guide to romance for countless readers, which has only been accentuated by the various film versions.

Readers are willing to forgive Gatsby for many aspects of his secret life and self-created personality in the novel, whether it is his Mafia ties or blatant adultery, because the romance is so overpowering and complete in his mind. Although hardened and always being called to the phone to deal with his faraway criminal underlings, for example, Gatsby is ultimately tender, shy, and anxious when it comes to his initial meeting with Daisy after the many years apart. His giddiness and embarrassment are palpable as he fidgets over the tea and cakes Nick purchased for the encounter and frets over whether or not he has sent over enough flowers. This is a commanding scene in the new *Gatsby* film and one many critics point to when evaluating DiCaprio's success as the title character.

In today's world of twenty-four-hour-a-day Lifetime movies and hundreds of cable television channels featuring romance-based content, in addition to the millions of romance and romantic novels sold annually, one could argue that the twenty-first-century Gatsby would get the girl. He would also deliver Tom the comeuppance he deserves . . . the kind of feel-good ending that audiences favor. Even though we understand that this is not the ending ahead for Gatsby—whether reading or rereading the book or seeing the film—we almost wish it were the case. The romantic impulse is too central to people's understanding of the world around them to think otherwise.

The sniffling and muted sobs you hear coming from those in the darkened theaters of America as DiCaprio and Mulligan play out the scenes in 3-D demonstrate how powerfully attuned to romance we all are. The Harlequin survey reveals how single females think about romance, while almost any other panoramic view of American culture shows similar results across mass media channels. Romantic love is a key aspect of our lives and a part of the meta-*Gatsby* influence this book envisages.

GATSBY: A ROMANCE

Returning to the 2012 Harlequin survey, we understand that romance— both as an idea and practical part of life—is critical in the lives of many single women. Perhaps a logical question is whether or not their responses indicate that the lack of romance is because men do not share in that notion or that (real-life) men simply cannot live up to the dreams of romance women promulgate. Yet, in at least partially answering that question, men are targeted as yearning for love, relationships, and commitment, too. As such, it is no stretch to conclude that romance, love, and all the tangents related to these ideas are significant as people define themselves and the world around them.

Looking across popular culture channels, it is easy to see that love and romance are central tenets of the entertainment business, which infers that the importance is mirrored in people's daily lives. The quest for romance is imbedded in our cultural DNA.

One simply needs to look to fairy tales and comic books to see the consequences of love and romance as it is presented in these texts. The Disney version of love, for example, almost always has true love winning the day against seemingly unfathomable evil. Thus, what saves the day for Sleeping Beauty and the kingdom as a whole is a prince who can not only defeat the evil witch, but also bring Sleeping Beauty back to life with true love's kiss, thus thwarting malevolence both physically and spiritually. Even media directed primarily at young boys carries underlying messages about love and romance. Superman, for instance, is largely self-defined by his secret love for Lois Lane, which he battles for with his cloaked identity as Clark Kent.

Jay Gatsby holds an obsessive love for Daisy at the core of his being and creates a world that he believes will wipe away the five long years the young lovers were apart. His commitment to an idealized romance gives new meaning to the old phrase "through hell or high water." Gatsby's willingness to fashion this mythic lifestyle to win her hand is more unequivocally declared in the 2013 film. Both the titular character and Jordan Baker directly address the notion, with the latter telling Nick, "He looked at her in a way that every young girl wants to be looked at."

What Fitzgerald created and Luhrmann emphasized is that at the heart of the American Dream is a significant other that one is willing to risk everything to love. It is ironic that Daisy is not more reviled or viewed as a villainous character across literary studies, because in the end her decision to stick with a sure bet versus taking a chance on love dooms Jay. She chooses a life of wealth, which ultimately costs Myrtle and Jay their lives. And, if we accept the film premise, this judgment also weighs heavily on Nick's teetering sanity.

According to noted literary scholar Harold Bloom, the deep connection between the American Dream and the romantic instinct exists. He explains, "Whatever the American Dream has become, its truest contemporary representative remains Jay Gatsby, at once a gangster and a romantic idealist, and above all a victim of his own High Romantic, Keatsian dream of love."[4] Thus, while we marvel at the spectacle of the life the young man creates, it is the vision and dream at the core of the novel that keeps one's heart racing. Boy meets girl, boy and girl fall in love, boy loses girl, boy gets girl, they live happily ever after: this is one of the primary cultural equations that occupies our lives and our minds across time.

Financial journalist Ben Stein, who moonlights as a television and film personality, makes an even stronger claim about the new film, explaining, "It's the best love story since *Gone with the Wind*. In some ways, it's better." While some critics find fault in the large party scenes and the 3-D special effects, Stein sees these items adding to the story line, which "makes everything like a fairy tale about money and love." For him, the tie between love and money is what fuels much of life, in addition to Luhrmann's strong adaptation. Referencing former junk-bond king Michael Milken, who later went to jail for his role in insider trading, Stein says, "One of the Milken people used to tell me, long ago, 'Don't forget. Money makes women fall in love.'" Though Stein admits that this is the family version of the financier's X-rated explanation, the thought holds true today, just as it did in Fitzgerald's day.[5] As a keen social observer and commentator, Fitzgerald knew this revelation about love and wealth intimately since his own lack of money, like the poor Jimmy Gatz, kept him from socialite Ginevra King and nearly wrecked his chances with Zelda.

SECRET CRUSH AND LOST, OBSESSIVE LOVE

One central theme that continues to draw readers to Fitzgerald's novel is that it centers on Gatsby's obsessive desire to reclaim lost love. At one point, he tells Nick that he has the power to relive the past, as if his aspirations are so immense that they will give him the power to physically yank back the hands of time. This is a feeling or emotion that is fresh in readers' minds as they contemplate the myriad of ideas contained in *Gatsby*.

The first time many young people experience *Gatsby* comes in a high school English class, often pushed on them as required reading. As a result of where they are in their lives and the central fulcrum primarily revolving around friends and the possibility of significant others, the force of Gatsby's love for Daisy can have consequences on their lives. Scholar Jonathan P. Fegley explains: "For most of our students, the intensity of first love is fresh in their minds, and some might even project a belief in the possibilities of love that rivals Gatsby's."[6]

This is the kind of romance that drives young people to romantic dramas directed at them, from *The Breakfast Club* in the 1980s to *The Notebook* in the 2000s. In each case, a poor boy gets the wealthy girl after a rocky chase and plenty of heartbreak along the way. These kinds of films have developed into classics that young women watch over and over again, which are often labeled "tearjerkers," because it is as if they are designed to make viewers cry. "In his love for Daisy, he evokes the love of a serf for a fair and beautiful princess, or of a poor man for the 'golden girl,'" explains scholar David Minter.[7] This same sentence could be used to describe *The Notebook*'s Noah and Allie or countless other romance-themed film couples that people can watch over and over again based on the ubiquity of DVDs, streaming capabilities, and the web.

It might be impossible to quantify the overall influence *Gatsby* has had on American culture, both directly and indirectly as a source of story lines, characterizations, and aesthetics. Yet, in some instances, the correlation is attributed and direct. For example, in mid-1990, *Gatsby* turned up with several other novels (Ernest Hemingway's *The Sun Also Rises*, D. H. Lawrence's *Women in Love*, and Gustave Flaubert's *Madame Bovary*) in a new advertising campaign for Calvin Klein's Obsession fragrance. Adding to the oddity, filmmaker and television show creator David Lynch directed the ads at a time when his quirky show *Twin Peaks* stood at the height of its popular culture influence. Klein, however, had a long history of eccentric commercials for Obsession. His madcap vision paid off, however, as sales at the time rose to more than $100 million annually, making it one of the top-selling perfumes in the world.[8]

The black-and-white spot opens with a close-up on the face of then-little-known actor Benicio Del Toro with the familiar Obsession logo in large white letters. The music is romantic yet melancholy, wailing horns that then dip behind the narrator. As the logo fades, "F. Scott Fitzgerald" appears in slightly smaller letters. As Del Toro turns his head, the narrator reads a passage about the first kiss between Gatsby and Daisy, the one that would change his life: "He knew that when he kissed this girl, and forever wed his unutterable visions to her perishable breath, his mind would never romp again like the mind of God."[9]

Quickly, actress Heather Graham—also before she became famous—appears in the Daisy role. Del Toro attempts smoldering intensity but actually seems scared. As they bend toward each other for the kiss, a sky full of stars is superimposed over the screen. Then, as they meet, a super close-up of their lips touching, followed by a blossoming white flower. As the commercial ends, "Obsession" appears, this time accompanied by a bottle of the fragrance.

Built around an interpretation of the novel it featured, each of the vignettes centered on the idea of passion, according to Calvin Klein executive Carmen Dubroc. "We wanted to use couples in love, so the ads would be more representative of the way more people live and love," she explained. "We've put romance in the place of promiscuity."[10] The loose idea of Gatsby as a model for passion might not jibe with the idea of a realistic portrayal of love, but the association between the novel and the perfume's moniker fits perfectly. The link is particularly apt when one considers the 1980s decade that had just ended and the unyielding tie between the obsession for wealth and love in that era.

GATSBY BELIEVED IN THE GREEN LIGHT

"So we beat on, boats against the current. . . ."[11] The end of *The Great Gatsby* is one of the best-known yet most maddeningly perplexing passages ever written. From the surviving manuscript facsimiles—lovingly compiled by the preeminent scholar Matthew J. Bruccoli—we know that

Fitzgerald did not engage in detailed editing of the ending from proof stage to publication as he did in other sections of the novel.[12] However, understanding how Fitzgerald pored over the manuscript, whittling each line to perfection, one can imagine the author searching for the exact words to end the book he knew would be his masterpiece. If I could have one conversation with Fitzgerald, the ending of *Gatsby* would be the topic: "So we beat on. . . ."

In reexamining the book's ending for details or inferences still unexplored, it is fruitful to interrogate the scene in its relationship to romance. The odd passage trips in and out of time but points to Gatsby's hope, which he wrapped in his love for Daisy. What made his future livable would be reuniting with Daisy. Yet, as Fitzgerald indicates, hope does not spring eternal: "year by year recedes before us." People do not give in or give up despite never quite catching up to their dreams, however, believing that the next morning's sunrise may provide the power and glory necessary for attaining these aspirations. In announcing "And one fine morning—," the author provides hope but does not complete the sentence, which may be, "—we will grasp the green light of our dreams." Optimistically, he claims, we continue to row against the tide, while the past remains fresh and our dreams become more remote.[13]

In the end, the optimism and romance at the heart of the novel contributes to its timelessness. Knowing, too, how Fitzgerald's personal history is sometimes interwoven into his fiction, the legend of the Jazz Age Fitzgerald commingles the line between *Gatsby* and reality, thus producing a more intense response to the novel. When we think of the green light and what it symbolized, it is not difficult to imagine Fitzgerald with his own beacon, whether it shone on winning the wild Southern belle or writing a major, important novel.

According to Arthur Mizener, there is a strong central link between Gatsby and his creator: "Fitzgerald was a man like Gatsby himself, at least in this, that he had a heroic dream of the possibilities of life and a need, amounting almost to a sense of duty, to realize that dream."[14] Writing in 1960, Mizener discussed how proud Fitzgerald would have been to know that his book sold well, "not out of vanity, but because his sense of achievement, his very sense of identity, depended on recognition."[15]

The kind of pride in accomplishment and determination in producing great work links Fitzgerald with Gatsby and also enhances the reader's understanding of the author's romanticism. There seems something almost hopelessly endearing about a person who cared so much, yet contained many flaws that made his pursuit of the romantic ideal more difficult. Maybe if there is a historical persona we almost think deserved to grow in stature and reputation after death it is Fitzgerald, who yearned for greatness in his own time but was cut down repeatedly by circumstances, his own missteps, and readers and critics who for the most part did not recognize the genius in their midst.

Bloom also draws a parallel between the creator and his creation, explaining, "Gatsby is the American hero of romance, a vulnerable quester whose fate has the aesthetic dignity of the romance mode at its strongest."[16] While the often vulgar and uncouth Jay Gatsby seemed vastly different from his creator on the surface, their romantic hearts seemed to beat as one.

NICK + JAY: A LOVE STORY

The final—and perhaps most interesting—romance in *The Great Gatsby* centers on Nick's deep love for Jay Gatsby. Despite the narrator's various claims to the contrary, such as his declaration of holding "unaffected scorn" for Gatsby, one senses deep affection and growing admiration as the events of that summer unfold.[17]

The reader cannot trust Nick's recollections to be completely truthful, but at the end of the novel after Gatsby's death, the tone changes. Nick becomes the center of the novel, from serving as a stand-in for Gatsby on various sinister phone calls from the man's underworld associates to hunting down Wolfsheim at his office in the city. He admits that in the tragic aftermath, "I found myself on Gatsby's side, and alone."[18]

After Gatsby is murdered, the story shifts to their relationship, so much so that Nick must set the shaky record straight by writing the book he is describing. Certainly, his story of Gatsby contrasts with the narrative that emerged immediately after his death, which Nick describes as "a nightmare—grotesque, circumstantial, eager and untrue."[19] Two years later, in retelling the story, Nick is still alone and on Gatsby's side.

Nick's love for Gatsby grows after the man's death, which allows him to express that emotion in a way that he could not when Gatsby walked beside him. Probably, such declarations would have been too much for

Nick and clashed with his conventional midwestern manners and world-view. He even goes into the room where Gatsby's dead body is laid out and talks with him, exclaiming, "I'll get somebody for you, Gatsby. Don't worry. Just trust me and I'll get somebody for you—" He even imagines Gatsby responding, "Look here, old sport, you've got to get somebody for me. You've got to try hard. I can't go through this alone."[20] Yet, with Nick at his side and later promoting him as a great man, Gatsby is not unaccompanied.

Nick's ability to transfer his feelings to Gatsby—even putting words in the dead man's mouth—reveals his yearning to do right by him, despite his internal sense of loss and regret. The imagined conversation speaks to the depths of Nick's emotional turmoil at the loss of his friend. It also addresses the guilt Nick certainly felt in not telling Gatsby how he felt more often. He takes great pride, for example, in telling the reader about the one compliment he gave him when he shouted across the lawn, "You're worth the whole damn bunch put together." But here Nick back-pedals a bit, explaining, "I disapproved of him from beginning to end," even though they had just spent the night talking after the accident and the unraveling of Gatsby's dream.[21]

Some commentators have interpreted Nick's love for Gatsby as ro-mantic or homosexual love. In early 2013, for example, novelist Greg Olear concludes that Nick is gay and in love with Gatsby. Olear reads a great deal into the manner that the narrator uses to describe each charac-ter, particularly in introducing Tom with "raw carnality," which can be construed as "decidedly erotic." From Olear's perspective, if Nick is gay and in love with Gatsby, it changes the way the novel must be read and assessed. He explains, "Then the entire novel operates as a rationalization of that misplaced love. Nick romanticizes Gatsby in the exact same way that Gatsby romanticizes Daisy."[22] Olear's analysis is interesting and sheds light on a new way to interpret the relationship between Gatsby and Nick, but there is a great deal of innuendo at play in his reading.

Fitzgerald's style using language to simultaneously explain and shroud events in mist and Nick's unreliable narration contribute to the possibility of one questioning his sexuality. A more concrete example, according to Olear, is the section of the novel that begins with Nick meeting Myrtle, Tom's mistress, and the party that ensues at the illicit couple's New York City love nest.

In one of the stranger episodes of the novel, Tom reacts to his mistress's shouting his wife's name over and over again by breaking her nose with a sharp, open-handed blow. While pandemonium breaks out in the small apartment, Mr. McKee, the feminine-looking photographer, wakes from his passed-out state and wanders toward the door, attempting to get back to his own flat downstairs. Oddly, Nick flatly states, "Taking my hat from the chandelier, I followed."[23] There is no rationale given for this, nor much indication that the two men even spoke to one another over the course of the drunken revelry.

On the surface, it seems that Nick is just uncomfortable with the chaos and Tom's violence. One must wonder, though, why follow Mr. McKee out? After a sexual-innuendo-laden conversation in the elevator ("Keep your hands off the lever"; "I didn't know I was touching it"), the next time we hear from Nick, some indeterminate amount of time has passed. Fitzgerald's intervention here is telling, too, since the passage begins with ellipses [. . .] and continues: "I was standing beside his bed and he was sitting up between the sheets, clad in his underwear, with a great portfolio in his hands."[24] One can imagine a scene in which after making love, McKee wants to show off to Nick by displaying his photography, which is the way he structures his world.

It is impossible to know what happened during that time, roughly between 10:00 p.m. and 4:00 a.m., however, because Nick jumps from the bedside and McKee in his underwear looking at his photography to the cold platform at Pennsylvania Station, where the man awakes drowsily waiting for the train back to West Egg. All the reader knows for sure is that Nick got drunk and then experiences gaps in time that he does not account for. Perhaps the narrator just blacks out or cannot recall the events of the evening. Yet Olear states flatly that Nick "hooks up with Mr. McKee" and the evidence may suggest that they did.[25] This cryptic scene in *The Great Gatsby* gives the contemporary reader pause because there are many markers there that would indicate that something took place in those mystery hours that Nick cannot or will not discuss.

Of course, questions regarding Nick's sexuality lead to similar queries about Fitzgerald's, since so many readers invert the author and his narrator. Furthermore, there were rumors of Fitzgerald and Hemingway engaged in a homosexual affair in the late 1920s, some of them started by Zelda, who in the midst of her madness used every possible target in attempts to demoralize her husband. She called into question his penis size, too, in a fight, claiming that he was too small to satisfy her. Hemingway later used the latter accusation against Fitzgerald in his posthumous memoir *A Moveable Feast*, saying that Fitzgerald asked him to look at it to prove Zelda wrong.[26]

Whether or not Fitzgerald held secret homosexual feelings and used Nick as a kind of surrogate to deal with those emotions, according to Matthew J. Bruccoli, "there is no evidence that Fitzgerald was ever involved in a homosexual attachment." A more realistic interpretation of his feelings about men, the great literary scholar explains, is that: "His close friendships with men were expressions of his hero worship and generosity."[27] Scholar Scott Donaldson also examines Zelda's charge, seeing it as a hurtful accusation that caused Fitzgerald to doubt himself, because he had always been considered too pretty and had an inquisitive mind that appreciated the feminine outlook, which he himself identified.[28]

***

One cannot deny the ties between Gatsby and the romantic idea as it has developed in America. Film critic Richard Brody of the *New Yorker* claimed that part of his fascination with the novel centered on its romantic core, "a vision of a rhapsodic and doomed romanticism that both captures the elusive shimmer of the so-called Jazz Age and rides on the back of another literary generation."[29]

Readers and audiences have shared this feeling, seeing Jay and Daisy as a kind of latter-day Romeo and Juliet, star-crossed lovers who cannot find ultimate happiness. Obviously, though, *Gatsby* cannot be boiled down that way, regardless of the way people have interpreted the book or tried to fix the films to emphasize this notion.

Returning to the recent Harlequin report on the state of romance in America, one can see how both the novel and film versions maintain popularity. Particularly in the Redford and DiCaprio movie vehicles, Gatsby's pining for his lost love gets slathered in Hollywood-style, overblown sentimentality. In putting the story on the big screen, movie types are saying, Do not fear, ladies, there is nothing disturbing about this rich creeper sidling his way into a married woman's life. Because it is lost love, Gatsby's actions are justified, particularly when we find that Tom Buchanan is an adulterous oaf.

Although the Luhrmann picture earned mixed reviews from professional critics who could not seem to figure out if they loved or hated the film, the romantic elements stood consistently at the fore, since the director centered the movie on the Jay/Daisy relationship. Ty Burr, reviewing for the *Boston Globe*, pointed to the "lushly swooning depiction of Jay and Daisy's affair" as both a strength and weakness: "touching and funny" and also "overindulged." In the end, Burr concludes that "Luhrmann wants to make the teenage girls cry (and mine sure did, snurfling happily beside me in the dark)."[30]

Perhaps the counterpoint one might raise is whether the focus on the romantic tie works, since popular culture clearly pivots on love, relationships, and romance. Fitzgerald himself could easily be labeled a romantic writer, in both his short stories written for popular audiences and the more serious writing that he felt comprised his novels. One of the most compelling aspects of Scott Donaldson's biography of Fitzgerald—the telling title: *Fool for Love*—is that he examines the author's compulsive need to "attract the attention and admiration of others."[31] While some might infer that this connoted a weak personality, the upshot is that it made Fitzgerald a skilled interpreter of people and their actions, which, in turn, helped him become a great writer.

The process of ingratiating himself meant that he had to concurrently and quickly assess the person who drew his attention. It put Fitzgerald in touch with others' emotions, though he also possessed the ability to turn into the devil on a dime when drunk. I contend that Fitzgerald's personality fueled his romantic vision as he yearned to engage with men and women. Gatsby's reaching for the green light and rowing against the tide ever hopeful of reaching his dreams is the character at his most romantic, because this is a view of romance at the center of one's worldview. It was Fitzgerald's, too.

11

A HOPE FOR READING AND THE QUEST FOR THE GREAT AMERICAN NOVEL

The Great Gatsby *is relevant for today's students. It gives us a much more clearer look on America before we were born. It provides us with history.* The Great Gatsby *does indeed make us think more about our future and what is really important in the end.*—Kalee Kesterson, junior, Greenfield (Tennessee) School[1]

The Great Gatsby *is not relevant to today's students for many reasons. One is being that the novel's themes and meanings are over most students' heads. It does not correlate or influence anything in the students' lives.*—Anonymous, junior, Greenfield (Tennessee) School

Books abound. There are books about writing books, books about reading books, books about how to read books better, and books about writers who write books. There are an endless number of genres, categories, and topics, yet at the end of the day, many people simply want to know which of these is the best book. Which book stands as the most important book ever?

This question may be unanswerable if one considers that each nation would have its own candidates and there is no cosmic judging body that could shuffle through them all to come up with a selection. For the United States, though, I would argue that *Gatsby* is that book, yet any number of comparable works could fit the bill. A person's outlook on such grandiose notions is driven by countless factors, certainly including personal experiences, education, and one's worldview. Obviously, to even have this conversation, we need to eliminate the primary texts of the world's major religions, which in my mind are in another category.

From a historical perspective, a rationale in the argument for *Gatsby* is its ubiquity in America's high school and higher-education system. As discussed in other places in this book, the way the novel has served as a mainstay in high school language arts classes and on college syllabi virtually guarantees that it is in the conversation about important books. Scholar Paul Lauter explains, "Education—like other cultural institutions—is an arena for struggle, and what is decided there significantly affects the political economy and important social arrangements . . . culture . . . is a significant way of constructing and mobilizing power."[2] Therefore, the education system is essential in understanding how people create points of view and think about the world around them.

The idea that we need books (and by extension, reading, which seems obvious, but is not if one has been inside a classroom recently) is logical and straightforward on the surface. However, in the public discourse about education, there is a decided lack of logic and sensibility. The victory of standardized management in the nation's K–12 schools has privileged test scores and worksheets over traditional education, such as deep reading of literature and nonfiction, as well as writing, which is virtually eliminated in the standardized world.

Despite the current national obsession with reading-test scores, for example, all the attempts to quantify and standardize reading have actually produced little or no improvement in reading ability as a whole. As a matter of fact, many educators would argue that the emphasis on testing has reduced the amount of time teachers can devote to reading without risking backlash for not teaching to the test. Writer Joy Hakim explains the root cause, saying:

> What we aren't doing in schools is exciting children with the printed page and wonders it can offer. We continue to present reading as a boring school subject that can't compete with television. Yet as any reader will tell you, it is TV that is ultimately boring, and books are what can transport you to other worlds.[3]

Hakim and other curriculum specialists point to the many causes for students not being energized by reading, and the use of standardized curriculum is one of the primary targets, even as other commentators push the blame off on parents, bad teachers, or socioeconomic challenges.

Concurrently, a general anti-intellectualism has swept the nation (though from another perspective, a simple argument could be that it has always existed and is merely more noticeable at this moment in our national history). One sees the devolution rearing its ugliness in public debate over critical issues. The result is that people and political parties are segregated. Rationality and common sense are out the window, replaced by incessant rigidity and shrill shouting.

In response to this state of affairs, I assert that the need for books and deep reading is more important than ever. For example, in contrast to earlier eras when nations had the ability to destroy one another and the planet, and at least worked toward ensuring that outcome would not come about through acknowledgment of the challenges, in today's world, people and nations would rather bury their heads and pretend that the problems we face do not exist. One simply needs to wade into the environmental battles regarding global warming or fracking to witness the termination of sane examination. It is as if audiences and stakeholders would prefer shouting and theatrics to wisdom.

Rather than realize that people and nations can only overcome problems by uniting against them, adversaries in the contemporary world believe they are scoring points by drawing lines they will not cross. There is no longer give-and-take, which creates a losing environment for the kind of critical thinking and problem solving today's challenges necessitate.

Noted Harvard professor Marjorie Garber explains that many readers pick up books, particularly older texts, "to shape ideas about identity, politics, gender, and power." As a result, "readers tend to identify with the major characters and to measure their actions and thoughts by the degree to which they imagine themselves in similar situations or with similar choices."[4] Deep reading and analysis provides, in part, the tools we need to combat this negative atmosphere.

We cannot deny that *Gatsby* is a key component in this discourse. Nor can we deny that the nation needs these kinds of texts. Now more than ever, reading is waging a losing battle with the bells and whistles of the Internet, thousands of cable TV stations, on-demand movies and shows, and the ubiquity of downloadable music. If reading a short, compelling novel that encompasses so many socioeconomic and cultural issues can help students deepen and strengthen their abilities to think and reflect about society's challenges, in my mind that is enough rationale for its continued place on high school and college syllabi now and well into the future.

***

What will become of *Gatsby* in the future, particularly as a part of the literary canon and its place on academic syllabi in the high school and college classroom? This chapter attempts to answer this important query. The early indications are that the new 2013 Baz Luhrmann–directed adaptation starring Leonardo DiCaprio as Gatsby has energized people about the novel and Fitzgerald. Perhaps, given the excitement regarding the movie, we can expect that it will keep *Gatsby* in the vanguard for at least the next decade. Undeniably, the new film ensures that language arts teachers and college instructors across the nation will have new fodder for classroom discussion and student assessment, since the novel and film differ enough to make such conversations useful.

This chapter (and the entire book, really) also addresses a classic chicken-and-egg question: Which came first, the canonization of *Gatsby* or the critical resurgence and enormous sales of the novel? We have ample evidence. For example, novelist and critic John Updike explains in his inimitable way, "Academia, intoxicated by his eternal undergraduate effluvium, has clasped Fitzgerald to its bosom."[5]

In clasping this question to my bosom, I thought it compelled study with actual students engaged with the book and various film adaptations. Obviously, it is one thing for the researcher to ponder what all this means, but quite stirring to hear from young people. As such, I worked with thirty high school students in eleventh grade at Greenfield School in Greenfield, Tennessee, a small town (population about 2,260) in the northwest part of the state, a far cry from the elite shores of Long Island. Teacher Denise Douglas reports that the small, K–12 school has 165 total students, with about 60 percent on free and reduced lunch.

Quincey Upshaw, a former high school teacher now studying for a doctorate in English and teaching at the University of South Florida, also provided insight into her experiences with the novel.[6] Upshaw taught in a much different environment than small-town Tennessee—an honors English class at East Lake High, a large high school in Florida's Pinellas County, near affluent Tarpon Springs. The students primarily came from upper-middle- to upper-class families with average incomes in the

$150,000 to $300,000 range. A handful of other teachers and former teachers who wished to remain anonymous also contributed to my thinking.

These student assessments provide the reader with additional insight into the novel's meaning (and the film's, too) for young people today and its potential role in their futures. The reasons why they make *Gatsby* part of their pedagogy gives a glimpse at the book's place in the high school classroom. I find that this material helps us contemplate the centrality of Fitzgerald's novel in curricula, which is itself under attack in a standardized management education culture. Education does not hinge on whether or not teachers assign *Gatsby*, but the system must focus on reading and writing, which one hopes the new Common Core Standards will facilitate rather than decimate.

THE GREAT AMERICAN NOVEL AND THE LITERARY CANON

For my money, the Great American Novel must be as elusive and enormous as the country it is supposed to represent. Nothing, then, comes as close to this expansiveness as *The Great Gatsby*. Yet there are many other contenders for the crown, from Melville's *Moby Dick* to the latest sprawling epic by today's hottest novelist.

The irony runs deep in labeling the novel as the undisputed king of American novels because on paper at least, Fitzgerald—an insecure, drunken, college dropout—had no business writing it. He did not even write it in the United States, for God's sake! Instead, after retreating to Europe to save money, he ground the text out between benders and attempts to keep Zelda on as short a leash as he could without being reduced to utter madness. The latter effort almost broke the couple into pieces, since her affair with French aviator Edouard Jozan destroyed something in her husband that he could never recapture. The affair and later psychotic breakdown she suffered took part of Scott, too. Scott Fitzgerald, though, is part of *Gatsby*'s lore. This self-delusional drunk . . . hack . . . writer for the slicks . . . for the paycheck . . . how did he do it?

The answer lies in the brilliance of the ideas contained at the heart of the book. According to scholars Jackson R. Bryer and Nancy P. VanArsdale, although they do not go as far as naming *Gatsby the* Great American

Novel, "It is a great American novel, portraying the traits, admirable and ugly, of an emerging and modern American character and American culture, influenced by the postwar era, the rise of a new generation of business and criminal tycoons, and the modernist movement in the arts."[7] These related topics come together so well in *Gatsby* that using the novel in the classroom opens the door to many of the central issues educated citizens must face.

Part of my response to someone who challenges my declaration of *Gatsby* as the Great American Novel—and many have emerged to question the notion in the wake of the 2013 film—is to essentially say, "Look at the scoreboard!" Tens of thousands of high school and college teachers over the course of the last handful of decades have assigned this novel because it helps them teach some aspect of life or theme that they find important for students to understand. *Gatsby*'s presence in high school and college classrooms all these years cannot be reduced to less than what it is.

In even addressing the question of a Great American Novel, however, the larger issue at stake is probably centered on the overall importance we place on reading and the humanities in general. We live in an age where these ideas are under attack from conservative and liberal forces that argue against canonization of particular texts.

Certainly, the rise and fall of "the" canon or "a" canon is important. From a cultural viewpoint, the identification or rejection of a common core set of guiding beliefs or principles helps us understand our own uniqueness, as well as the common bonds that tie us to one another. Yet others would argue whether a set of literary texts could hold up under the continual onslaught of new voices and new experiences entering the fray as the nation and world transforms.

There are many good and other not-so-valid explanations for why a writer or specific work goes in or out of fashion at a given moment in history. One solid rationale is that books are part of the mass media entertainment industry and therefore subject to the fickle nature of consumers. Certainly Fitzgerald understood this idea; he continually obsessed over potential audiences, the people who bought books and magazines, and how he needed to shape his work (particularly his short stories) to meet their demands. At the same time, Fitzgerald always worried about his novels being viewed as serious literature and something apart from his short work.

Watershed historical events or moments can also sweep a writer into or out of the spotlight, according to literary scholar Morris Dickstein. His assessment of Fitzgerald's place in the canon ties it to larger events taking place in the nation. For example, in the Depression and war-filled 1940s, Fitzgerald became "simply irrelevant." In modern times, Dickstein contends, the move by scholars to recognize traditionally neglected writers has moved focus away from those traditionally associated with the canon: "To many professors Fitzgerald has simply become one of the dead white males, more a burden than a revelation."[8] These examples demonstrate how large-scale cultural waves impact the fate of particular authors.

I believe that the existence of a literary canon has consequence as we confront the challenges ahead and place the past in context. Great works of fiction assist us in finding commonality within our precious American individuality, even if the work in question does not contain a requisite number of ethnicities, perspectives, or diversity-based views. In other words, I see the literary canon as broad, deep, and adaptable. The keepers of the canon—primarily individual high school teachers and college faculty—should remain under constant vigilance to ensure that it contains books representative of the American experience.

In addition, one should not limit the canon based on the needs of the current education system or individual educators. Or, to put in more pointed language, the canon should not be limited because a seventh-grade teacher or tenured professor feels that he or she only has a certain amount of time to get through some subset of material. As a matter of fact, I would argue that we should base learning around these seminal texts and reading, rather than the school calendar or semester length. Too often in our current education system the success or failure of a school district and its teachers is based on the students' performance on standardized tests. Thus, the notion of preparing students for the exams trumps teaching them to be productive citizens with higher-order critical-thinking skills.

Scholar Mark William Roche addresses the idea of canonical texts by asking the question, "How does literature help us not only enlarge our individual frames of reference but also enhance our understanding of the collective concerns of an era—in our era, technology and ecology?"[9] This query juts right to the very heart of why a canon is necessary and that exposure to it in the American education system—even radically redefining the system itself—would make for a wiser, more prepared citizenry.

Importantly, too, the idea of a literary canon does not mean that only those who possess a "literary bent" partake in the work.

Canonical texts that illuminate ideas or individuals from fields outside literature may have a profound impact on the way the specialist approaches his profession and life's work. The same effort scholars and educators have made in pushing diversity into the canon could unfold in other areas, too. Roche is speaking primarily about multiculturalism, but his thinking would work across disciplines as well: "We might be especially attentive to works that don't simply replicate our feelings and anxieties but give us entirely different perspectives, including works from other ages and cultures."[10]

One cannot properly address the existence of the Great American Novel or the debate about whether or not it exists without thinking about the future of the book, which at this point in history hinges on the e-book. Although books abound, there is also a concurrent diminishing of physical books taking place. The increasing popularity of e-books, spurred by the ability to read books electronically on Amazon's Kindle reader, Barnes & Noble's Nook, or Apple's iPad, is quickly changing the book industry, from the way authors write to the distribution and sales channels. One only needs to think back to the demise of bricks-and-mortar retailer Borders to understand how different the business is from the past.

Therefore, as we ponder education, reading in the future, and the possible role *Gatsby* may play in this new environment, the fate of books as physical objects is important, as is the transition to e-books. For instance, *Publishers Weekly*, a magazine devoted to charting the industry, reported that sales of print books dropped 9 percent in 2012. Moreover, the Association of American Publishers reported that e-book sales comprised some 22.5 percent of the book industry's net revenue.[11] The drop in print books is not surprising, given the ubiquity of handheld electronic devices that enable people to access books via the web. However, the fact that more than one in every five dollars of profit is derived from electronic texts is surprising.

Although it is hard to imagine that *Gatsby* will not make a successful transition to e-book status, particularly given its importance in college and high school curricula and the boost the novel will receive from the release of the 2013 film and later DVD, other classics might have greater difficulty. E-book buyers, for example, do not necessarily need a librarian's help in finding titles or the advice of traditional book critics, especially in an era where newspapers are less important in setting the cultural agenda. As a result, e-books and their publishers might draw readers to the latest celebrity tell-all biography or trashy autobiography and away from classic texts by William Faulkner, Toni Morrison, or Ernest Hemingway.

ASSIGNING *GATSBY* IN THE AGE OF STANDARDIZED MANAGEMENT

"I remember so vividly the first time I read the book, the language was unlike anything I had ever read (and I read a ton!) and I was just blown away by it," explains Quincey Upshaw, as mentioned earlier a former high school honors English teacher in Florida. Her personal experience with the novel, as a matter of fact, led her to assign the book later as a teacher, in hopes of getting her students into it the way she experienced it. Sometimes it worked, others not so much. Upshaw explains, "I saw that same reaction in many of my sophomores over the years. Some would tell me it was now their favorite book. Others would contact me about it years later to tell me how reading it had changed their lives. Again, others just slept. Such is the life of a high school teacher."

If one were to survey high school and college instructors who use Fitzgerald's novel in their classrooms, Upshaw's story would be duplicated countless times. Fitzgerald produced what scholar James L. W. West III calls "one very teachable gem of a novel . . . which in form and language fell perfectly in line with the concerns of the postwar New Critics."[12] The concurrent forces of physically greater numbers of students in the education system, a publisher looking for sales, and scholars driving the intellectual importance of the book makes this outcome seem inevitable, though no one orchestrated these events to take place together.

In 1989, *USA Today* reporter Dan Sperling wrote about a survey conducted by the Center for the Learning & Teaching of Literature at the University at Albany, SUNY, that revealed that high school reading lists had not really changed much in the last quarter of a century. While *Gatsby* did not top the list of required reading (the sacred spot reserved for Shakespeare's *Romeo and Juliet*), it placed fourth, which meant that some 54 percent of 322 public high schools surveyed posted it as required reading. Further, the study showed that required texts were virtually the same whether at private, religious-based, or independent schools. At that time, schools with large minority populations also read the same texts. [13]

While some critics question whether a literary canon should or can exist, other thinkers are addressing the primacy of standardized management systems that many argue undervalues deep reading and writing. What has emerged under standardized management in the recent past is a complex bureaucracy that exists to keep the multibillion-dollar system in the hands of corporations. One really cannot comprehend K–12 education without assessing standardized management and its consequences.

In January 2002, several months after the September 11 bombings that rocked the United States and sent reverberations through the global community, President George W. Bush signed No Child Left Behind (NCLB) into law. Senator Edward Kennedy (D-Mass.) and Representative John Boehner (R-Ohio) stood on each side of Bush, smiling among attendees publicizing the new legislation. Television cameras whirred and cameras clicked, broadcasting the event as a bipartisan display of unity for a tense nation still in the grips of the terrorist attacks.

At its core, NCLB seemed logical: the much-ballyhooed legislation implemented a series of reading- and math-based standardized tests designed to measure students' ability in these subjects versus their grade level (dubbed "adequate yearly progress" or AYP). Under the new program, schools across the country would be able to compare student achievement and get meaningful data regarding learning outcomes. Perhaps more importantly, NCLB set up penalties for districts that did not score well enough. Overall, NCLB proponents believed that the new legislation would concentrate efforts on improving America's schools, particularly for poor and minority students, while simultaneously providing incentives for good districts to become even better.

Fast-forward to today and opinions regarding NCLB are almost completely negative and range from labeling it merely flawed at one end of the spectrum to an utter failure at the other. Not mincing words, Senator Michael Bennet (D-Colo.), Denver's former school superintendent, told a national newspaper, "If you called a rally to keep No Child Left Behind as it is, not a single person would show up." [14] In response to this kind of overt disapproval that Bennet displays and calls from education reform leaders nationwide, President Barack Obama initiated his own standardized test program, called "Race to the Top," and allowed individual states to seek waivers from some parts of NCLB. The question is whether or not these new actions will simply replace one faulty system with another.

While NCLB may be slowly dismantled, refurbished under a different guise, or scrapped wholesale, the challenge for educators—where they have and will continue to face constant attack—is in the new environment that results from ten years of relentless battle between every participant in the fight over standardized testing. Regardless of whether pro-testing or anti-testing forces claim victory, the ghost of NCLB will continue to place standardized testing at the center of all improvement efforts.

In other words, the death of NCLB will not end the battle for educators and others opposed to what scholar Nel Noddings and others call "high stakes testing" or "tests that involve significant consequences."[15] Among America's educators and other interested audiences, the wholesale adoption of standardized management is simply defined as "teaching to the test." The idea is that NCLB testing places enormous constraints on teachers, which results in them teaching to the particular test, hoping that it will lead to higher test scores, thus avoiding the challenges faced if test scores are not met.

The wider criticism about NCLB is that the rigorous preparation and testing program is creating a generation of students so focused on getting the right score that they lose invaluable critical-thinking and creative skills. In addition, there are important areas not tested that can sometimes fall to the wayside in a school's march toward lifting test scores, such as writing, science, and social studies.

What is taking place in K–12 classrooms, as a result of standardized management, is that teachers have to sneak writing and deep reading into their courses, even though it could have detrimental consequences on student test results. Scholar James G. Henderson's alternative to standardized management is to emphasize "transformative education," which centers on teaching students via subject, self-, and social learning. Utilizing this ideology, Henderson and Richard D. Hawthorne see educators teaching the whole student, rather than identifying testing shortcomings. They ask us to imagine an alternative to high-stakes testing and its fruitful outcomes: "Imagine teachers who help their students change into people who can think for themselves, who can engage life imaginatively and fully as life-long learners, and who can embrace democracy as a vibrant way of living."[16]

The gap between teaching to the test and preparing students to become vibrant community members in a democratic society is enormous. Helping students to perform well on standardized tests tells us nothing about the student's ability to perform nuanced critical thinking, to problem solve, or to think deeply about subject matter. "Education . . . is a moral enterprise," according to Philip W. Jackson. Its "bottom line," he says, "aims at improvement. It seeks to make everyone it touches, teachers as well as students, better than they are now . . . tries to leave the world a better place."[17]

Transformative education—as a means of redirecting classroom efforts, unifying communities, and battling entrenched standardized management curriculums—is a construct that enables educators to reimagine their work, lives, and consequences on students. Rather than high-stakes testing with punitive negative consequences for educators, Kathleen R. Kesson and Henderson explain, "Education in the United States should be oriented towards the historic problem of preparing citizens for life in a democratic society."[18]

America's schools have an alternative to standardized management dictatorship, one that is not only more logical and inspirational but also easily adapted to the public relations warfare necessary within educational reform efforts today. The bottom line is that educating young people for lives as democratic learners who exhibit higher-order critical-thinking skills prepares them for lives in the information age. Contrast this aspiration with scoring *adequately* on standardized tests (in schools generally labeled as *failing*) and one can envision the path to a brighter future for the nation's schools and students.

Perhaps in an era of bullet-point presentations and content created for the short attention span of web readers, the idea that reading is important across a person's entire life span is as antiquated as manual typewriters and public pay phones. Yet I contend that deep reading and analysis of novels like *Gatsby* are critical in students' overall learning, as well as the kind of meaningful writing assignments that enable kids to engage with topics that influence their lives. Scholar Marjorie Garber contends, "So reading any literary work involves a kind of stereo-optical vision: one eye on the image of the past, the other on the present, the two eyes then combining them into a vivid single picture."[19]

More than just based on how it can be interpreted, *Gatsby* is also employed in high school and college curricula because of the way it is read as a poetic, lyrical novel. Teachers enjoy *Gatsby* for its contradictory use of language and hope that students will engage with the writing style itself.

Yet there is an ambiguity that confounds readers used to being given the answers in today's world of short attention spans. According to writer R. Clifton Spargo, "Fitzgerald's take on the American dream is, in the end, a cautionary tale. And yet, for all his resistance, Nick starts to sympathize with Gatsby and his quest—and the reader gets drawn in. There may be something pathetic in Gatsby's class striving, but there's something innocent about it, too."[20] Spargo's summary emphasizes the duality in the novel that attracts (or perhaps confuses) so many readers. Scholar Anthony Larson explains that from a reader's perspective, the "mystery only deepens as the reader advances in the novel, coming to the increasingly evident truth that Gatsby is a con-man, liar, and small-time gangster." Yet, according to Larson and other critics, "this contradiction/tension is at the heart of the novel and is its driving force."[21]

As narrator, Nick is the center of everything taking place and he cannot be trusted. Ultimately, a thoughtful reader might conclude that Gatsby himself is a fiction. Personally, I feel that one way to read the novel is to suppose—like in Chuck Palahniuk's *Fight Club*—that the dashing, elegant Gatsby is a persona Nick creates to woo Daisy from her brute husband and unfulfilling life. In this reading, Gatsby is Tyler Durden and Nick is Palahniuk's unnamed narrator, presenting a quasi-reality in which he gets the girl. Rather than battle Tom Buchanan physically, Nick invents a suave, ideal man who can hold his own via wealth and military heroics. Larson wisely asks, "Where does the voice of Nick the narrator end and where does that of Gatsby, the great liar and thief, begin?"[22]

Rather than provide easy answers, Fitzgerald layers the narrative in ambiguity and misdirection. The novel itself becomes a kind of puzzle, where according to Larson, "the reader is off once again, hunting down Gatsby's lies and faults so as to better judge him in the end."[23]

Secondary education played a pivotal role in establishing *Gatsby* as the Great American Novel. Surely it could not have achieved this status without decades of readers—as a matter of fact, decades of people *forced* to read the novel as part of their high school studies. Once educators bought into selling *Gatsby* en masse, it did not take long for others to recognize its importance.

In a standardized education system, one wonders about the future of *Gatsby* as part of high school curricula. Yet there is hope in that the novel is included as a primary text for high schools in the new Common Core Standards guidelines. The upside here is that teachers will be able to teach the novel, but the downside centers on whether it will be the novel itself or an abridged version of the text or some other form that bastardizes the language and nuance of the book. Often, alternative versions are provided for students deemed "struggling readers," which many critics believe is exactly the opposite tack teachers should take.

Returning to Upshaw's experience as a student reading *Gatsby*, and then assigning it in her classroom, that passion for the text compelled her to use it because she wanted to see the students get that same wow factor. The fact that Fitzgerald's novel has traversed the fickleness of the general public, stays on countless syllabi over time, and continues to enthuse teachers and students is profound. Upshaw also sees the long-term consequences of reading Gatsby via how past students engage with the text. She explains:

> I would urge them to read the book again at 20, then again at 25. I promised they would understand more about it and themselves if they did. The crazy thing is, I have a dearly beloved former student who is now a creative writing MFA student and she told me she did this, and I was right. I love being told I'm right by students as much as the next teacher, but the important part is that, for some students, this book really is life changing. Through the years they can see more of themselves in the characters and they comprehend more of the richness of Fitzgerald's language as their own minds deepen.

GATSBY IN HIGH SCHOOL: A CASE STUDY

For Greenfield School teacher Denise Douglas, teaching *Gatsby* in the same small, rural Tennessee town she grew up in is important in an attempt to open her students' minds to what is taking place around them and will influence them in the future. Her feeling here played out over and over again in the answers the students provided to interview questions. In general, they understood how studying the themes in both the novel and 2013 film might prepare them for facing life's current and future challenges.

The issue that resonates with her students foremost, Douglas explains, is the emotion and "issue of unfaithfulness," which they see in their own lives. "This helps some to really identify with the book even though they do not identify with the wealth. It's the relationships of the characters that get them so emotionally involved in the book," she says.

Reading over the students' responses, I am struck by their optimism and general hope for the future, a kind of innocence that as adults many of us begin to ignore. While some of these interpretations are not necessarily in line with what takes place in the novel, Douglas's students demonstrate that although they are only sixteen- or seventeen-year-old high school juniors, they comprehend how *Gatsby*'s broader themes might influence their thinking. Jeremy Lannom, for example, claims that the novel "proved to me that anything you want to achieve is possible," while Taylor Alderson sums up, "Money isn't everything" and McCall Scates says, "The novel made me think of how I want to plan my future to be the most successful I can be."

Overall, 33 percent of the students agreed or strongly agreed (four or five on a five-point scale) that the novel changed their thinking about themselves and 50 percent claimed the same on their thinking about society. Interestingly, the figures increased when the students were asked about the Luhrmann film. Some 53 percent said the film changed their thinking about themselves, while the number jumped to 65 percent when examining society. For example, student Savannah Ricketts explains that the book "helped me by being more aware of the people around me and not to get too caught up with someone that you don't see the real them. Don't fool success for happiness." In commenting on the film, her classmate Logan Galey concludes, "The movie gave me a better understanding of the society in which they lived in. The movie put it into real life and gave us a better perspective on that time in history." However, students also demonstrated keen insight by disliking *Gatsby*. "I found the characters unlikeable and un-relatable. They are all unhappy, but they refuse to change their current situation," explains Lauren Rush.

In assessing the novel (70 percent) and the 2013 film (88 percent) overall, a strong majority of students rated them highly. Given the star quality of the Hollywood film, the higher rating for the film is no surprise. These particular students might have also been more attracted to the emotional and romantic parts of the film, since Douglas thought that was the aspect most familiar to them in their own lives. Jessica Boettner pins her assessment on hope, explaining, "To me, hope has always been a grand feeling. . . . Now I understand the consequences of too much hope and idealism. One must be a little realistic . . . and protect oneself from some of the heartache of things gone wrong."

Clearly, for these students, the combination of reading the novel and viewing both the 1974 and 2013 film adaptations proved important. Douglas explains what she sees in her students' attitudes, saying:

> None of them can ever understand Daisy or how she could stay with Tom over Gatsby, but none of them have been married or have children. They also don't understand the carelessness of rich people . . . because they have only seen people that affluent in movies and books. They do understand very well how fake people can be and how selfish people can be. They understand how when things are good you have lots of friends, but when things take a turn for the worse you find out who your true friends are. They experience these things time and time again throughout their high school years. And, unfortunately, will continue to experience after because such is life.

Her thoughts shine through the comments by Kayla Totty, who says the novel taught her to "live your life to the fullest and what you do to other people will come back on you." Her classmate Brody Stanford relates, saying, "I will try not to dwell on the past and focus on the future." Brittany Ricketts concludes, explaining, *"The Great Gatsby* is relevant for today's students because there are people that still think like Tom and Daisy. People still only care about themselves and what is going to happen to them."

In the end, Douglas hopes *Gatsby* demonstrates to her students "how important it is to be true to themselves and not live their lives trying to be something they aren't just because they think it will make them popular." She sees great significance in the "careless people" theme for the young people, as well as a perspective on the American Dream that remains important: "I hope it also shows them not to let go of their dreams because they are so important, but at the same time not to cling so tightly to the past that it rips away their future." Wisely, her student Bethany Cole explains, "Some dreams are worth risking everything for, while others are not, and the difficult part of life is distinguishing them."

Any fan of *Gatsby* and the K–12 education system will get a smile when they read about one of former high school teacher Quincey Upshaw's favorite moments in teaching Fitzgerald's novel. She describes a particular connection a student presented, which showed her how the book helped build students' thinking skills. The incident took place the semester after the students read *Gatsby* and then turned to *All Quiet on the Western Front* (1930) by Erich Maria Remarque. According to Upshaw, "A student said to me once as we were reading *All Quiet*, 'Man, I bet Gatsby saw some of this stuff.'" For the class the connection was instant and powerful; she says, "That basically blew the collective mind of the class and we had an awesome discussion that day about how the carnage of World War I would have affected Gatsby's outlook on the world." Watching young people make these kinds of links between important texts is incredibly fulfilling for teachers, as well as the students in their classrooms. A student who makes this kind of connection based on critical and contextual thinking is the type of person one would like to have as a physician, business leader, nonprofit executive, scientist, or teacher educating the next generation of students.

There is a long-term benefit for both teachers and students in interactions with works of art like *Gatsby*. According to famed education scholar Maxine Greene, "Aesthetic questioning heightens awareness." For the student, "such involvement heightens our consciousness of the mystery . . . discloses possibilities we could not have anticipated before." Yet it is teachers as guides (and in this call, I would say both formal and informal teachers) "who have thought about their own experiencing, their own moments of joy . . . make significant choices . . . because they *know* . . . they have 'been there'; they are committed to opening doors."[24] Those of us committed to teaching Gatsby are the arbiters of its future and our students' transactions with the text. We are the guides, opening doors for them to enter into a new world of possibilities that exist for those honed in critical- and contextual-thinking abilities.

***

Although I argue that *Gatsby* is the Great American Novel, that assertion does not mean that novelists should not strive to replace it or that scholars and critics should discontinue efforts to prove that some past work should rise to surpass it. Some writers, like Norman Mailer, spoke about the desire to write the Great American Novel, while others, like John Updike and Joyce Carol Oates, kept churning away in its pursuit, as if talking about it were too presumptuous. Yet the goal remains central to the national consciousness. In my mind, it is an eternal quest, just as the argument for or against a particular novel can be pursued forever.

While I take this stand, some people wonder if there continues to be a place for the Great American Novel. Those arguing this point often cite the seemingly endless recession that has gripped the middle class since the mid-2000s. The stark reality of millions of homes ripped out from under hapless homeowners is too much evidence supporting the notion that the American Dream is dead. Others claim that the definition of "American" is now too multifaceted to encompass all it implies in one set of ideas. Without the quest for the American Dream, therefore, there can be no Great American Novel.

Another argument against the Great American Novel is that there is no longer a place for it in a world that in many respects now seems so anti-American. Layered within is the notion that America itself really is not all that great anymore. Proponents of this position cite various rationales, spanning from the way the country churns through the global oil supply and its resulting environmental damage to the nation's global aggression as symbolized by the so-called "war on terror" and its subsequent human rights violations.

Writer Julia Ingalls, however, sees the quest as worthy. She asks, "Is the Great American Novel still relevant? It can be, provided that novelists are able to recapture the spirit of the Great American journey without glossing over the realities of the 21st century."[25] This answer provides space for contemporary novelists to confront the challenges laid out by opponents, while still acknowledging that the American experience holds many aspects that are unique, even if the system itself seems strikingly divided between the wealthy and the not wealthy, with the supposed middle class shrinking to nonexistence.

Novelist and poet George Garrett does not take a stance for or against the Great American Novel, but he does speak to *Gatsby*'s importance for writers, explaining, "I have never known an American writer, of my generation or of the older and younger generations, who has not placed *Gatsby* among the rare unarguable masterpieces of our times."[26] Garrett's thinking on this point mirrors the way many academics and teachers perceive the novel. Scholar Nancy P. VanArsdale concludes:

The book requires the reader to consider larger questions of American identity and American destiny. Readers must participate with Nick in questioning whether Jay Gatsby achieved greatness by remaining steadfast to his dream of marrying Daisy, and why, in America, wealth appears to trump other core values: love, trust, friendship, and honesty.[27]

As a result, *Gatsby*'s place within the American literary canon and as an important teaching tool seems secure. Just as in Fitzgerald's day, the topics VanArsdale mentions demand to be addressed by an educated public, not only for the ideas that are derived, but as a device in creating an intelligent mind.

12

BOOM, BUST, REPEAT: POWER, GREED, AND RECKLESSNESS IN CONTEMPORARY AMERICA

America was going on the greatest, gaudiest spree in history and there was going to be plenty to tell about it. The whole golden boom was in the air—its splendid generosities, its outrageous corruptions and the tortuous death struggle of the old America in prohibition.—F. Scott Fitzgerald, "Early Success," 1937

Although he claims to loathe being labeled a politician while in college, Nick Carraway often serves as prosecuting attorney, judge, and jury in *The Great Gatsby*. His revision and narration of Gatsby's greatness includes continual reexamination of the major players involved in the events as they unfolded that climactic summer. At the end of the story, Nick reserves his harshest verdict for Daisy and Tom, calling them "careless people" who "smashed up things and creatures," and then forcing "other people [to] clean up the mess they had made."[1] This declaration is one of Fitzgerald's severest criticisms of the rich and demonstrates his complicated feelings about wealthy people, regardless of Ernest Hemingway's celebrated and much-discussed accusation that his friend and rival favored or had a sycophantic longing for them.

The "creature" that Daisy and Tom break to bits is Gatsby himself, employing their combined power and wealth to destroy him—first his dream of a future with his lover, and then physically as Tom sells him out to George Wilson. In one sense, the "mess" that is left is Nick's to clean up by telling the titular character's story. Yet, here again, Nick assumes the politician's role, simultaneously recasting Gatsby as great and as someone he ultimately claims to scorn. This equivocal stance adds mystery and nuance to the story and exemplifies Fitzgerald's skill in keeping the reader guessing throughout the book, essentially forcing the reader to address the basis and validity of Gatsby's greatness.

Nick assesses his cousin and her husband harshly—as reckless individuals—and by doing so, indicts that generation of the rich, who believed that they could live in a lawless manner with few or no consequences for their actions. What is interesting in Nick's final encounter with Tom in New York City is that there is clearly a moment where the power structure of their relationship flips. Once Nick correctly surmises that Tom sent Wilson on his deadly journey, he could have provided an account of what actually happened the night Myrtle died, particularly that Daisy was the driver. Given Tom's self-claimed emotional breakdown at her death and having to clean out the apartment afterward, Nick's restraint at this juncture reveals itself as another example of his abilities as a politician or the comprehension that delivering this devastating news will not change Tom's or Daisy's true nature. In other words, whatever it does to Tom personally, the news will merely serve as another speed bump on their marital road. Wealth is their indestructible bond.

In the end, it seems as if Nick's secret is also broken up by Tom and Daisy's basic childishness, which, combined with their wealth, provides a form of insulation in contrast to his "provincial squeamishness."[2] What Nick quickly surmises is that the rules do not encompass people like the Buchanans. They can act however they want, if they are willing to retreat to the world of the ultrarich at any sign of trouble in the "real" world. In exchange, they must sublimate their emotional lives to that faux society where a different set of rules exists almost beyond Nick's understanding.

In contrast to the gaudy environs of the wealthy, Nick views himself as a realistic and thoughtful person. For example, he can live among the ultrarich, attending their parties and serving as a collaborator in their intrigues, but justify it all based on his midwestern decency and renting a cheap home tucked into an unnoticed fold. As a result, he does not reveal Daisy's secret, which Gatsby took to the grave, because in doing so he would become as reckless as them.

Here, Nick's restraint, Gatsby's greatness, and the Buchanans' immorality intersect at the intellectual heart of the novel. Fitzgerald's condemnation of the rich and their irresponsibility finds no truer home than when Nick decides that no good could come of Tom knowing the truth about his lover's death. Fitzgerald is basically demonstrating that the narrator's squeamishness about the rich and their actions (though they often seem glamorous and alluring) can only result in everyone else bending to the will of the wealthy.

***

One could reasonably argue that a novel rarely has the power to rouse great change in its own day (perhaps Upton Sinclair's *The Jungle* is a rare exception). Yet, if *Gatsby* had reached more readers or achieved the sales figures and media attention that Fitzgerald's *This Side of Paradise* attained, perhaps people might have realized the potential outcome of the rampant speculation that took place in the mid-1920s. Much of early twentieth-century history would need to be rewritten to think that the book could have prevented the Great Depression, but looking back now, readers can certainly see it as a warning. Maybe Fitzgerald simply wrapped the book in too pretty a package given the seriousness of its message. The illicit sexuality and promiscuity of *Gatsby*, for example, obviously did not grab at the public's heart (or stomach) the way Sinclair did in illuminating the evils of the Chicago meatpacking industry almost two decades earlier.

This chapter looks at the enduring legacy of greed and recklessness in American society, which is a key takeaway from *Gatsby*. Portraying this aspect of our culture is one of Fitzgerald's great triumphs. As a matter of fact, Fitzgerald's impressions and ideas about wealth have often been misconstrued, whether Hemingway's early miscalculation or numerous students diving into the novel for the first time.

Scholar Ronald Berman, however, deftly assesses Fitzgerald's thinking, explaining, "He is not concerned with the idea that wealth corrupts: instead, he works with the idea that wealth reveals."[3] According to literary scholar Brian Way, Nick's observations about Daisy and Tom reveal the depths of their corrupt way of life. Tom's racism and Daisy's melancholy move the reader from comprehending the "restlessness and futility of their lives" to its "element of brutality and arrogance." Fitzgerald satirizes the rich deftly via Tom and his leaps to action. Way explains, "Tom's style of physical dominance, his capacity for exerting leverage, are not expressions merely of his individual strength but of the power of a class."[4]

The power of this class in contemporary society is all but complete. The primary downside to this centralized power is that it breeds a kind of hubris and recklessness that takes shape in entities and individuals that exist only to make money and solidify their power; everything else is inconsequential. In this kind of environment, most people become pawns, a form of walking ATM aimlessly spending money on unnecessary consumer trinkets because some commercial or marketing gimmick exclaimed that life would be better by owning it. This is the mind-set vicious capitalism necessitates. Like Tom Buchanan, one simply takes from those weaker or lower on the financial order then fights like hell to protect what's gained.

POWER AND HUBRIS

Many of today's corporate giants exude extravagance and overindulgence. These episodes fill magazines and television news reports and fuel a great deal of popular culture. Yet, vulgar displays of wealth take place in small organizations as well and in small towns across the nation. In a country so fixated on wealth and showing off, there are countless illustrations.

For example, a close friend worked for one of the largest financial institutions in the world as it completed a round of layoffs (dubbed "downsizing" in corporate jargon to alleviate or hide that it stands for mass firings), essentially getting rid of thousands of employees. While these people's lives went into immediate turmoil, one company executive commenced a leadership retreat at a fancy coastal resort town. While sipping drinks and celebrating the company's fortunes one evening—since mass layoffs often result in stock price gains—the highlight of the night took place, a $25,000 fireworks show. One's mind races to Gatsby's Long Island mansion and the hundreds gathered there, craning their necks as the nighttime sky filled with light. While many friends and associates would cash paltry severance checks, the select few drank champagne and patted themselves on the back for a job well done.

Despite meta-*Gatsby* and the way it has been employed across culture to condemn such folly, it would be a mistake to not at least question whether Fitzgerald portrayed the rich so well that many people misinterpret the novel as championing that lifestyle. In other words, what percentage of readers, whether high school students or adults, view the book as an aspirational text, just as many business students idolized the Gordon Gekko character from Oliver Stone's film *Wall Street*, despite its satirizing the industry? The onus for interpreting meta-*Gatsby* is everyone's responsibility but primarily falls to the nation's high school and college educators. There is a level of vigilance necessary to ensure that Fitzgerald's warnings about wealth and the dark side of the American Dream are central to readers' and viewers' thinking.

An engaged reader need look no further than Fitzgerald's two masterworks—*Gatsby* and *Tender Is the Night*—to understand how he felt about wealth. In each novel, the author clearly does not emulate or venerate those who are fantastically wealthy simply because they have money. This common perception of Fitzgerald—accentuated by Ernest Hemingway's cruel use of his onetime close friend as a prop in the short story "The Snows of Kilimanjaro"—launched the wrongheaded idea that Fitzgerald worshipped the affluent, but this idea does not hold up if one actually reads the author's work. Nor does it come through in examining his life. Fitzgerald had been around wealthy people most of his early adulthood, not only as a teenager in St. Paul, Minnesota, but also as a college student at Princeton. What Fitzgerald held, instead, is a keen insight into the role of money in rich people's lives.

What is striking is that in writing to Hemingway, Fitzgerald provides the key to his thinking on this issue. In the letter, he bitingly tells Hemingway that he does not "want friends praying aloud over my corpse," then asks that his name be removed whenever the story appeared in a collected book of stories. After praising Hemingway (certainly Fitzgerald knew his request would have to come with some sugar added given the younger man's immense ego and competitiveness), the last line, added in after Fitzgerald's signature, is revealing. The author explains, "Riches have *never* fascinated me, unless combined with the greatest charm or distinction."[5]

The exchange and several after it explain the Fitzgerald/Hemingway complicated relationship more than what either man honestly felt about those with money, but Fitzgerald demonstrated again and again in his work what he really thought. Gatsby and Tom seem to represent the two extremes in Fitzgerald's thinking. Gatsby is heroic, a "Son of God," because he uses his wealth to pursue an idea. Tom, on the other hand, is a racist xenophobe who shows the abuse of inherited wealth that results in intellectual laziness and self-entitlement.

Famed literary critic Arthur Mizener discusses Fitzgerald's unique vision of wealth as it linked to greatness (possibly embodied in Gatsby?), saying, "For the rich who made the most of their unique opportunity to live the life of virtue with the maximum imaginative intensity, Fitzgerald felt something like hero worship."[6] Those who chose not to live a life of integrity earned the author's complete scorn for what Mizener labels "the brutality of unimaginative, irresponsible power."[7]

Certainly one of the traits that differentiates Gatsby and Buchanan is the "intensity" of their dreams. The former is driven to unimaginable ends to win his lost love, while the latter is floating through life, yearning for the lost days of Yale football. Nick sees how deflated Tom has grown, explaining that he represented "one of those men who reach such an acute limited excellence at twenty-one that everything afterwards savors of anti-climax."[8]

Fitzgerald's special insight into the wealthy is on display throughout *The Great Gatsby*, which his editor Max Perkins at Scribner's picked up on right away. Assessing the novel in its earliest form, the famed editor calls it a "wonder" and says it contains "a great deal of underlying thought of unusual quality."[9] Moreover, after reading it another time, he picks out the creation of Tom Buchanan as a highlight of the novel: "marvelously palpable and vital—I would know Tom Buchanan if I met him on the street and would avoid him." Ironically, in the same letter, Perkins sees Gatsby as "somewhat vague . . . his outlines are dim." [10] Fitzgerald continued to transform the central character as the book progressed through galley drafts and proofs, which led to the full embodiment of the vision, but regardless, it is Tom that seems most real to Perkins. Mizener uncovers an alternative way of interpreting the novel through the lens of Tom and Daisy as "a history of the slow but steady decline of Nick's admiration for them, as the full evil of their moral irresponsibility is revealed to him and he loses interest in their glamour."[11]

What is striking about Tom as well is that his hubris comes with a large helping of insecurity. His list of fears, like many wealthy people today, runs deep and runs the gamut from minorities to the newly wealthy who like to show off their riches. This reminds me of a story an acquaintance told me about a former chief executive at a large global bank who used to pop into a local bar during the height of the Great Recession. With him were two giant bodyguards in imposing black suits and sunglasses, just like the movies. Even if the bar was virtually empty, the tycoon sat in the corner, nervously looking around the room, by himself, while the bodyguards hovered nearby. The image harkens to a modern-day Tom Buchanan, relishing in his status but also afraid that something sinister might lurk in the darkened saloon. When he got up to use the bathroom, the towering hulks shielded the entry, barring anyone else from using the facilities while Nero did his business.

GREED

What individuals and families lost in the Great Recession will be debated and scrutinized by economists and business analysts for a long time. Currently, the standard line is that trillions of dollars of personal wealth disappeared. While no one has determined the exact amount of loss, the reverberations continue to rock the nation from both socioeconomic and cultural perspectives. Unfortunately, in the six years since the Great Recession took hold, little evidence exists that demonstrates the world could not again fall prey to the forces of greed that sparked the catastrophe.

The subprime mortgage crisis placed an anchor around the neck of an otherwise teetering American economy already groping under the weight of a costly overseas war against terrorism in Iraq and other parts of the Middle East. "Recession"—the dreaded r-word—crept back into the national consciousness. While the experts debated whether the country had already entered a recession or not, politicians devised "stimulus packages" designed to force spending money into the pockets of cash-strapped Americans. On a daily basis the news never seemed to improve, ranging from massive layoffs at various global corporations to declining numbers of jobs created. People who turned to Wall Street for some indication of the nation's economic status found themselves in the midst of roller-coaster swings.

As with most aspects of popular culture, perception soon became reality. The more the media reported on the recession, the more steam the idea gained. People's fears about their jobs, the economy in general, and an unsettled situation in Iraq and Afghanistan made them apprehensive about spending money. Historically, when consumers turn off the spigot, the national economy reels. In early 2008, the gloomy outlook forced President Bush to address the situation: "Obviously the housing market is creating deep concern. And one of the real problems could be that if people, as a result of the value of their homes going down, kind of pull in their horns."[12]

A poll conducted by the Associated Press in February 2008 revealed that 61 percent of the public believed that the United States stood in the midst of its first recession since 2001. The facts provided evidence to the national mood. In 2007, the economy had its weakest year overall since 2002, expanding a mere 2.2 percent. The real estate fiasco triggered the anemic growth, with builders dropping spending by almost 17 percent. People also took home less pay in 2007, with average weekly earnings actually falling 0.9 percent when adjusted for inflation.[13]

Despite mounting hard evidence, many economists joined President Bush in stating that the American economy was not in a recession. However, the threat of more fiscal challenges on the horizon led Congress and the president to work on an economic stimulus package that would provide tax rebates for individuals and tax cuts for businesses. In the rush to "solve" the monetary problems, however, relatively few people questioned how the nation would pay for the $168 billion rescue package. It turned out to be via costly overseas loans from foreign countries and by printing money by the truckload.[14]

Writer Matthew O'Brien, looking back on the economic crisis, lays the blame at former Federal Reserve chairman Alan Greenspan's feet. If one reads between the lines, greed is the culprit, not necessarily by Greenspan personally, but among the legions of players in the financial market that benefited from creating the housing bubble. O'Brien explains:

> Where the Fed really failed was as a regulator. It could have gone after the predatory lending in the subprime world, if it had wanted to. At least one Fed governor suggested doing so. Greenspan rebuffed him . . . if the Fed had clamped down on the endemic fraud in the mortgage market, it's not difficult to imagine the run-up in housing prices being much more muted. After all, if the problem had been low interest rates, prices should have skyrocketed across the board. That prices only skyrocketed for housing tells us that something peculiar was going on there, namely an abdication of any regulatory oversight.[15]

Repeated efforts by the Federal Reserve to manage the economy, through interest rate cuts and other cash-infusion measures, had little consequence on individual households distressed by layoffs, credit challenges, and real estate woes.

The industries suffering the most widespread job losses during the Great Recession indicate the state of the overall national economy: construction, financial services, manufacturing, retailing, and business services. The snowball effect of the housing crunch, combined with costly overseas wars, stretched the economy's effort at stability. In an increasingly unstable environment, executives reacted by cutting overhead, which usually resulted in massive job losses.

What Fitzgerald identified in the 1920s, according to scholar Brian Way, is the Wizard of Oz qualities of Gatsby, a flimflam man of the sort that has since only grown and dominated the nation, from the door-to-door salesmen of the 1950s to the late 1990s web gurus with dreams of paper millions piped together on little more than a hope and a prayer. Way explains:

> That Gatsby should have brought to life all this miraculous shimmering ephemeral beauty and excitement places him among the great artist-showmen of America—the architects who designed the World's Fairs and Expositions; the circus ring-masters . . . directors of Hollywood epics and musicals . . . and media men who . . . turned the Apollo moon-shots into the best television entertainment ever made. [16]

The contemporary business world is filled with the kind of hucksters that Fitzgerald anticipated in the novel. There seems to be a touch of the sinister even in sources we are educated to trust, whether politicians or businesspeople. For example, from the mid-1990s until its financial collapse in late 2001, Enron stood as a darling of the business media, ranging from one of *Fortune* magazine's "World's Most Admired Companies" to an organization studied in business schools nationwide for its innovation and success. Enron, led by chief executive Jeff Skilling and chairman Ken Lay, also fooled finance professionals, receiving glowing reports from analyst firms that bought and sold enormous blocks of stock for investors, retirement funds, and 401(k)s. Billions of dollars were at stake in these decisions, and Enron duped all the major players in perhaps the largest Ponzi scheme in history. Enron's stock, which at one point traded for ninety dollars a share, plummeted to fifty cents a share, not really even worth the price of the certificate it would have been printed on.

When the Enron collapse began, it unraveled faster than anyone could have imagined. Bankruptcy and mass layoffs took place quickly, while some employees lost their retirement funds in the meltdown. On May 25, 2006, a jury found Lay and Skilling guilty of conspiracy and fraud. For journalists Bethany McLean and Peter Elkind, who helped break the Enron fraud, the guilty verdicts had "positive implications," including offering "a measure of consolation—or retribution—for those employees who lost everything in Enron's bankruptcy. And it reinforces a critical notion about our justice system: that, despite much punditry to the contrary, being rich and spending millions on a crack criminal defense team does not necessarily buy freedom." [17]

At the heart of Enron's criminal activity was the deliberate manipulation of company stock to make the company more valuable on paper than in reality. Top executives then sold millions of dollars of essentially worthless stock for profit, when they knew the price was a sham. The unfortunate aspect of every underhanded financial plot is that someone is left holding the bag. In this case, it turned out to be Enron employees and investors.

The Enron scandal serves as the most shocking downfall in an era of high-profile corporate collapses. The others spanned a variety of industries and included some of the more prominent corporations in America. Like Enron, these were considered top-notch businesses. Accounting firm Arthur Andersen fell apart in the wake of serving as Enron's public accounting agency. Although the company collected revenues of $9.3 billion in 2001, some eighty-five thousand Andersen employees either left the firm or lost their jobs in the downfall.

Adelphia Communications, founded by the Rigas family, grew into the fifth-largest cable company in the United States. Members of the Rigas family hid debt and essentially allocated themselves millions of dollars in undisclosed loans. John and Timothy Rigas were found guilty of securities violations after federal officials determined that they stole $100 million in company money. Other stunning disintegrations included Tyco chief executive Dennis Kozlowski and WorldCom founder Bernard Ebbers. Both leaders, seen as innovative leaders prior to the scandals, ended up in jail for bilking investors. Ebbers, for example, had $400 million in undisclosed loans. [18]

In 2006, on average, these leaders at the nation's largest five hundred corporations made $15.2 million. Countrywide, which is well known for its television commercials and web advertising pushing home financing, paid executive Angelo Mozilo a $1.9 million salary and $20 million in stock awards based on performance, while he sold another $121 million in stock options. This took place as the company lost $1.6 billion in 2007 and its stock dropped 80 percent. Mozilo told the committee, "As our company did well, I did well." Representative Henry Waxman (D-Calif.) viewed the disparity between company results and CEO compensation as "a complete disconnect with reality."[19]

The greed and hubris of so-called leaders like Skilling and Mozilo is shocking under any microscope, but perhaps more important, these types of individuals pull entire companies with them into fraudulent activity. Writer Gerald Russello, for example, discusses the consequences of Enron within the broader context of contemporary America, explaining:

> Enron is in many ways the quintessential American story. It joins a rags-to-riches tale of a company and its founders (Mr. Lay, for example, was a preacher's son from the Midwest) to a Gatsby-esque fall from economic and political grace. It also has a lot of lessons to teach as American corporate culture recovers from the shock of a chain of disasters, of which Enron remains the most resonant.[20]

While it is difficult to comprehend, people continue to be duped by such charismatic, yet evil, leaders. Part of the ongoing value of *Gatsby* and meta-*Gatsby* ideas across culture is that we should know better.

RECKLESSNESS

As the 1990s rushed toward an end, *Time* magazine writer Adam Cohen wrote an article comparing and contrasting two of the era's towering figures: President Bill Clinton and Bill Gates, Microsoft chief and then the world's richest man. At the time, despite their combined power and wealth, both faced intense scrutiny, Clinton on the heels of the affair with intern Monica Lewinsky (perhaps a modern-day Myrtle Wilson?) and Gates fighting antitrust allegations that threatened his company's stranglehold on the nation's computer software.

Interestingly, Cohen discloses that the two iconic figures did not get along well, which the writer identified as growing out of generational differences. Clinton and Gates, although of the same generation, were born at each end of the baby boomer era. The president represented the hippie mentality of the 1960s, while Gates stood for the me-first and antigovernment mentality of the 1970s.[21]

Cohen also examines where the two paralleled, particularly a shared and legendary internal drive to get what each wanted. Each man understood from an early age the parameters of power and went about attempting to attain and keep it. "Both have limitless drive and self-absorption, and a willingness to push the rules to the edge—or past it—to get what they want," Cohen writes. However, too often their determination led to circumventing existing rules and what Cohen calls "a strained relationship with the truth." Clinton's need to connect with people, according to the writer, led to the affair with Lewinsky, while Gates's desire for power led to his company's monopolistic actions and the resulting fallout that would weaken Microsoft at the dawn of the Internet age.[22]

Given their shared single-mindedness and blatant grabs for power, Cohen compares both Gates and Clinton to Gatsby. He even notes that the Microsoft head had a quote from Fitzgerald's novel inscribed on the ceiling of his library in the $60 million mansion he designed and had built outside Seattle. Ironically, Gates seems to have totally missed the point of the quote, which signifies Gatsby's inability to achieve his dream. Cohen, however, concludes, "The two Bills are already modern Gatsbys of a sort, having achieved their very different versions of the American Dream. Whether their flaws, like the original Gatsby's, pull them down remains to be seen."[23]

In hindsight, we realize that despite the great challenges Clinton and Gates faced in the late 1990s and early 2000s, both men emerged essentially unscathed. As a matter of fact, in contemporary America, Clinton and Gates have achieved iconic status, both revered in many quarters for their philanthropic and humanitarian work. Perhaps in comparison to Gatsby, each real-life leader might be an example of a potential "what if," typifying the kind of life the fictional character might have aspired to if real and having undergone a change of heart from his criminal past to a do-gooder future.

More important for this study, Cohen's use of Gatsby as a barometer for Clinton and Gates demonstrates the cultural significance of the novel.

In his use, "modern Gatsbys of a sort" means that one is Gatsby-esque if one has achieved one's personalized version of the American Dream. The article also reinforces the notion that even if one rises up, any "flaws" might pull him or her back toward earth.[24]

Yet it is primarily in where their dreams lead that separates would-be Gatsby figures from Fitzgerald's creation. Many celebrities, whether in business, politics, or another profession, actually seem more like Tom Buchanan types. Their ruthlessness—both Gates and Clinton flaunting the system for their own gain—dictates that they win and others bend to their will, just like Tom's manipulation of those around him. Tom is so controlling that he is able to convince Nick that he should feel sorry for him, which justifies the narrator not telling Tom that Daisy actually drove the death car that killed his mistress. Nick condemns both the Buchanans for their wanton behavior, but he does not deliver the blow that might rock Tom from his self entitlement bubble.

***

One of the lasting images of the Great Depression in popular culture is that Wall Street traders in gleaming skyscrapers jumped from their office windows en masse as they realized that their fortunes were lost. Over the years, researchers have discovered that the image does not necessarily fit reality.

Rather than an epidemic, suicide in New York City and nationwide spiked upward, just slightly more than the trend that had been on the rise since the mid-1920s. Examining census statistics for 1925, for example, revealed that 12.1 people per 100,000 across the nation committed suicide and 14.4 in New York. By 1932, the year with the highest overall average, the nationwide figure rose to 17.4 (up 44 percent) and New York reached 21.3 (up 40 percent). The data are not insignificant, particularly if one factors in many other suicides that were probably reported as deaths to save the surviving family members from shame. Yet researchers looking deeper into the topic have provided greater clarity on the issue. Overall, less than 2 percent of the deaths during the Depression were from suicide.[25]

Jumping ahead to the Great Recession of the late 2000s, researchers have concluded that the suicide rate in the United States accelerated, totaling about 1,580 additional suicides per year on average from 2008 to

2010. Sociologist Aaron Reeves and his research team also discovered that the unemployment rate corresponded with increased suicides. As a result, they deduce that "there is a clear need to implement policy initiatives that promote the resilience of populations during the ongoing recession."[26] What these figures further indicate is that there is a human price to be paid when preoccupation with power and money outruns logic, compassion, and dignity.

As a nation, we need to address the corruption of individuals and entities and how that relates to the broader capitalist system. One of the most pertinent questions is simply this: Is there morality in such a system?

Innovation fuels America's global military and economic power, as well as the nation's culture. Yet, the constant demand for "more" and "faster" ratchets up anxiety. In the new millennium, general nervousness about the economy continues to spread like cancer a little bit more each day. Small signposts are all over that indicate large problems on the horizon. Soaring gas prices, for example, serve as a daily yardstick. For sale signs and the empty homes they mock fill the nation's streets, cul-de-sacs, and suburban enclaves, constantly reminding hardworking (but scared) citizens that chaos is an inch away.

In examining the heady topics of this chapter, one asks that the full power of Fitzgerald's novel be appreciated for its deft examination of the issues at the core of a consumer capitalist society. While many aspects of our current economic system would baffle Fitzgerald, he provided insight into people's motivations and aspirations as if we could in some way chart how and why a person would act given the opportunity to fulfill his or her version of the American Dream. *Gatsby* demonstrates that Wall Street is no less corrupt than the Mafia underworld (and both are greased on illegal bootlegged alcohol), America's aristocrats are as lowly as its dirt poor, and dreams are attained and lost based on consequences that seem like fate but are more likely at the hands of human nature. Here, Fitzgerald tells us, here are the keys to understanding it all. He asks that we use them wisely, but still we career off the road, axle destroyed, and wheels off the track, yet mesmerized by the loud splash of horns filling the night sky.

13

THE GREAT GATSBY (2013): THE FILM

My big job was to try to illuminate the book. It's fascinating to me, the power of that book . . . the story is aspirational. Gatsby's a sign, a symbol, for us all.—Baz Luhrmann, in an interview, April 2013

Holed up in a passenger car on the Trans-Siberian Railway, more or less detoxing after the glitz, glamour, and spotlight of a new movie opening, famed director Baz Luhrmann drank red wine and listened to a recording of *The Great Gatsby* on his iPod. By the end of the audio version, he realized that someday he had to bring the novel to life on film, despite what many observers believed were lackluster adaptations in the past.[1] Jump ahead more than a decade and Luhrmann's film—starring Leonardo DiCaprio in the title role and Carey Mulligan as Daisy Buchanan— opened in the United States on May 10, 2013, prior to its starring slot launching the Cannes Film Festival a week later.

Like many big-budget films, the whispers and rumors of how Luhrmann would cast and shoot the film swirled and flowed through Hollywood and across the globe in the year before the film flickered across the big screen. The anticipation grew steadily, along with an aura of wonder, particularly after rumors leaked that Hollywood golden boy DiCaprio would star. Another wave of publicity and titillation sparked when people learned that the movie would feature a sound track of current artists reinterpreting and performing 1920s music—those close to the film let it be known that rapper and mogul Sean "Jay-Z" Carter would serve as musical director.

Commentators speculated from the beginning about what a Luhrmann version of *Gatsby* would look like and how his influences would transform the film. The director himself added to the intrigue since his films are often sweeping epics or over-the-top historical pieces that mix anachronistic music with larger-than-life visuals. The Australian director, for example, had great success adapting one literary icon for contemporary viewers—*William Shakespeare's Romeo + Juliet* (starring a young Leonardo DiCaprio)—and won both critical acclaim and box office financial success with the romp *Moulin Rouge!* Adding to the suspense in the lead-up to the release, people also debated the use of 3-D in the film, which Luhrmann thought would intensify the relationships between the characters and heighten their emotional responses to situations.

Known for meticulously recreating his historical films, Luhrmann and wife Catherine Martin spent countless hours drawing on images and photos of the 1920s to ensure that the movie would replicate the era. Hundreds of extras, for example, fill the party scenes with exuberance, dancing, and drinking. One writer called the film "visually stunning," while Mulligan explains, "The way Baz portrays the disgusting, overblown insanity of these parties is perfect. . . . It's exactly representative of what people were doing in the mid-Twenties. They were going crazy."[2]

It is not a stretch to proclaim that the new *Gatsby* film sparked a wave of *Gatsby* mania, particularly in the time between the film's original release date in the December 2012 holiday season and its eventual distribution in May 2013. Yet, amid the craze of product tie-ins and screaming fans slobbering over DiCaprio or Mulligan, others raised significant points about the role of the new film as a reflection and interpretation of contemporary American culture.

***

I contend that the 2013 film and its subsequent DVD release will reinvigorate global interest in *Gatsby* (and to some degree, Fitzgerald), which makes it critical that this chapter examine the wave of *Gatsby* mania washing over the globe. While this entire book is an argument for why the novel has been so central to interpreting and establishing the themes at the heart of American life, one would be remiss in not recognizing how influential big box office films are in contemporary culture. The Luhrmann version is a case study in the significance of film as a cultural touchstone.

For example, my own viewing of the film took place at the very first showing on a Friday afternoon at a large multiplex in a Cleveland suburb. Although the theater stood relatively empty—it was a Friday afternoon, after all—a small busload of urban high school students flowed into the stadium seating just before the string of trailers began. Clearly, they were on a school-sanctioned field trip, since their teacher reminded the group about cell phone use and proper manners while the film played.

From this concrete evidence and other anecdotal examples drawn from teachers around the country, countless teachers and college instructors led authorized or informal group trips to see the film the first weekend it opened. I have heard from many teachers that they purposely paired the reading and study of Gatsby in their classrooms with the film opening to add a bit of extra incentive for their students. In addition, when the DVD is released and people can purchase the disc, one can only imagine how extensively it will be used in the nation's classrooms. There is little doubt that a generation of *Gatsby* readers will also be *Gatsby* viewers. The teacher in my heart of hearts just hopes that students continue to read the novel, not just attempt to crib its contents by watching the film version.

The sense one gets from talking to teachers and college professors who have assigned the book to coincide with the film release is that they believe that the novel addresses meaningful issues. Therefore, by extension, the film will also play a role in students' overall learning processes. I think we can also move this line of thinking beyond the high school or college classroom and surmise that moviegoers will reflect on the film's subject matter as it relates to the wider world.

Many critics and commentators view *Gatsby* as particularly important at this point in history, a significant era that features challenges internationally and domestically, from post-9/11 society and the wars in the Mideast to the lingering economic difficulties worldwide and America's real estate and banking meltdowns. In a newspaper interview several weeks before the opening, for example, Luhrmann discussed the timing of the film and its relevancy for current audiences, claiming, "In that moment before the financial crisis of 2008, I remember thinking that something wasn't quite right. The greed and wealth were very reminiscent of *The Great Gatsby*. I thought, 'The time is right to make this film.'"[3]

GATSBY MANIA

As soon as Hollywood stars Leonardo DiCaprio and Tobey Maguire were rumored to play the lead roles in *Gatsby* the picture took on an aura of glamour, intrigue, and expectation. This *Gatsby* had to be truly great, which meant everything associated with the film had to be bigger than life. While filming took place in Australia, stills were released showing scenes from the Wilsons' garage in the valley of ashes, heightening the great expectations and setting off a new wave of chatter. It was as if the talk about the film grew into its own industry.

The celebrity media drove the fascination, especially after Warner Bros. decided to push the release date from December 25, 2012, to the following summer. Initially, the speculation turned negative with wags determining that the delay must be based on bad internal reviews. Soon, though, reporters learned that pushing the film back allowed Luhrmann to get the 3-D special effects right and continue building the star-studded sound track. In addition, a summer release with its high-profile status enabled Warner Bros. to bulk up its list of films, which included *The Hangover: Part III* and the rebooted Superman film, *Man of Steel*.

Gatsby fever grew astronomically as time progressed toward opening night. While the general U.S. release occurred on May 10, 2013, nine days earlier on May 1 fans could watch a star-laden premiere at the Lincoln Center in New York City via a streaming web feed. In this celebrity-obsessed age, such events not only give consumers anywhere in the world access to the hoopla, but also create new and interesting content that will then be used to fill the marketing and social media buckets, which demand fresh content at all times. Both during and after the event, clips were in heavy rotation on several social media sites and available on YouTube.

Instead of the traditional red carpet, celebrities and others associated with the film sallied down a black carpet with gold trim that matched the marketing theme for the film posters and trailers featuring an art deco, gold "JG," the main character's monogram. While fans lined up on-site to watch the stars arrive, virtual fans saw it all via streaming video. Organiz-

ers and marketers planned the event to feature the film's corporate partners. So, the backdrops where stars, musicians, and others were photo-
graphed were sponsored by Brooks Brothers and Tiffany & Co. Moreover, the entire world premiere event and streaming video was sponsored
by the new Samsung Galaxy cell phone (quite an anachronistic touch in
advertising a film set in the 1920s).

The mix of today's technology juxtaposed against a film set in the
early twentieth century remained on display at the gala. Repeatedly, hosts
Asha Leo and Marc Istook referred to the film's Instagram site, Facebook
page, and Twitter feed, the latter using both @GatsbyMovie and #Gats-
byPremiere to direct fans to the scrolling comments. Throughout the
show, Asha Leo used an iPad to keep track of the social media as it
unfolded, quoting Twitter feeds and basically announcing the online material as if she were doing play-by-play at a sporting event. For example,
one fan on Twitter said that she read the novel the day of the red carpet
affair and cried in anticipation of the film version. Many of the thousands
of other tweets focused on fashion and how the celebrities looked. A
similar tweeting tidal wave took place around the debut of the film at the
Cannes Film Festival a week later.

While the hosts used information gathered from the web to fill airtime
until the stars appeared, not only did the many fans gathered at the site
watch themselves being broadcast on giant video screens, but they also
were shown holding their cell phones high above their heads to film the
actors. The synergy of watching via the Internet as Leo and Istook talked
about streaming feeds and comments and then seeing the fans onsite
watching themselves on-screen and taping the gala with their cell phones
created a surreal moment of life in the twenty-first century.

In another interesting twist, the way the hosts spoke about the film
revealed the way *Gatsby* is woven through culture. For example, Leo had
already seen the film, while Istook had not. While glancing up and down
from the ubiquitous iPad she held throughout the show, at one point Leo
declared the film "a tragic love story." Since he had not viewed the
movie, however, Istook focused on the special effects, which seemed to
interest him more, emphasizing that 3-D gave Luhrmann the "technology
necessary to bring F. Scott's vision to life."

One wonders how much of their reactions were based on each playing
a specific gender role and what commentary like this portends for *Gatsby*
in the future. For her, the love story aspect of the film took center stage,

while he highlighted the 3-D filming, which one might expect—the female focusing on emotion, with the male sticking to technology. Will the
Luhrmann version in some ways usurp the novel as a quicker and easier
method of engaging with Fitzgerald's ideas versus the actual process of
reading the novel?

Gatsby mania surfaced all over the globe, not just in the United States.
The film scored major media coverage as it opened the Cannes Film
Festival. In addition, numerous special events around the world took
place to celebrate. In London, for instance, Harrods department store
announced that it would open a unique cocktail bar to celebrate the film's
release in the United Kingdom. From May 9 to 20, Harrods shoppers
could sip 1920s cocktails in a vintage bar setting reminiscent of the era.
Another, the nightclub Libertine, in London's West End, held a *Gatsby*-
themed party hosted by official film sponsor Moët & Chandon champagne three days before the film opened in the UK on May 16, 2013. The
party, which the club deemed a "saucy, alluring evening of glamour and
excess," required 1920s attire and featured live jazz music, dancers doing
period numbers, and a burlesque performance.[4]

The explosion of interest in *Gatsby* as a film starring DiCaprio and
filmed by director Luhrmann colliding with the utter pervasiveness of the
novel itself and then adding on top the intense historic interest in the
1920s adds up to a unique popular culture phenomenon that may never
again be rivaled. I am not sure if anything else could rival the combined
effect of *Gatsby*, which begins for many people as early as ninth grade (at
thirteen or fourteen years old), carries into college, often includes one or
more of several film versions at some point, may involve CliffsNotes, and
rereading as an adult.

The utter craze the movie accelerated is evidenced by the way the
novel itself sold before and after the film release. Scribner's reissued a
paperback with the original cover art, as well as a film-inspired version
with the cast and gold-and-black film logo. As a result of interest driven
by the movie, the novel spent time atop Amazon's best-seller list before
being dropped to number two by megaseller Dan Brown's new novel
Inferno. One needs to look no further than the global media world for
further evidence of the *Gatsby* rage. For example, a Google news search
conducted several days after the Cannes opening resulted in 116 million
hits on "Great Gatsby." While much of this content centered on the film
and reviews from all around the world, many writers and commentators

set out to reexamine or analyze the novel and/or the film for contemporary audiences. Clearly from this research we find that what the Luhrmann and DiCaprio picture will do is further enhance and solidify the many meanings (and misunderstandings) about the novel, opening the ideas up to current and future generations of readers and viewers.

BRAND FEVER

The images are splashed across popular culture: short skirts, sequins, bobbed hair, double-breasted suits, and slicked-back hair—the Roaring Twenties, the height of the Jazz Age. Unlike some decades that go in and out of style, the 1920s have remained fashionable, whether the era is the setting for a movie or novel or a person dresses up as a flapper or gangster at Halloween. The Hollywood/Internet hype machine and the enduring popularity of the 1920s collided as the Luhrmann film opened. As a result, the merchandising and product launch machine went into overdrive.

Yet, even with a blockbuster film, there seems to be a limit to how much marketing people can take. Writer Misty Harris contrasted those who called *Gatsby* "the most stylish movie ever made" with "the film's multi-channel marketing [that] has demonstrated all the subtlety of Liberace's piano."[5] Numerous high-end brands created partnerships with the studio, such as Brooks Brothers and Tiffany & Co., as well as Moët & Chandon champagne and the Plaza Hotel in New York City. In the new world order of blockbuster films, though, these splashy product tie-ins are necessary to offset the massive costs of making movies.

A film release in today's popular culture world is an event. Yet it is much more than celebrities and stars walking the red carpet. Countless divergent forces compete with one another, from video generated for YouTube and the inevitable CD release to the mountain of product tie-ins mentioned above and content driven by interviews and commentary. What the movie studios hope is that the resulting media convergence will overcome the typical white noise produced in a culture that churns on and on nonstop.

The idea behind convergence is that lines between media channels and consumerism no longer exist. One might ask, for example, how viral marketing on YouTube differs (if at all) from traditional advertising.

What is clear, though, is that all these channels are now essential marketing tools. The goal of the marketers is to deepen and extend the tie between fans and brands. Scholar Quentin Vieregge explains, "Brands do not simply label products anymore, they define our identities and help us relate to our communities."[6] Given the enduring fascination with the Jazz Age and the hype surrounding *Gatsby*, the opportunity presented a dream scenario for companies hoping to gain from the synergy.

People do not just interact with brands they cherish; they consume them, particularly if the item is linked to a celebrity. Thus, the idea that a person could dress like Jay Gatsby or wear jewelry similar to Daisy's compels consumers to buy. The companies that produce the merchandise, in turn, use events like the film release in an attempt to stand above the seemingly endless cloud of marketing, advertising, sales, and informational touch points demanding something from consumers—their attention, money, memory, or engagement. Imagine the millions of impressions that were created just in the release of *Iron Man 3* and *Gatsby* in successive weekends as the early summer season kicked off. Not only is the resulting blur of information stultifying, but these franchises are also competing against one another for space on the viewer's mental screen.

As we all know, the Internet plays a central role in how brands interact with consumers and potential stakeholders. Every artist, actor, musician, and brand ambassador in a converged culture operates in a setting that enables constant interaction with consumers across numerous media outlets, but the idea that everyone is always adding to the system creates a situation in which people cannot decipher or distinguish the messages.

What *Gatsby* had going for it in this high-stakes setting is that millions of people had read or at least heard of the novel, so the film's marketers did not have to start from scratch. Furthermore, the use of established film stars basically ensured that people would pay attention to some degree. Vieregge sees storytelling as a central element here, saying, "The brands that catch our attention are those that tell stories about who we are, our community, and how the brand ties us to our community."[7] In other words, the story already existed, as did people's relationship with the book or an earlier film, which then strengthened the marketing efforts. In total, these influences lead to greater exposure, thus greasing the marketing gears that keep the popular culture industry churning.

In addition to playing up the star-filled cast and timeless story, *Gatsby* marketers launched a Facebook page that just after the movie hit the box office tallied more than six hundred thousand "likes." More importantly, the page gave fans a way to engage with the film, from taking part via commenting to running special contests and giveaways. A fan art contest, for example, allowed participants to create their own versions of *Gatsby*, which resulted in beautiful pieces that were then shared on the Facebook page. Another tool gave fans the ability to create themselves as 1922 avatars. From the perspective of consuming the brand, these opportunities gave people the option of engaging with the film in a number of ways, based on one's own preferences.

Pulling fans into the creative process and then giving them a chance to interact plays on the general narcissism of Americans today. With You-Tube, for instance, consumers realize that they can create and recreate their own versions of popular culture items. Movie execs then walk a thin line between protecting copyright and artistic integrity versus the chance to drive viewers, listeners, and others interested in the work.

YouTube also played a significant role in advertising the film, as it does with all new work these days. Some 760,000 videos appeared when searching "Great Gatsby" the day the film opened the Cannes Film Festival. These results ranged from brief clips made by fans discussing their eagerness to see the film to authorized trailers and the entire sound track. Many clips were interviews with various stars and musicians associated with the Luhrmann film. Others were tangential, hoping to play off the hype, such as the piece demonstrating "Daisy's Dance" as a cardio work-out (received about ninety thousand views). Another video showcased a makeup tutorial that promised to help women look like flappers from the Jazz Age and it rang up more than sixty-five thousand views in just six days. A competitor in the makeup video category hit thirty-one thousand in the same time frame. Some companies also sponsored videos/ads, including Tiffany & Co., which forged a close relationship with the film based on the jewels featured in the movie.

CRITICAL RECEPTION

From my perspective, the critical reception of the Luhrmann film corroborates the thesis of this book. First, I think the wildly undulating reviews demonstrate not only that people have deep-rooted ideas about the book and movie, but also that balancing their expectations against these notions produces rather strong opinions. Second, since everyone seems to have a judgment about what *Gatsby* means or how it should be interpreted, the mass media commentators are adding a level of both analysis and misinformation into the overall gist of the idea of meta-*Gatsby*. In this view, the critics are acting as educators, both interpreting the film and adding to the reader's or viewer's sense of what it all suggests. As a matter of fact, I think the film is going to become more central to how people think about meta-*Gatsby*, regardless of what the critics conclude are the strengths and weaknesses of Luhrmann's version.

The distance between a novel of ideas and a novel of action is what makes Fitzgerald's masterpiece so elusive and difficult to film. Gatsby's place in the action is at the core here. In the novel, Fitzgerald keeps the titular character submerged. However, Hollywood requires that his story be central. For some readers, too, this dichotomy either results in one loving or hating the book. People simply do not realize that *Gatsby* is a novel of ideas masked within a novel of action. Thus, we have a story that begins in flashback and seems to end with the main character's death and funeral, but even here Fitzgerald takes us back to Nick from a current perspective.

Just like a person would experience memory in reality, Nick is haphazard with times and dates, which accentuates the timelessness of summer and the ideas at the heart of the book. The cloaking that occurs is the result of Fitzgerald's ability to manage these intricacies, as well as his beautiful writing style. Using Nick as a narrator enables Fitzgerald to emphasize the storytelling aspects while concurrently casting the unreliability in that recounting. Because Nick is all over the place in retelling the story and weaving it with his own judgments of the action, the reader finds room for interpretation that other novels try to force. Thus, *Gatsby* lives on into the twenty-first century in a way that other books of that era have not.

As a result, the film versions of *Gatsby* look beautiful and are shot brilliantly, but yet they still collapse as the physical depiction of the romance between Jay and Daisy takes precedence over the idea of romance. The former is what filmmakers create in an assessment of what filmgoers want to see, but the latter is what Fitzgerald actually produced and has kept readers returning to the novel.

Certainly the Hollywood star system has an impact here. Movie producers cannot hire actors like Robert Redford and Leonardo DiCaprio for millions or tens of millions of dollars to play iconic roles and then keep them offscreen for two-thirds of the film, as Fitzgerald does in the novel. Thus, adapting the book to film necessitates that Gatsby becomes the central figure in the story, much more concrete and "real" than the author ever intended.

In the latest adaptation, critics generally applauded DiCaprio's performance and felt that it is one of the film's highlights. At the other end of the spectrum, though, commentators see Tobey Maguire's Nick as a weakness, as well as the new asylum story line Luhrmann introduced to show him telling the story. But, even here, the reviewers are mixed in assessing these specific scenes and characters. Perhaps noted film critic David Edelstein's review sums up the general consensus: "Why I Sort of Liked *The Great Gatsby*."[8] Richard Lawson, reviewing for the *Atlantic*, stands in for many commentators, declaring, "His [Luhrmann's] *Gatsby* ultimately proves an overly simple, and decidedly unthoughtful, stagger through familiar territory. It's not without its merits, though."[9]

For other reviewers, the film's flaw was structural and centered on the notion that the 3-D special effects and wild party scenes detract from the seriousness of the work. For example, reviewing the movie for the *Cleveland Plain Dealer*, Joanna Connors discusses her frustration, explaining that under Luhrmann's direction, *Gatsby*

> is what you would expect. . . . It is all spectacle, and no introspection. It's gorgeous and overwhelming and packed to the very edges of the frame with activity and lush, showy production design. . . . I found the 3-D distracting and completely at odds with the material—except, perhaps, during the extravagant bacchanals at Gatsby's mansion.[10]

While generally liking the scenes, Edelstein still chimes, "The Deco extravagance of the big party scenes is enthralling. Luhrmann throws money at the screen in a way that is positively Gatsby-like, walloping you intentionally and un- with the theme of prodigal waste."[11]

The reason I find the critical reception of the latest adaptation so important is that it demonstrates how smart people both interpret and misinterpret the novel (as they have in print and other media for many decades). For example, *Slate*'s Dana Stevens calls *Gatsby* "the story of a supremely unsubtle man given to bold gestures and flashy set pieces."[12] From my perspective, every aspect of this statement could be challenged, yet in having *Slate* as a platform for publishing this review, Stevens is influencing a large audience of readers who may or may not have the ability or experience to evaluate such statements.

I do not want to place too much emphasis on the judgment of a handful of reviewers, but the collective reviews across traditional and online media in widely read venues have a shelf life of their own. Just as a good or bad teacher could irrevocably harm or benefit a student, reviewers have power. The influence of thousands of reviews of the film and comparisons to the novel will shape the conversation about meta-*Gatsby* in our culture.

THE FILM

This book is not about my evaluation of Luhrmann's *Gatsby* or the novel itself. However, some insight into the film might be valuable as readers think about its place as a part of meta-*Gatsby*. While most reviewers read the novel (ironically, those that did not often admitted so or claimed that they had not read it in a long time), I think a scholarly assessment is useful, particularly since I have read the novel upward of a hundred times, listened to it narrated a couple dozen times, and read much of the academic criticism produced about Fitzgerald and his work.

Personally, my epiphanic moment came while watching the streaming video of the movie premiere described above. Something clicked and I determined right then and there that I would watch the movie as a movie and attempt to divorce myself from my scholarly interest. In other words, I would look at the film as its own distinct entity. What I found by getting out of my own way intellectually is that the film was breathtaking in its sweep, particularly from an emotional perspective. The cast, under Luhrmann's direction, nailed the power of Fitzgerald's masterpiece, ultimately bringing the novel to life in a way that had not been done previously.

Luhrmann and cowriter Craig Pearce add many details to the film in an attempt to flesh out Jay Gatsby, which accentuates the dark side of a 1920s gangster. For example, Gatsby lashes out or reacts in several instances that demonstrate he is barely keeping his façade together. More specifically, in the famous scene at the Park Plaza Hotel when Daisy ultimately chooses her life with Tom, Gatsby attacks Tom Buchanan, screaming wildly and raising his fist and ready to strike before regaining his composure. Beautifully, though, while Gatsby attempts to rein himself in, his hair is disheveled and symbolizes his violent streak and wildness just below the surface. At another point, it seems as if Gatsby is having difficulty maintaining his place as Meyer Wolfsheim's figurehead leader and balancing his affair with Daisy.

In what I see as a nod to contemporary culture, Luhrmann and Pearce also emphasize Gatsby's celebrity, making his fame and fortune front-page fodder. One headline zips across the 3-D screen and asks: "Where Did the Money Come From?" Without diluting the mysteriousness surrounding the main character, the film invites the viewer to question the link between wealth and fame, as well as the centrality of celebrity in the modern world.

This version of *Gatsby* also plays to today's moviegoers by serving up many details in a more heavy-handed manner. One glaring example focuses the way Tom repeatedly points out that the newly rich Gatsby and his faux friends are different than the respectable, patrician old-money East Eggers who have pedigree and class. At one point he declares that he and others like him are "born different" because money is "in our blood." Perhaps the most direct demonstration involving Tom is that the film shows him telling George Wilson about Gatsby and insinuating that the garage owner should kill him. The change from the way Fitzgerald portrayed the events leading up to Gatsby's death does not make Tom any less guilty or complicit, but it does give the filmmakers a chance to quicken the film's pace. Personally, while I understand the need to explain the action more directly (after all, before films even begin, audiences are told half a dozen or more times to not talk and silence their cell phones), removing the subtleties allows viewers to outsource their thinking more than I would like to imagine.

What this new version of *Gatsby* nails is the grandiosity of the novel and its deep emotion. When Jay enters Nick's bungalow to see Daisy for the first time, the character's nervousness and anxiety surge like an electric shock through the theater. It is a palpable emotion, nearly making the viewer uncomfortable at his ache. And, while some critics thought that DiCaprio overplayed the use of "old sport," coming off a bit too smart-alecky, the awkwardness of the phrase harkened one back to Fitzgerald's declaration (via Nick) that Jay Gatsby was a young roughneck with just enough fake formality to be simultaneously laughable, yet convincing.

***

Undeniably, the Luhrmann version of *Gatsby* is now the standard adaptation of the novel. This status is weighty, because viewers now and in the future will use the film as a means for interpreting, assessing, and contextualizing the book and vice versa. One can imagine generations of high school and college teachers lamenting the differences between the two, collectively smacking their foreheads each time a student makes reference to an aspect of the film in a paper about the novel.

From a broader perspective, however, a more positive outcome is that future readers and/or viewers will have additional tools to engage with the ideas contained in each. Scholar Arthur Frank, discussing the role of storytelling, explains:

> To think about a story is to reduce it to content and then analyze that content. Thinking with stories takes the story as already complete; there is no going beyond it. To think with a story is to experience it affecting one's own life and to find in that effect a certain truth of one's life. [13]

In the case of *Gatsby*, we have already identified the multitude of ways it has become a cultural touchstone. Thus, the new film not only adds to the folklore but extends and broadens its many meanings—it is a new and critical part of meta-*Gatsby* that people all over the globe will have at their disposal as they rethink its meaning in their lives.

CONCLUSION: *GATSBY* IS AMERICA

F. Scott Fitzgerald was one of the best writers who ever lived. The ultimate reason for the Fitzgerald revival, then, is that great writing will always find its permanent audience . . . every year people read Fitzgerald for the first time and are never quite the same after the exposure to his "heightened sensitivity to the promises of life."
  Matthew J. Bruccoli, 2003

I regard Scott Fitzgerald as the most generous, and the most grateful of American writers. And The Great Gatsby *still strikes me as the most perfectly crafted work of fiction to have come from America.*—Tony Tanner, 1996

Scholar Ray B. Browne (1922–2009) wrote about popular culture and folk studies throughout his long, distinguished career. He believed in the significance of probing these disciplines, despite the academic snobbery he faced from others who felt researching how common people lived was beneath them or unimportant. To Browne, however, folk and popular culture were significant and had consequences for how people lived their lives and the ways they viewed themselves as citizens. He called folk studies, for example, "society's way of life, the timeless and world-wide comparative attitudes toward the problems of life and those people's ways of adjusting to and coping with those problems." In the end, he felt that understanding culture might lead to people developing solutions "for the benefit of all society." This lofty goal remained central to Browne's work, as well as the generations of scholars who studied with him or have attempted to follow his teachings.[1]

What this book underscores, in the Browne tradition of popular culture studies, is that a work of art like *Gatsby* can have a transformative influence on people's lives by serving as a tool for them to better comprehend themselves, the society around them, and their possible futures. Rather than dismiss Browne's ideology as Pollyannaish, as some critics might, I concur with his rationale for the humanities when he states:

> The humanities are those aspects of life that make us understand ourselves and our society. They are a philosophical attitude and an approach to thinking and behaving which interpret life in a human context. In other words, the humanities humanize life and living, make it more understandable and bearable and human.[2]

Given its omnipresence in the nation's classrooms, educators in high schools, colleges, and universities obviously recognize the novel's practicality across many central ideologies at the heart of good citizenship and social responsibility.

What is also increasingly clear is that in its long life, *Gatsby* moved beyond mere novel, or any kind of label one might place on it as a great book, to function as a part of American folklore. Furthermore, for better or worse, the mythic status of Scott and Zelda is included in this transformation: he the drunken (but angelic) genius; and she, his zany, madcap flapper wife. Like all powerful folklore narratives, there is a community aspect in the novel's service to society and culture, which includes and extends beyond the common ideas and misperceptions of the book.

In other words, *Gatsby*'s place within American folklore is not dependent on readers or audiences understanding where the legend of Scott and Zelda weaves in and out of reality or that Gatsby was not throwing parties to demonstrate his wealth. Rather, the power of the book is conveyed through its central themes, which keep it fresh and evocative long after one would naturally expect it to lose its power. These topics run a broad gamut from the hero's journey to the ethics of wealth and living a just life. The central theme, though, that turns *Gatsby* from important novel to part of the nation's folklore is its personification of the American Dream.

Some folklorists might quibble with placing *Gatsby* within the folklore label, given that it is a more formal cultural production than the kinds of traditions or material culture that many scholars study, such as regional oral history or music. That point noted, however, I counter that over time the novel has taken on new meaning for contemporary audiences while simultaneously drawing us back to a vanishing era in American history, which can be mechanically reproduced in film and television but in reality becomes more distant by the moment. And, though this book concentrates on formal pieces of mass media to prove its thesis, an enterprising scholar could conduct the kind of oral history necessary to demonstrate *Gatsby*'s influence on a more intimate scale.

Generations of high school and college students have been assigned *The Great Gatsby* once or more in their educational experience for use as a text defining the American experience. If we assume that countless numbers of students actually read the novel or, conversely, were forced to sit listening to class discussions about it even if they did not, its symbols and ideas have found expression in popular culture. Perhaps it is too idealistic to believe that as a result *Gatsby* plays an important role in people's worldviews, but I chart toward having confidence in people's critical-thinking abilities. Scholar Richard M. Dorson explains:

> A tale is not a dictated text with interlinear translation, but a living recitation delivered to a responsive audience for such cultural purposes as reinforcement of custom and taboo, release of aggressions through fantasy, pedagogical explanations of the natural world, and applications of pressures for conventional behavior.[3]

Although the novel could have disappeared as merely a relic of a bygone era, *Gatsby* now exemplifies Dorson's thinking above. Taken as a whole, the text itself, the film versions, and other forms of mass communications that have used it as an inspiration have transformed Fitzgerald's book into a living document that enables interested audiences to create, build, and strengthen their perspectives.

***

This book's conclusion speaks to *The Great Gatsby* and its titular figure as something more deeply rooted than the typical literary work, or even those books under consideration as the fabled Great American Novel, to its place as a part of our national folklore or Americana. As I parse through this thinking, however, I am not exactly sure what Fitzgerald would have thought of such a claim. He meant *Gatsby* to be his literary masterpiece and to establish his place in the upper echelon of American writers, which it has done. He certainly knew *Gatsby* was a great book, despite mediocre sales (by his standards) and mixed critical reviews. Yet I am not sure any writer could imagine that a single work—particularly one of only about fifty thousand words—might have the kind of impact Fitzgerald's novel has had on the nation.

The research that shores up the claim of *Gatsby*'s move into part of Americana reveals both its reach and influence over the course of the last ninety years. Granted, thousands of generic uses of the novel have filled mass communications outlets during that same period. These misappropriations, however shocking, do challenge our common understanding of the book. Yet, even then, what interesting company for a work of literature, particularly when *Gatsby* becomes a stand-in or filler for the American Dream and its corollary rags-to-riches narrative.

Fitzgerald's novel and the American Dream work together in concert to keep both at the forefront of people's minds. Anecdotally, I think it would be difficult to find someone who did not immediately have an image or impression pop into his or her mind when hearing the word "Gatsby." Given the blockbuster expectations of the 2013 film, this influence will certainly solidify and spread. By creating marketing copy and campaigns to sell "classic" novels to new audiences, scholar Marjorie Garber says, publishers and others recreate and repackage texts that highlight "dilemmas with which the reader is tacitly invited to identify."[4] This is at least in part the rationale for having rapper and hip-hop mogul Jay-Z score the 2013 film version of *The Great Gatsby*.

GATSBY AS AMERICAN

Jay Gatsby is a deeply flawed hero, like so many other antiheroes all the rage in contemporary popular culture, such as Dexter Morgan, a serial killer who only murders bad guys, on the hit Showtime series *Dexter*, or *Mad Men*'s Don Draper, who possesses many Gatsby-esque traits, like changing his identity to create a new version of himself yet still not finding happiness or contentment. That this kind of fictional character is popular now, in an era dominated by massive societal upheaval brought on by terrorism, warfare, and economic instability, brings to light some ideas about our cultural mind-set.

America's popular culture heroes often do not operate within a black-and-white code, like superheroes of the past. Instead, they acknowledge or are forced to operate within the gray spaces that exist in both day-to-day life and extraordinary situations. Some of this transformation reflects the vibrations radiating through history, for example, mirroring the rise and fall of individual politicians and larger political parties. As a result, the public is accustomed to looking for the fallibility in those we emulate, recognizing that those we place on a pedestal often have flaws that may be revealed upon greater scrutiny.

The current fascination with reality television and obsession with everything related to celebrity has also transformed what it means to be a hero. The line between hero and celebrity is blurry, at best. The idea of being celebrated outruns whatever it is that a person is being recognized for doing. Attaining the spotlight is more important than what one does in the glare. Reality television pulses through the broader culture, showing that every moment of a person's life is up for scrutiny, criticism, and abuse. The medium also demonstrates that once in the spotlight, life becomes one enormous game show. Points are won and lost based on duplicity, deception, false fronts, and ill-begotten alliances against one's enemies.

Amazingly, *Gatsby* fits into today's cultural climate and may be used as a vehicle for understanding our moment in time, just as it has for decades. Writer William Voegeli discusses how the fictional character fits within contemporary thinking, explaining, "Gatsby is not Everyman. He is an American, and the struggle to fashion a life guided by practical wisdom in America faces special challenges that make his story even more poignant . . . something moral, the principles on which the American experiment is founded, and something material, the place where it unfolds."[5] It is the commitment to their own sense of righteousness that drives many popular culture antiheroes. Like Gatsby, they live by a code that they are sure has justifiable ends, even if the means take them into areas outlawed by traditional society and laws.

Gatsby wears a mask with multiple consequences. Sometimes his mask enables him to get closer to his dream, while at other junctures his guise covers his fraudulent life and dubious focus on wealth. In contrast to Gatsby, Tom wears no mask. As a result, he seems a more "real" figure, stooping to the depths of a serial adulterer, elitist, and racist.

Gatsby's lies all seem to have meaning, while Tom's lies just make him sinister.

Fitzgerald's creation of two central figures of this magnitude breathes timelessness into the novel, because Americans love dreamers, even if they are ultimately revealed to be frauds, while simultaneously begrudgingly admiring powerful figures like Tom, even if they are shortsighted morons. I think many people would lump today's corporate and business leaders, if not many politicians, into the latter camp.

Many similarities also exist between the 1920s and post-Vietnam and post-Watergate America, which makes the novel seem like a prediction. Scholar Thomas C. Foster compares Fitzgerald's 1920s with today, explaining that each is filled with "a bunch of seedy people with challenged ethics" and "greed and corruption were rampant."[6] Current readers can definitely relate to the sinister nature of business and the illegal world of gangsters in the pre-Depression era and find fingers of that time reaching into the days of the dot-com rise and crash and the Great Recession of 2008, which feels like it will never end. According to Foster, Fitzgerald "presents all this as a perversion of the American Dream, which traditionally has had to do with freedom, opportunity, space to build a life, but which has been replaced by grasping, win-at-all-costs materialism."[7]

We know that Gatsby is doomed, because unforeseen (almost predestined) forces rise up to stamp down dreamers. Few people—real or fictional—get everything they want, even when it seems so close. From a lifetime of popular culture influences, from blood-splattered movies and television shows to the sensationalism of the news industry, today's reader will recognize that Gatsby getting gunned down is more poignant than Fitzgerald could have ever imagined. One can almost visualize a similar scene today: a wealthy celebrity found murdered, the body of his stalker found nearby, dead of suicide. The resulting pictures would end up in a trashy tabloid and inevitably on the web in full-colored gruesomeness.

FITZGERALD AS AMERICAN

Fitzgerald's immaculate insight into Jay Gatsby revealed, according to critic Alfred Kazin, the author's "tragic moodiness" and "a burst of self-understanding" that set the book apart from those of his 1920s contemporaries (and writers ever since).[8] It took a special comprehension of the lives of the wealthy and the lives of ordinary people to create such a broad swath. "Fitzgerald could sound the depths of Gatsby's life because he himself could not conceive any other," he explains. "Out of his own weariness and fascination with damnation he caught Gatsby's damnation, caught it as only someone so profoundly attentive to Gatsby's dream could have pierced to the self-lie behind it."[9]

Kazin's idea captures the strength and beauty of the novel and may actually reveal why it has such staying power. Fitzgerald, despite his claims of not really understanding Gatsby as he created him, desperately identified with the dreams the character espoused. He knew the pain of losing the girl and the joy in attaining her.

Even deeper, however, Fitzgerald understood the dual role of insider-outsider that enabled him to go deeply into the minds of his characters as they played out their goals and aspirations. The ability to capture Myrtle and Tom, for example, and then reveal how modern life could bring them together and eventually result in tragic consequences necessitated that Fitzgerald hold innate command of the people that inhabited the world in the 1920s.

Critic and biographer Arthur Mizener explains Fitzgerald's important turn, saying, "His use of a narrator allowed Fitzgerald to keep clearly separated for the first time in his career the two sides of his nature, the middle-western Trimalchio and the spoiled priest who disapproved of but grudgingly admired him."[10] Even more important, though, his characters had to have timelessness, too, the ability to transcend the age in which they were created and become akin to myths. As a result, Mizener contends, Gatsby himself could be an idealist and a brassy thug. Fitzgerald's brilliance is in creating him with parts of both but still enabling the reader to view the character as more, as the kind of person who could embody the American Dream, even if it is fulfilled illegally.

Ironically, Fitzgerald himself, the literary wunderkind and global celebrity, seemed to become more American or realistic in some strange sense after the commercial failures of *The Great Gatsby* and *Tender Is the Night*. His overarching narrative arc changed from American success story to rags-to-riches-to-rags, which our national culture embraces, although he was not as poor as he remembered growing up and certainly had many advantages that others did not. The fall from grace, however, which began with the mediocre sales of *Gatsby*, changed Fitzgerald. Morris Dickstein discusses the author's transformation from literary and celebrity prince to "representative man," which led to him producing more "introspective" work. The result, Dickstein explains, was that the great novelist "virtually invented the confessional mode in American writing." Because of the "Crack-Up" essays in Esquire, later writers felt free to explore the genre, including Norman Mailer in *Advertisements for Myself* (1959).[11]

Writing about Fitzgerald in late 1963, critic Malcolm Cowley assesses the author's life as similar to one of his artistic creations, even greater than that perpetuated by Jay Gatsby. There is a certain duality, he concludes, between the study of *Gatsby* in high schools all over the nation and the author's life becoming "a legend like that of Poe or even that of Davy Crockett."[12]

Much of Fitzgerald's commitment to the American Dream for those who have studied his career is represented by two interrelated facts: first, he survived as a freelance writer; second, he built his career as the years went along to finance his mentally ill wife and provide his daughter with a first-rate education. Although Fitzgerald lived an exulted life in the early years, no one should overlook the hardship of the second half, particularly given his family responsibilities. "We should not forget that the publishing industry is a classic form of capitalism . . . a variety of gambling," explains noted literature scholar James L. W. West III. "For the first half of his career, F. Scott Fitzgerald was a good horse to bet on; the only problem was that there weren't all that many ways to wager."[13]

THE FUTURE OF READING *GATSBY*

Let's be completely honest in our assessment, some part of *Gatsby*'s success as a classroom text is its length. American high school teachers and university faculty appreciated the combination of thematic power, lyrical writing, and its novella-like dimensions. Based on practicality, Fitzgerald's novel could easily fit within a section or portion of a marking period or semester, thus providing teachers and instructors broad flexibility in using it as a required or secondary text. This ability, though hampered in today's standards-driven K–12 education environment, has provided generations of teachers a text that is both enjoyable reading and manageable within the grading period.

Yet, in stark contrast to its diminutive size, Fitzgerald's novel is over-flowing with ideas and concepts that (again) make it almost perfect in a high school or college course. Simply put, there are not more than a handful of novels in the history of the English language that can be ably taught to ninth graders *and* advanced graduate students. The ubiquity of *Gatsby*, then, virtually guarantees its lasting impact on American culture and society. It is an übertext, one basically universal across age groups and the broader popular culture.

Writers provide readers with guideposts that help one understand what it is to navigate life's uncertainties. Without literature, our quest for self-fulfillment or the American Dream not only is lonelier but also contains greater ambiguity. Great works, according to William Mark Roche, en-able students to become lifelong learners. He explains, "Ideally, students are brought to the point where they learn not only an interpretation of a given work, but—far more important—also the strategies they must em-ploy to interpret works as yet unread."[14] When this synergy takes place, he comments, student and teacher/critic become one another's "partner in conversation."[15]

Literature, according to scholar Frank B. Farrell, "maintains a strong and fertile tension between its world-directed functions, in which it is bringing some truth of the world into view, and the internal functions through which its elements achieve a complex, self-maintaining order and connectedness, an aesthetic rightness."[16] If one accepts Farrell's conclu-sion, then the joy of reading *Gatsby* is intimately linked to it being used as a part of curricula now and in the future.

Teachers use *Gatsby* as a guide for addressing central themes and issues with their students. They also employ the novel as a guide for how one should aspire to write. Critic Clive James calls the author's prose style "ravishing." Further examination of that poetic nature, he believes, demonstrates the connection between Fitzgerald as a novelist and person, a mix of "anguish with its enchantment. . . . He wrote that way because he was that way: the style was the man."[17]

It is fitting that John Updike, a writer often mentioned in the same breath as Fitzgerald for his luminous style, offers uncanny insight into *Gatsby*'s staying power, and thus, why readers will continue to value the novel:

The novel's significant elements—Gatsby's shimmering parties, the
Buchanans' opulently chaste household, the wilderness of ash heaps
where Dr. Eckleburg's giant eyes preside, the overripe torpidity of
summer Manhattan, Wolfsheim and his world of crime, Tom and his
burly wealth, the downtrodden and violent Wilsons, the apparition of
pathetic Henry Gatz at the end—are carried to the point of caricature
but with the reward of a penetrating vividness . . . as bright and plau-
sibly implausible as a movie.[18]

GATSBY, CLASS, RACE, AND CONTEMPORARY AMERICA

Fitzgerald's near-perfect depiction of Tom is one of the aspects of the
novel that creates an enduring link between the book and contemporary
America. As readers, we can identify with the portrayal of a rich man's
extravagance and his insistence of personal self-righteousness, despite
wrongheaded thinking on just about every account, whether it is how the
family should be structured, race, or morality.

As a matter of fact, one could argue that we expect this kind of irra-
tionality from those in positions of power, particularly when they do not
have to account for their authority or they surround themselves with
lackeys that serve to insulate them from reality. As scholar Jonathan P.
Fegley explains, "More Machiavellian than Platonic, Tom regards himself as the last standard-bearer of both Western civilization and the
American family even as he engages in an adulterous affair with the wife
of a garage mechanic he sees as being beneath any regard."[19]

When Tom lashes out at Myrtle after a long day and night of drinking
and partying, Fitzgerald shows the violence that can erupt between the
classes. He strikes his mistress in a fit of rage and does not have to take
responsibility for the pain he delivers because he controls the entire faux
environment via his bankroll. Representing inherited wealth and the
white race, Tom uses his hard body as a cruel lever to keep those beneath
his contempt in their places. And, when that fails, as it does on that last
fateful afternoon with George Wilson, Tom outsmarts the lesser man,
deliberately pointing him to Gatsby in West Egg. He has no remorse for
the act that later takes place.

Many corporate chief executive officers are a modern manifestation of
the sanctimoniousness Fitzgerald embodies in Tom Buchanan. Pulitzer
Prize–winning author Chris Hedges draws parallels between this kind of

self-congratulating narrative and its consequences across culture, explaining:

> Sadism dominates culture. It runs like an electric current through reality television and trash-talk programs, is at the core of pornography, and fuels the compliant, corporate collective. Corporatism is about crushing the capacity for moral choice and diminishing the individual to force him or her into an ostensibly harmonious collective.[20]

Moreover, Tom's brand of elitism—equating wealth with the ability to discern the essence or truth at the heart of any issue or topic—drives modern political and business narratives. There is only opposition in this environment, a basic "us" versus "them" setting that eliminates common ground. One sees this mode of thinking unfold in any number of venues, from the way advertisers market "organic" or "natural" foods to the political battles over scientific issues like global warming and theories of evolution.

Another central facet is that the harsh, realistic portrayal of the wealthy and the ends they will go to retain their status remains significant in class relations today. Tom and Daisy, according to scholar David Minter, "have been born into that world and have no intention of relinquishing their hold on it."[21] In their eyes, no boundaries or limitations exist when it comes to protecting their sacred wealth, or as Minter explains, "The very rich of the twenties were set apart by their determination to claim as their own the rights of casual indifference to the consequences of their action . . . they became expert in protecting themselves from the competition of those who tried it."[22] Certainly, Fitzgerald sensed the deep schism wealth caused in his own time. His astute writing on the subject, then, gains power in its relevancy for generations of readers.

THE FUTURE OF *GATSBY* AND THE AMERICAN DREAM

In a short piece published prior to the release of the 2013 remake of *Gatsby*, Hollywood star Leonardo DiCaprio admitted to not connecting with the novel while in high school. He explains, "It was a world I didn't quite understand, had never been exposed to and didn't connect with." In preparing to star as the famous character, however, the actor read it about twenty-five times over four years. After rethinking the book, he noted that it is "quite beautiful and tragic at the same time" and that he found "a direct correlation between Gatsby and America today and the financial crisis we're now going through."[23] Although not typical, DiCaprio's use of the novel to spark his own creativity demonstrates its importance.

DiCaprio's experience with Fitzgerald's masterpiece over time is enlightening and might provide clues to how the novel is resituated within popular culture and academic studies on the heels of the Baz Luhrmann–directed film. If the film is as popular over the long run as critics and audiences expect, then the film and novel will work together, creating a kind of collaborative connection in which the success of one drives the other and vice versa. For instance, what high school or college student won't see the film on DVD or online rental when the novel is used in the classroom? Just like the book driving sales of CliffsNotes versions for shortcutting the actual reading, the film will open an entirely new audience to the topics it weighs.

The changes Luhrmann and the actors made while filming might launch a new avenue of study for teachers who hope to engage their students. According to the director, with DiCaprio as lead, "Gatsby moves from being the most charismatic, charming and attractive man to someone who is obsessive, dark and complex."[24] One does not have to hold a doctorate in English to see how this change in the film stands apart from what resides on the pages of Fitzgerald's novel.

For a more dramatic example of the transformation from page to screen, one can look to the scene where Gatsby confronts Tom Buchanan in the suite at the Plaza Hotel. Via Luhrmann and DiCaprio, Gatsby lunges at the man, grabbing him by the shirt with both hands, and then cocking his fist and shouting in his face in anger. Gatsby, here, loses control and is filled with rage. Fitzgerald's version, in contrast, has Gatsby virtually speechless as he realizes that his dream is destroyed. Tom's victory over the man leaves Daisy shaken, which leads to her driving the car that will eventually kill Myrtle Wilson and ultimately Gatsby, too. It is arguably the penultimate scene in the novel, but is not violent. One can already hear the debates taking place in classrooms across the nation regarding this scene, attempting to determine which is stronger and more appropriate, which may just speak to the age each was produced in more than anything else.

DiCaprio's ability to link the 1920s with today's economic challenges also indicates the novel's timelessness and use as a way of interpreting the present day. Certainly, the over-the-top depiction of Gatsby's life in the new film is going to cause many viewers to think about similar stories they have heard about rich businessmen and celebrities in the new millennium, whether the young millionaires in the technology sector or the old-school titans at the head of venture capital firms or investment banking units.

The simple fact that one of the central themes in *Gatsby* revolves around wealth and the place of money in one's life adds to the novel's legacy for later generations. Gatsby holds immaculate parties in a cavernous mansion filled with celebrities, endless supplies of food and alcohol (in the midst of Prohibition), and riotous music and dancing. He does so in hopes that Daisy will wander by and marvel at the spectacle. She and Tom, however, are ensconced in their own modern-day castle across the bay. He is off riding horses or gallivanting in New York City with his mistress, while she is cooped up, wondering exactly what it is people do with their free time, what it is that they plan.

Since the novel basically pits two megarich white men against one another in a struggle over a woman, who while beautiful, does not seem all that attractive as a person, some contemporary readers might wonder why anyone necessarily cares in today's world. William Voegeli answers the call, centering the power of the book on this morality play in Nick's mind, explaining, "The moral drama of *The Great Gatsby* involves coming to our own judgment about why Gatsby is fundamentally admirable for Nick, while Tom is fundamentally contemptible."[25] Fitzgerald's ability to keep the reader interested is important when looking at the issue, since both men have bad sides, ranging from adultery to law breaking, and ultimately both prove to be liars and manipulators of the first order.

The idea of why we care as individual readers and as a nation is a kind of mixture of these many threads, running from our love affair with nostalgia and depictions of the past through our fascination with wealth and power to the ambiguity about the title character as he pursues a warped American Dream. The great Alfred Kazin is one of the few literary critics bold enough to attempt to define the novel's power over contemporary readers. In Fitzgerald's writing, he sees "a moment's intimation and penetration; and as Gatsby's disillusion becomes felt at the end, it strikes like a chime through the mind."[26] What *Gatsby* does for us as readers is to present situations that we can understand and relate to, regardless of the era we inhabit. As a result, Fitzgerald's masterpiece is not diminished by time, but instead, empowered by its lasting vitality and appeal to the ideas and tenets that reside at the heart of what it means to be human.

Historian Jim Cullen finds that *Gatsby* is powered by Fitzgerald's sophisticated understanding of these factors as they express themselves in the American Dream: "What makes the *American* Dream American is not that our dreams are any better, worse, or more interesting than anyone else's, but that we live in a country constituted of dreams, whose very justification continues to rest on it being a place where one can, for better and worse, pursue distant goals."[27] Although no literary critic, DiCaprio pointed to the fiber of *Gatsby* that we can all attach to, that sense of beauty and tragedy that not only makes the novel important, but for many people marks life itself.

***

The Great Gatsby represents a kind of magic—no matter how many times it is read, the reader uncovers, discovers, or is led to some new image, thought, or understanding. According to historian Cullen, Fitzgerald's ideas about duality fuel the novel's staying power as a tool for developing critical-thinking skills and understanding the American Dream on a deeper level:

> The problem with the American Dream . . . is not exactly that it's corrupt or vain. Indeed, the great paradox of *The Great Gatsby* is that even as Gatsby pursues his dream through instruments of fraud and adultery there is a deeply compelling purity about his ambition, especially given the smug pieties of those around him . . . any American Dream is finally too incomplete a vessel to contain longings that elude human expression or comprehension.[28]

The book's enduring brilliance, then, is in Fitzgerald's ability to pack all of America and the American Dream as its unifying ideology in this slim volume, as if each new visit bequeaths a shiny new additional prize. In this light, the novel is more like the greatest movie ever filmed because it never fails to astonish or seem as fresh as when one first cracked the spine.

What remains to be seen is whether the new film propels *Gatsby* back into the national consciousness for more than a veritable nanosecond in the great American hype machine of marketing, publicity, and advertising that we realize serves the popular culture engine in the Internet era. This is the blockbuster age, for goodness' sake, so the blip that the movie causes as it ripples through the Twitterverse and Google search algorithms may peak and fall pretty quickly, whether it is ultimately judged a flop or a global hit.

If one thinks back to the hype surrounding the slew of big-ticket movies that turned into megablockbusters, say, any of the recent superhero flicks, such as *The Avengers* or *The Dark Knight Rises*, the narrative arc of prerelease marketing, launch, postrelease gross revenue expectation, which is later revived briefly for DVD/Blu-ray sale and then award season/possibly Academy Award nomination, defines the lifeline of most films. This cycle happens so quickly in the technology age that it flits within the wider canvas of life, taking up a moment's notice before it slips off the screen forever.

As a culture connoisseur, John Updike realized the way film bested the page, which must have been a crushing conclusion for a writer whose best work never received good movie treatment. He explains, "Even a very lame movie tends to crush a book. When I try to think of *The Great Gatsby*, I get Robert Redford in a white suit . . . Mia Farrow in a floppy pastel hat, or Alan Ladd floating dead in an endless swimming pool, before I recover, via Fitzgerald's delicate phrasing . . . the hair in the gangster Wolfsheim's nostrils."[29] The validity of Updike's feeling is being played out with the new film version of *Gatsby*, which will probably result in Leonardo DiCaprio replacing Redford as the vision of the character in the mind's eye of generations of new and future readers.

Since the film has already done well in the U.S. market, streaking past the $100 million mark after two weeks, one might also consider if the movie's greater long-term consequence will be in how it is used in conjunction with the novel as a teaching tool. Also, its global bearing might also be of great interest, since the nations around the world who have bought into the *Gatsby* craze may use the film as a barometer of assessing the United States.

Yet, from one perspective, it would be great if the film generates new and interesting questions about the nation and the American Dream. According to Roche, the power of a novel like *Gatsby* resides in the queries that are generated as a result of reading. He explains, "If literature and literary criticism are no longer anchored in the idea that the object of interpretation and evaluation is to garner a window onto an ideal sphere, why should we continue the enterprise?"[30] Deep in my gut, I know that Fitzgerald's novels and many others matter as readers continue the journey toward greater understanding of themselves and society.

Gatsby: The Cultural History of the Great American Novel is a biography of *The Great Gatsby* that examines how Fitzgerald's slim work grew in both critical stature and sales to become one of the most significant achievements in twentieth-century fiction. More importantly, I introduce the idea of meta-*Gatsby*, the manifestation of its enduring influence, which demonstrates—in part—why I feel that the book is the Great American Novel. My hope is that by reading this book, others will better comprehend what makes *Gatsby* great and, more importantly, how the novel helps us make sense of our own lives and times.

NOTES

PREFACE

1. Joanne Berger DuMound, "*The Great Gatsby* Arrives at Berea High School," *Cleveland.com*, January 30, 2013, http://www.cleveland.com/berea/index.ssf/2013/01/post_14.html (accessed January 30, 2013).

2. Louise M. Rosenblatt, *Literature as Exploration*, 5th ed. (New York: Modern Language Association, 1995), 276.

3. Mark William Roche, *Why Literature Matters in the 21st Century* (New Haven, Conn.: Yale University Press, 2004), 8.

4. Matthew J. Bruccoli, ed., *F. Scott Fitzgerald: A Life in Letters* (New York: Simon & Schuster, 1994), 315.

5. Matthew J. Bruccoli and Margaret M. Duggan, eds., *Correspondence of F. Scott Fitzgerald* (New York: Random House, 1980), 545.

6. Bruccoli and Duggan, *Correspondence of F. Scott Fitzgerald*, 545.

7. Charles Poore, "Two New Views of Fitzgerald and His Works," *New York Times*, July 20, 1963, 17.

8. Arthur Mizener, *The Far Side of Paradise: A Biography of F. Scott Fitzgerald* (New York: Houghton Mifflin, 1965), 85.

INTRODUCTION: WHY *GATSBY* MATTERS

1. Mark William Roche, *Why Literature Matters in the 21st Century* (New Haven, Conn.: Yale University Press, 2004), 10.

2. Center for Media Research, "9.9 Billion Video Ad Views in February," *Research Brief Newsletter*, May 6, 2013, http://www.mediapost.com/publica-

tions/article/199678/99-billion-video-ad-views-in-february.html#axzz2 UbwV6Xn8 (accessed May 6, 2013).

3. Jonathan P. Fegley, "'If I Couldn't Be Perfect I Wouldn't Be Anything': Teaching Becoming and Being in *The Great Gatsby*," in *Approaches to Teaching Fitzgerald's* The Great Gatsby, ed. Jackson R. Bryer and Nancy P. VanArsdale (New York: Modern Language Association, 2009), 131.

4. Harold Bloom, ed., *F. Scott Fitzgerald's* The Great Gatsby, new ed. (New York: Chelsea House, 2010), 5.

5. Roche, *Why Literature Matters*, 207.

6. Frank B. Farrell, *Why Does Literature Matter?* (Ithaca, N.Y.: Cornell University Press, 2004), 11–12.

7. Roche, *Why Literature Matters*, 257.

8. Lawrence R. Samuel, *The American Dream: A Cultural History* (Syracuse, N.Y.: Syracuse University Press, 2012), 167.

9. Quoted in Samuel, *American Dream*.

10. Farrell, *Why Does Literature Matter?*, 13.

11. Farrell, *Why Does Literature Matter?*, 13.

12. Roche, *Why Literature Matters*, 211.

13. David Lodge, *Language of Fiction: Essays in Criticism and Verbal Analysis of the English Novel* (New York: Columbia University Press, 1966), 80.

14. Lodge, *Language of Fiction*, 81.

15. Jane Mount and Thessaly La Force, *My Ideal Bookshelf* (New York: Little, Brown, 2012), xiii.

16. Roche, *Why Literature Matters*, 236–37.

17. Jason P. Leboe and Tamara L. Ansons, "On Misattributing Good Remembering to a Happy Past: An Investigation into the Cognitive Roots of Nostalgia," *Emotion* 6, no. 4 (2006): 596.

18. F. Scott Fitzgerald, *The Great Gatsby*, ed. Matthew J. Bruccoli (New York: Cambridge University Press, 1991), 20.

19. Alfred Kazin and Ted Solotaroff, *Alfred Kazin's America: Critical and Personal Writings* (New York: Harper Perennial, 2004), 119.

20. Kazin and Solotaroff, *Alfred Kazin's America*, 118.

21. Matthew J. Bruccoli and Judith S. Baughman, eds., *F. Scott Fitzgerald in the Marketplace: The Auction and Dealer Catalogues, 1935–2006* (Columbia: University of South Carolina Press, 2009), xvii.

22. Bruccoli and Baughman, *Fitzgerald in the Marketplace*, xviii.

23. Morris Dickstein, ed., *Critical Insights:* The Great Gatsby (Pasadena, Calif.: Salem Press, 2010), 4.

24. Quoted in Matthew J. Bruccoli, ed., *F. Scott Fitzgerald's* The Great Gatsby: *A Documentary Volume*, vol. 219 of *Dictionary of Literary Biography* (Detroit: Gale Group, 2000), 310.

25. George Garrett, "Fire and Freshness: A Matter of Style in *The Great Gatsby*," in *New Essays on* The Great Gatsby, ed. Matthew J. Bruccoli (New York: Cambridge University Press, 1985), 115–16.

26. Charles Scribner III, "Publishing—Past Imperfect," in *The Professions of Authorship: Essays in Honor of Matthew J. Bruccoli*, ed. Richard Layman and Joel Myerson (Columbia: University of South Carolina Press, 1996), 72.

27. Kazin and Solotaroff, *Alfred Kazin's America*, 120.

28. Kazin and Solotaroff, *Alfred Kazin's America*, 120.

29. Farrell, *Why Does Literature Matter?*, 18.

30. Ray B. Browne, "Redefining the Humanities," in *Eye on the Future: Popular Culture Scholarship into the Twenty-First Century*, ed. Marilyn F. Motz et al. (Bowling Green, Ohio: Bowling Green State University Popular Press, 1994), 252.

31. Philip Hensher, "*Great Gatsby*: A Story for the Modern Age," *The Telegraph* (London), May 23, 2012, http://www.telegraph.co.uk/culture/film/film-news/9284394/Great-Gatsby-a-story-for-the-modern-age.html (accessed March 30, 2013).

32. Maxine Greene, *Variations on a Blue Guitar: The Lincoln Center Institute Lectures on Aesthetic Education* (New York: Teachers College Press, 2001), 206–7.

33. Bruce Bahrenburg, *Filming* The Great Gatsby (New York: Berkley, 1974), 26.

34. Bloom, *Fitzgerald's* The Great Gatsby, 5.

I. A LITERARY STAR ROARING THROUGH THE TWENTIES

1. "Fire and Explosion Rock 42D Street," *New York Times*, April 3, 1920, 1.

2. Matthew J. Bruccoli, *Some Sort of Epic Grandeur: The Life of F. Scott Fitzgerald*, 2nd revised ed. (Columbia: University of South Carolina Press, 2002), 128.

3. Quoted in Nancy Milford, *Zelda: A Biography* (New York: Harper & Row, 1970), 61–62.

4. Quoted in Milford, *Zelda: A Biography*, 62.

5. Kirk Curnutt, ed., *A Historical Guide to F. Scott Fitzgerald* (New York: Oxford University Press, 2004), 3.

6. F. Scott Fitzgerald, *Afternoon of an Author: A Selection of Uncollected Stories and Essays* (Princeton, N.J.: Princeton University Press, 1957), 84–85.

7. Fitzgerald, *Afternoon of an Author*, 85.

8. Fitzgerald, *Afternoon of an Author*, 85.

9. Jackson R. Bryer, "F. Scott Fitzgerald 1896–1940: A Brief Biography," in *A Historical Guide to F. Scott Fitzgerald*, ed. Kirk Curnutt (New York: Oxford University Press, 2004), 29.

10. From Fitzgerald's personal clipping file, in Matthew Bruccoli, Scottie Fitzgerald Smith, and Joan P. Kerr, eds., *The Romantic Egoists: A Pictorial Autobiography from the Scrapbooks and Albums of F. Scott and Zelda Fitzgerald* (Columbia: University of South Carolina Press, 2003), 59.

11. Morris Dickstein, *A Mirror in the Roadway: Literature and the Real World* (Princeton, N.J.: Princeton University Press, 2005), 78.

12. Bryer, "F. Scott Fitzgerald," 30.

13. Bruccoli, *Epic Grandeur*, 131.

14. Arthur Mizener, *The Far Side of Paradise: A Biography of F. Scott Fitzgerald* (New York: Houghton Mifflin, 1965), 159.

15. Bruccoli, *Epic Grandeur*, 161.

16. Ruth Prigozy, "Introduction: Scott, Zelda, and the Culture of Celebrity," in *The Cambridge Companion to F. Scott Fitzgerald*, ed. Ruth Prigozy (Cambridge: Cambridge University Press, 2002), 11.

17. Bruccoli, *Epic Grandeur*, 189.

18. Bruccoli, *Epic Grandeur*, 141.

19. Matthew J. Bruccoli and Margaret M. Duggan, eds., *Correspondence of F. Scott Fitzgerald* (New York: Random House, 1980), 112.

20. F. Scott Fitzgerald, *The Great Gatsby*, ed. Matthew J. Bruccoli (New York: Cambridge University Press, 1991), x–xv.

21. Mizener, *Far Side of Paradise*, 178.

22. For a detailed examination of Fitzgerald's writing and revising process, please see Matthew J. Bruccoli, ed., *F. Scott Fitzgerald's* The Great Gatsby*: A Documentary Volume*, vol. 219 of *Dictionary of Literary Biography* (Detroit: Gale Group, 2000), 7, 67–75.

23. Fitzgerald, *Gatsby*, ed. Bruccoli, xix.

24. Bruccoli, Smith, and Kerr, *Romantic Egoists*, 240.

25. Quoted in Fitzgerald, *Gatsby*, ed. Bruccoli, xx.

26. Quoted in Fitzgerald, *Gatsby*, ed. Bruccoli, xx–xxi.

27. Quoted in Bruccoli, *Epic Grandeur*, 132.

28. Alfred Kazin and Ted Solotaroff, *Alfred Kazin's America: Critical and Personal Writings* (New York: Harper Perennial, 2004), 117.

29. Quoted in Scott Donaldson, *Fool for Love: F. Scott Fitzgerald* (New York: Congdon & Weed, 1983), 66.

2. BREAKING BAD: FITZGERALD'S DEMISE, 1925–1940

1. Quoted in Morris Dickstein, *A Mirror in the Roadway: Literature and the Real World* (Princeton, N.J.: Princeton University Press, 2005), 80.

2. Matthew J. Bruccoli, *Some Sort of Epic Grandeur: The Life of F. Scott Fitzgerald*, 2nd revised ed. (Columbia: University of South Carolina Press, 2002), 410–11.

3. Matthew J. Bruccoli, ed., *F. Scott Fitzgerald: A Life in Letters* (New York: Simon & Schuster, 1994), 320.

4. Bruccoli, *F. Scott Fitzgerald*, 322.

5. Arthur Mizener, *The Far Side of Paradise: A Biography of F. Scott Fitzgerald* (New York: Houghton Mifflin, 1965), 336.

6. Clive James, *Cultural Amnesia: Necessary Memories from History and the Arts* (New York: Norton, 2007), 209.

7. Matthew Bruccoli, Scottie Fitzgerald Smith, and Joan P. Kerr, eds., *The Romantic Egoists: A Pictorial Autobiography from the Scrapbooks and Albums of F. Scott and Zelda Fitzgerald* (Columbia: University of South Carolina Press, 2003), 185.

8. Bruccoli, *Epic Grandeur*, 327.

9. Scott Donaldson, *Fool for Love: F. Scott Fitzgerald* (New York: Congdon & Weed, 1983), 114.

10. Elaine P. Maimon, "F. Scott Fitzgerald's Book Sales: A Look at the Record," *Fitzgerald/Hemingway Annual* 5 (1973): 166–67.

11. Donaldson, *Fool for Love*, 196.

12. Matthew J. Bruccoli with Judith S. Baughman, *Reader's Companion to F. Scott Fitzgerald's* Tender Is the Night (Columbia: University of South Carolina Press, 1996), 4.

13. F. Scott Fitzgerald, *Tender Is the Night* (New York: Scribner, 1934, 1962), 179.

14. Fitzgerald, *Tender Is the Night*, 174.

15. Fitzgerald, *Tender Is the Night*, 177.

16. Fitzgerald, *Tender Is the Night*, 177–78.

17. Fitzgerald, *Tender Is the Night*, 192.

18. Ernest Hemingway, *A Moveable Feast* (New York: Scribner, 1964, 2003), 181.

19. Matthew J. Bruccoli and Margaret M. Duggan, eds., *Correspondence of F. Scott Fitzgerald* (New York: Random House, 1980), 545.

20. Bruccoli and Duggan, *Correspondence*, 545.

21. Bruccoli and Duggan, *Correspondence*, 552.

22. Alfred Kazin and Ted Solotaroff, *Alfred Kazin's America: Critical and Personal Writings* (New York: Harper Perennial, 2004), 124.

23. James, *Cultural Amnesia*, 210.

3. *GATSBY* REBORN, 1941–1963

1. Charles Scribner III, "Publishing—Past Imperfect," in *The Professions of Authorship: Essays in Honor of Matthew J. Bruccoli*, ed. Richard Layman and Joel Myerson, 68–77 (Columbia: University of South Carolina Press, 1996), 72.

2. Morris Dickstein, ed., *Critical Insights:* The Great Gatsby (Pasadena, Calif.: Salem Press, 2010), 3.

3. Matthew Bruccoli, Scottie Fitzgerald Smith, and Joan P. Kerr, eds., *The Romantic Egoists: A Pictorial Autobiography from the Scrapbooks and Albums of F. Scott and Zelda Fitzgerald* (Columbia: University of South Carolina Press, 2003), 216.

4. Matthew J. Bruccoli, *Some Sort of Epic Grandeur: The Life of F. Scott Fitzgerald*, 2nd revised ed. (Columbia: University of South Carolina Press, 2002), 484.

5. Jackson R. Bryer, "The Critical Reputation of F. Scott Fitzgerald," in *The Cambridge Companion to F. Scott Fitzgerald*, ed. Ruth Prigozy, 209–34 (Cambridge: Cambridge University Press, 2002), 210.

6. Quoted in Bruccoli, Smith, and Kerr, *Romantic Egoists*, 240.

7. Leo Gurko and Miriam Gurko, "The Essence of F. Scott Fitzgerald," *College English* 5, no. 7 (1944): 374.

8. Gurko and Gurko, "Essence of F. Scott Fitzgerald."

9. Gurko and Gurko, "Essence of F. Scott Fitzgerald," 375.

10. Alfred Kazin and Ted Solotaroff, *Alfred Kazin's America: Critical and Personal Writings* (New York: Harper Perennial, 2004), 121.

11. Elaine P. Maimon, "F. Scott Fitzgerald's Book Sales: A Look at the Record," *Fitzgerald/Hemingway Annual* 5 (1973): 168–69.

12. Wheeler Winston Dixon, "The Three Film Versions of *The Great Gatsby*: A Vision Deferred," *Literature Film Quarterly* 31, no. 4 (2003): 290.

13. Bosley Crowther, "*The Great Gatsby* (1949)," *New York Times*, July 14, 1949, http://movies.nytimes.com/movie/review?res=9502E6DC123CE53 ABC4C52DFB1668382659EDE (accessed February 14, 2013).

14. Matthew J. Bruccoli, Arlyn Bruccoli, and Park Bucker, *The Matthew J. and Arlyn Bruccoli Collection of F. Scott Fitzgerald at the University of South Carolina: An Illustrated Catalogue* (Columbia: University of South Carolina Press, 2004), 31.

15. Bruccoli, Bruccoli, and Bucker, *Collection of F. Scott Fitzgerald*, 240.

16. William H. Young and Nancy K. Young, *The 1950s* (Westport, Conn.: Greenwood, 2004), 21.

17. Maimon, "Book Sales," 169–70.

18. Maimon, "Book Sales," 170.

19. Maimon, "Book Sales," 173.

20. James L. W. West III, "Fitzgerald's Posthumous Literary Career," *Journal of Scholarly Publishing* 28 (1997): 98.

21. Bruce Bliven, "The Revolution of the Joneses," *New York Times*, October 9, 1960, SM28.

22. Bliven, "Revolution of the Joneses," SM120.

23. Arthur Mizener, "*Gatsby*, 35 Years Later," *New Yorker*, April 24, 1960, http://www.nytimes.com/books/00/12/24/specials/fitzgerald-gatsby60.html (accessed December 19, 2012).

24. Mizener, "*Gatsby*, 35 Years Later."

25. Maimon, "Book Sales," 173.

26. Richard Anderson, "*Gatsby*'s Long Shadow: Influence and Endurance," in *New Essays on* The Great Gatsby, ed. Matthew J. Bruccoli (New York: Cambridge University Press, 1985), 25.

27. Scribner's, Advertisement, *New York Times*, February 14, 1960, BR23.

28. Lewis Nichols, "In and Out of Books," *New York Times*, January 8, 1961, BR8.

29. Charles Poore, "Two New Views of Fitzgerald and His Works," *New York Times*, July 20, 1963, 17.

30. Bryer, "Critical Reputation," 210.

4. A GRAND ILLUSION, 1964–1980

1. Richard Severo, "For Fitzgerald's Works, It's Roaring 70's," *New York Times*, March 3, 1974, http://www.nytimes.com/books/00/12/24/specials/fitzgerald-roaring.html (accessed December 20, 2012).

2. Severo, "It's Roaring 70's."

3. Quoted in Severo, "It's Roaring 70's."

4. "Mia's Back And *Gatsby*'s Got Her," *People*, March 4, 1974, http://www.people.com/people/archive/article/0,,20197613,00.html (accessed January 2, 2013).

5. Edward J. Rielly, *The 1960s* (Westport, Conn.: Greenwood, 2003), 24.

6. David F. Trask, "A Note on Fitzgerald's *The Great Gatsby*," *University Review* 33, no. 3 (March 1967): 197–202. Repr. in *Novels for Students*, ed. Diane Telgen, vol. 2 (Detroit: Gale, 1998). Literature Resource Center.

7. Trask, "Fitzgerald's *The Great Gatsby*."

8. Joshua B. Freeman, *American Empire: The Rise of a Global Power, the Democratic Revolution at Home, 1945–2000* (New York: Viking, 2012), 188–90.

9. Andrew Turnbull, "Speaking of Books: Perkins's Three Generals," *New York Times*, July 16, 1967, 2.

10. "The People's Choice," *New York Times*, February 26, 1967, BRP18.

11. "The People's Choice," *New York Times*, February 26, 1967, BRP18.

12. "The People's Choice," *New York Times*, February 25, 1968, BRA26.

13. "The People's Choice," *New York Times*, February 16, 1969, BRA28.

14. "Mia's Back."

15. Bruce Bahrenburg, *Filming* The Great Gatsby (New York: Berkley, 1974), 8.

16. Bahrenburg, *Filming* The Great Gatsby, 21.

17. Quoted in Gene D. Phillips, "*The Great Gatsby* (1974)," in *The Francis Ford Coppola Encyclopedia*, by James M. Welsh, Gene D. Phillips, and Rodney F. Hill (Lanham, Md.: Scarecrow Press, 2010), 121.

18. Phillips, "*The Great Gatsby* (1974)," 121.

19. George Frazier, "Scott Fitzgerald: The *Gatsby* Legend," *Saturday Evening Post*, May 1974, 60.

20. Frazier, "Scott Fitzgerald."

21. Frazier, "Scott Fitzgerald," 62.

22. Roger Ebert, "*The Great Gatsby*," *Chicago Sun-Times*, January 1, 1974, http://rogerebert.suntimes.com/apps/pbcs.dll/article?AID=/19740101/RE-VIEWS/401010315 (accessed January 31, 2013).

23. Ebert, "*The Great Gatsby*."

24. Vincent Canby, "They've Turned *Gatsby* to Goo," *New York Times*, March 31, 1974, http://www.nytimes.com/books/00/12/24/specials/fitzgerald-gatsby74.html (accessed December 19, 2012).

25. Donald A. Yates, "The Tragic Experience," review of *F. Scott Fitzgerald: A Critical Portrait*, by Henry Dan Piper, *New York Times*, November 21, 1965, BR14.

26. John H. Allan, "Interest Rates Surge for Bonds," *New York Times*, August 7, 1966, 1; C. D. B. Bryan, *The Great Dethriffe* (New York: Dutton, 1970), 30.

27. Robert Gorham Davis, "Is Our Past Becoming Irrelevant?" review of *The Urgent West: The American Dream and Modern Man*, by Walter Allen, *New York Times*, March 16, 1969, BR4.

5. ALL THAT GLITTERS, 1981–2000

1. Bob Batchelor and Scott Stoddard, *The 1980s* (Westport, Conn.: Greenwood, 2007), 10.

2. Quoted in Gil Troy, *Morning in America: How Ronald Reagan Invented the 1980s* (Princeton, N.J.: Princeton University Press, 2005), 209.

3. Jack Boozer, "Wall Street: The Commodification of Perception," in *Cultural Power/Cultural Literacy: Selected Papers from the 14th Florida State University Conference on Literature and Film*, ed. Bonnie Braendlin (Gainesville: University Press of Florida, 1991), 76–77.

4. F. Scott Fitzgerald, *The Great Gatsby*, ed. Matthew J. Bruccoli (New York: Cambridge University Press, 1991), 72.

5. Kurt Eichenwald, "Wall Street Cutting Muscle Now," *New York Times*, November 9, 1990.

6. Arnold Weinstein, *Morning, Noon & Night: Finding the Meaning of Life's Stages through Books* (New York: Random House, 2011), 6.

7. Simon J. Bronner, *American Folklore Studies: An Intellectual History* (Lawrence: University Press of Kansas, 1986), 125–26.

8. Anthony R. Dolan, "Don't Count the Gipper Out," *New York Times*, July 10, 1987, A35.

9. Dolan, "Don't Count the Gipper Out," A35.

10. Anthony Lewis, "*The Great Gatsby*," *New York Times*, August 6, 1987, A27.

11. Anthony R. Dolan, "An Ascendant Conservative's Advice to Grim, Rejected Liberals," *New York Times*, August 25, 1987, A20.

12. Weinstein, *Morning, Noon & Night*, 6.

13. Nicholas Carr, *The Shallows: What the Internet Is Doing to Our Brains* (New York: Norton, 2011), 3.

14. Carr, *The Shallows*, 4.

15. Quoted in "Reagan's 'Scrooge'?" *Newsweek*, December 19, 1983, Lexis-Nexis Academic (accessed December 23, 2012).

16. Alfred Kazin and Ted Solotaroff, *Alfred Kazin's America: Critical and Personal Writings* (New York: Harper Perennial, 2004), 485.

17. Kent Cartwright, "Nick Carraway as an Unreliable Narrator," *Papers on Language and Literature* 20, no. 2 (Spring 1984): 218–32. Repr. in *Twentieth-Century Literary Criticism*, ed. Linda Pavlovski, vol. 157 (Detroit: Gale, 2005). Literature Resource Center.

18. Cartwright, "Nick Carraway."

19. Cartwright, "Nick Carraway."

20. Charles Bremner, "Is the American Party Over?" *Times* (London), September 30, 1989.

21. Bremner, "Is the American Party Over?"

22. Russell Baker, "Too Far from West Egg," *New York Times*, August 23, 1989, A21.

23. Lynne Helm, "Timeless Treasures," *Baltimore Sun*, October 14, 1990, 17.

24. George Will, "Fitzgerald Conjures Echoes from Jazz Age," *St. Louis Post-Dispatch*, December 20, 1990, 3C.

25. Carter Coleman, "Riding a Ghost Train, *Gatsby*-Style," *Los Angeles Times Book Review*, June 9, 1996, 10. Repr. in *Contemporary Literary Criticism Select* (Detroit: Gale, 2008). Literature Resource Center.

26. Steven Oxman, "A&E Finds *Gatsby* Elusive," *Variety*, January 15, 2001, 60.

27. Quoted in Lewis Beale, "Great *Gatsby* Expectation," *New York Daily News*, January 14, 2001, 6.

28. Paul Lewis, "*Ulysses* at Top as Panel Picks 100 Best Novels," *New York Times*, July 20, 1998, E1.

6. *GATSBY* TODAY, 2001–PRESENT

1. Richard Brody, "Why *The Great Gatsby* Endures," *New Yorker*, April 30, 2013, http://www.newyorker.com/online/blogs/movies/2013/04/the-great-gatsby-the-raw-material.html (accessed May 1, 2013).

2. Philip Hensher, "*Great Gatsby*: A Story for the Modern Age," *Telegraph* (London), May 23, 2012, http://www.telegraph.co.uk/culture/film/film-news/9284394/Great-Gatsby-a-story-for-the-modern-age.html (accessed March 30, 2013).

3. Hensher, "*Great Gatsby*."

4. Leigh H. Edwards, *The Triumph of Reality TV: The Revolution in American Television* (Santa Barbara, Calif.: Praeger, 2013), 177.

5. F. Scott Fitzgerald, *The Great Gatsby*, ed. Matthew J. Bruccoli (New York: Cambridge University Press, 1991), 49.

6. Clive James, *Cultural Amnesia: Necessary Memories from History and the Arts* (New York: Norton, 2007), 209.

7. Paul Krugman, "For Richer: How the Permissive Capitalism of the Boom Destroyed American Equality," *New York Times Magazine*, October 20, 2002, E62.

8. Krugman, "For Richer," E65.

9. Krugman, "For Richer," E65.

10. "Apple's Taxes Expose the Rotten U.S. Code," *Bloomberg*, May 21, 2013, http://www.bloomberg.com/news/2013-05-21/apple-s-taxes-expose-the-rotten-u-s-code.html (accessed May 21, 2013).

11. Krishnamurthy Sriramesh and Dejan Verčič, *Culture and Public Relations: Links and Implications* (New York: Routledge, 2012), 2.

12. "Outsourcing Trends to Watch in 2007," *Fortune*, September 3, 2007, S2.

13. Evan Osnos, "Reading *Gatsby* in Beijing," *New Yorker*, May 2, 2013, http://www.newyorker.com/online/blogs/comment/2013/05/reading-gatsby-in-beijing.html (accessed May 20, 2013).

14. "*Gatsby*'s Influence Reaches Chinese Fashion," *Jing Daily*, May 22, 2013, http://www.jingdaily.com/gatsbys-influence-reaches-chinese-fashion/26871/ (accessed May 23, 2013).

15. Osnos, "Reading *Gatsby* in Beijing."

16. Quoted in Chloe McConnell, "How to Write about America," *New Yorker*, October 1, 2011, http://www.newyorker.com/online/blogs/festival/2011/10/how-to-write-about-america.html (accessed January 2, 2013).

17. Ray B. Browne, "Popular Culture as the New Humanities," in *Popular Culture Theory and Methodology: A Basic Introduction*, ed. Harold E. Hinds Jr., Marilyn F. Motz, and Angela M. S. Nelson (Madison: University of Wisconsin Press, 2006), 75.

18. Brendan Riley, e-mail to the author, March 29, 2012.

19. Brian A. Cogan, e-mail to the author, March 28, 2012.

20. Quoted in Whitney Pastorek, "David Duchovny," *Entertainment Weekly*, 947 (2007): 21–22, Academic Search Complete (accessed December 24, 2011).

21. Robert Bianco, "Duchovny Delights in *Californication*," *USA Today*, August 13, 2007, http://usatoday30.usatoday.com/life/television/reviews/2007-08-12-californication_N.htm?csp=34 (accessed August 13, 2007).

22. Richard Huff, "Duchovny Says His Heel Has a Soul, Too," *New York Daily News*, September 25, 2009, LexisNexis Academic Solutions (accessed December 24, 2011).

23. Matthew J. Bruccoli, ed., *F. Scott Fitzgerald: A Life in Letters* (New York: Simon & Schuster, 1994), 320.

24. James, *Cultural Amnesia*, 210.

25. Philip Norman, "The New Great Gatsbys," *MailOnline* (U.K.), June 15, 2012, http://www.dailymail.co.uk/news/article-2160115/The-new-Great-Gatsbys-Why-F-Scott-Fitzgeralds-book-relevant-Twenties.html (accessed March 30, 2013).

7. THE AMERICAN DREAM

1. "All for Love," *Time*, December 31, 1965, 20, Academic Search Complete, EBSCOhost (accessed December 23, 2012).

2. "No. 9," *Time*, June 8, 1962, 25, Academic Search Complete, EBSCOhost (accessed December 23, 2012).

3. Sam Hodges, "Teflon Tycoon," *Mobile (Ala.) Press-Register*, December 19, 2001, http://www.al.com/specialreport/mobileregister/boykin_08.html (accessed February 23, 2013).

4. Sam Hodges, "Frank Boykin: The Politician," *Mobile (Ala.) Press-Register*, December 17, 2001, http://www.al.com/specialreport/mobileregister/boykin_15.html (accessed February 23, 2013).

5. Hodges, "Teflon Tycoon."

6. Hodges, "Teflon Tycoon."

7. Lawrence R. Samuel, *The American Dream: A Cultural History* (Syracuse, N.Y.: Syracuse University Press, 2012), 1.

8. Brad Tuttle, "Southwest Airlines: We're Not Really about Cheap Flights Anymore," *Time*, March 26, 2013, http://business.time.com/2013/03/26/southwest-airlines-were-not-really-about-cheap-flights-anymore/ (accessed April 9, 2013).

9. Arthur Mizener, "The Real Subject of *The Great Gatsby*," in *Readings on F. Scott Fitzgerald*, ed. Katie de Koster (San Diego: Greenhaven Press, 1998), 85.

10. Anthony Larson, "*Gatsby* and Us," *Critical Horizons* 4, no. 2 (2003): 285.

11. Larson, "*Gatsby* and Us," 286.

12. Jim Cullen, *The American Dream: A Short History of an Idea That Shaped a Nation* (New York: Oxford University Press, 2003), 179.

13. Cullen, *American Dream*, 179.

14. Carolyn Kellogg, "Last Gasp of the Gatsby House," *Los Angeles Times*, April 20, 2011, http://latimesblogs.latimes.com/jacketcopy/2011/04/last-gasp-of-the-gatsby-house.html (accessed April 1, 2013).

15. Kellogg, "Last Gasp."

16. Terry Castle, "Home Alone," *Atlantic*, March 2006, http://www.theatlantic.com/doc/200603/house-porn (accessed March 30, 2010).

17. Marcelle S. Fischler, "Gatsby Would Feel at Home," *New York Times*, March 28, 2010, RE9.

18. Stuart Ewen, *Captains of Consciousness: Advertising and the Social Roots of the Consumer Culture* (New York: Basic Books, 1976, 2001), 8.

19. Susan Strasser, *Satisfaction Guaranteed: The Making of the American Mass Market* (New York: Pantheon, 1989), 204–6.

20. Michael Schudson, *Advertising, the Uneasy Persuasion: Its Dubious Impact on American Society* (New York: Basic Books, 1984), 151.

21. Arthur Asa Berger, *Ads, Fads, and Consumer Culture: Advertising's Impact on American Character and Society* (Lanham, Md.: Rowman & Littlefield, 2004), 35.

22. Marius Bewley, "Scott Fitzgerald's Criticism of America," in *F. Scott Fitzgerald: A Collection of Critical Essays*, ed. Arthur Mizener (Englewood Cliffs, N.J.: Prentice Hall, 1963), 127.

23. David F. Trask, "A Note on Fitzgerald's *The Great Gatsby*," *University Review* 33, no. 3 (March 1967): 197–202. Repr. in *Novels for Students*, ed. Diane Telgen, vol. 2 (Detroit: Gale, 1998). Literature Resource Center.

24. Brian Sutton, "Fitzgerald's *The Great Gatsby*," *Explicator* 59, no. 1 (Fall 2000): 37.

25. F. Scott Fitzgerald, *The Great Gatsby*, ed. Matthew J. Bruccoli (New York: Cambridge University Press, 1991), 117.

26. F. Scott Fitzgerald, "The Crack-Up," in *The Crack-Up*, ed. Edmund Wilson (New York: New Directions, 1965), 69.

27. John F. Callahan, "F. Scott Fitzgerald's Evolving American Dream: The 'Pursuit of Happiness' in *Gatsby*, *Tender Is the Night*, and *The Last Tycoon*," *Twentieth Century Literature* 42 (Fall 1996): 376.

28. Fitzgerald, *Gatsby*, 19–20.

29. Fitzgerald, *Gatsby*, 153.

30. Fitzgerald, *Gatsby*, 154.

31. Richard L. Trumka, "Why Working People Are Angry and Why Politicians Should Listen," *Vital Speeches of the Day*, June 2010, 269.

32. Alan Abramowitz and Ruy Teixeira, "The Decline of the White Working Class and the Rise of a Mass Upper-Middle Class," *Political Science Quarterly* 124, no. 3 (2009): 417.

33. Gail McDonald, *American Literature and Culture, 1900–1960* (Malden, Mass.: Blackwell, 2007), 78.

8. WEALTH AND POWER

1. William Voegeli, "*Gatsby* and the Pursuit of Happiness," *Claremont Review of Books* (2003): 70.

2. F. Scott Fitzgerald, *The Great Gatsby*, ed. Matthew J. Bruccoli (New York: Cambridge University Press, 1991), 99.

3. Alexander Nazaryan, "Huge Incoherent Failures," *New York Daily News*, March 9, 2011, http://www.nydailynews.com/opinion/huge-incoherent-failures-doomed-mansion-great-gatsby-fitzgerald-america-article-1.120545 (accessed January 24, 2013).

4. David Minter, *A Cultural History of the American Novel: Henry James to William Faulkner* (New York: Cambridge University Press, 1994), 114.

5. March 4, 1938, *F. Scott Fitzgerald: A Life in Letters*, ed. Matthew J. Bruccoli with the assistance of Judith S. Baughman (New York: Touchstone, 1995), 352.

6. Gary Cross, *An All-Consuming Century: Why Commercialism Won in Modern America* (New York: Columbia University Press, 2000), 5.

7. Cross, *All-Consuming Century*, 17.

8. Joshua B. Freeman, *American Empire: The Rise of a Global Power, the Democratic Revolution at Home, 1945–2000* (New York: Viking, 2012), 124.

9. Steve Kemme, "King of the Bootleggers," *Cincinnati Enquirer*, August 1, 2011, http://cincinnati.com/blogs/ourhistory/2011/08/01/king-of-the-bootleggers/ (accessed May 4, 2013).

10. Kemme, "King of the Bootleggers."

11. Kemme, "King of the Bootleggers."

12. Edward Iwata, "Former CEO of National Century: Man of Mystery," *USA Today*, December 18, 2002, 1B.

13. Iwata, "Former CEO of National Century," 1B.

14. Iwata, "Former CEO of National Century," 1B.

15. Daniel Gross, "Membership Has Its Penalties," *Newsweek*, January 2, 2009, http://www.thedailybeast.com/newsweek/2009/01/02/membership-has-its-penalties.html (accessed March 30, 2013).

16. Eric Olsen, "The Great American Novel—What Is It, and Who Cares," *Portland Book Review*, February 4, 2012, http://portlandbookreview.com/2-4-12-the-great-american-novel-what-is-it-and-who-cares/ (accessed January 24, 2013).

9. CELEBRITY . . . AN OBSESSION

1. Larry Z. Leslie, *Celebrity in the 21st Century: A Reference Handbook* (Santa Barbara, Calif.: ABC-CLIO, 2011), xiii.

2. Leslie, *Celebrity in the 21st Century*, xiii.

3. F. Scott Fitzgerald, *The Great Gatsby*, ed. Matthew J. Bruccoli (New York: Cambridge University Press, 1991), 150.

4. Marshall Fishwick, Introduction to Icons of America, ed. Ray B. Browne and Marshall Fishwick (Bowling Green, Ohio: Popular Press, 1978), 4.

5. Michael Specter, "The Age of the Sage (or Is It Money Talking?)," *New York Times*, January 4, 1998, WK5.

6. Quoted in Nancy Milford, *Zelda: A Biography* (New York: Harper & Row, 1970), 67.

7. "The $1.7 Trillion Dot-Com Lesson," *CNNMoney*, November 9, 2000, http://money.cnn.com/2000/11/09/technology/overview (accessed November 15, 2000).

8. "UN Report Cites Global Internet Growth Despite Economic Woes," *USA Today*, November 18, 2002, http://www.usatoday.com/tech/news/2002-11-18-global-net_x.htm (accessed November 19, 2002).

9. Ruth Prigozy, "Introduction: Scott, Zelda, and the Culture of Celebrity," in *The Cambridge Companion to F. Scott Fitzgerald*, ed. Ruth Prigozy (Cambridge: Cambridge University Press, 2002), 24.

10. Jackson Lears, *Fables of Abundance: A Cultural History of Advertising in America* (New York: Basic Books, 1994), 10.

11. Lears, *Fables of Abundance*, 10–11.

12. Stuart Ewen, *Captains of Consciousness: Advertising and the Social Roots of the Consumer Culture* (New York: Basic Books, 1976, 2001), 51.

13. Charles Goodrum and Helen Dalrymple, *Advertising in America: The First 200 Years* (New York: Abrams, 1990), 106.

14. Goodrum and Dalrymple, *Advertising in America*, 131.

15. Kirk Curnutt, ed., *A Historical Guide to F. Scott Fitzgerald* (New York: Oxford University Press, 2004), 5.

16. Fitzgerald, *Gatsby*, ed. Bruccoli, 50.

17. "Kings of Leon Play at Billionaire's Caribbean New Year's Eve," *WRTV Indianapolis*, January 3, 2013, http://www.theindychannel.com/entertainment/kings-of-leon-play-at-billionaires-caribbean-new-years-eve_22646991 (accessed January 8, 2013).

18. Brian Kendall, "Golf with the Stars in a Celebrity Pro-Am," Canadian Golf Traveller, November 5, 2012, http://canadiangolftraveller.com/golf-with-the-stars-in-a-celebrity-pro-am/ (accessed January 8, 2013).

19. Clive James, *Cultural Amnesia: Necessary Memories from History and the Arts* (New York: Norton, 2007), 210.

20. Stephen Gundle, *Glamour: A History* (New York: Oxford University Press, 2008), 156.

21. John Updike, *More Matter: Essays and Criticism* (New York: Random House, 1999), 538.

22. Updike, *More Matter*, 539.

10. IS ROMANCE TIMELESS?

1. Harlequin Enterprises, "Harlequin Romance Report—2012 Survey Results," Harlequin Media Center, February 9, 2012, 1–2.

2. Harlequin, "Harlequin Romance Report."

3. Ronald Berman, The Great Gatsby *and Fitzgerald's World of Ideas* (Tuscaloosa: University of Alabama Press, 1997), 160.

4. Harold Bloom, ed., *F. Scott Fitzgerald's* The Great Gatsby, new ed. (New York: Chelsea House, 2010), 5.

5. Ben Stein, "*The Great Gatsby* in 3-D, the Third Dimension Is Money," *Forbes.com*, May 17, 2013, http://www.forbes.com/sites/schifrin/2013/05/17/ben-stein-great-gatsby-101/ (accessed May 19, 2013).

6. Jonathan P. Fegley, "'If I Couldn't Be Perfect I Wouldn't Be Anything': Teaching Becoming and Being in *The Great Gatsby*," in *Approaches to Teaching Fitzgerald's* The Great Gatsby, ed. Jackson R. Bryer and Nancy P. VanArsdale (New York: Modern Language Association, 2009), 137.

7. David Minter, *A Cultural History of the American Novel: Henry James to William Faulkner* (New York: Cambridge University Press, 1994), 111.

8. Kim Foltz, "The Media Business: Advertising; A New Twist for Klein's Obsession," *New York Times*, August 15, 1990, http://www.nytimes.com/1990/08/15/business/the-media-business-advertising-a-new-twist-for-klein-s-obsession.html (accessed November 15, 2010). The commercial can be viewed at YouTube, either searching via keywords or at http://www.youtube.com/watch?v=Lv_5sVCuXQ8.

9. F. Scott Fitzgerald, *The Great Gatsby*, ed. Matthew J. Bruccoli (New York: Cambridge University Press, 1991), 101.

10. Quoted in Foltz, "Media Business."

11. Fitzgerald, *Gatsby*, ed. Bruccoli, 154.

12. Matthew J. Bruccoli, ed., The Great Gatsby*: The Revised and Rewritten Galleys* (New York: Garland, 1990), 189.

13. Fitzgerald, *Gatsby*, ed. Bruccoli, 154.

14. Arthur Mizener, "*Gatsby*, 35 Years Later," *New Yorker*, April 24, 1960, http://www.nytimes.com/books/00/12/24/specials/fitzgerald-gatsby60.html (accessed December 19, 2012).

15. Mizener, "*Gatsby*, 35 Years Later."

16. Bloom, *Fitzgerald's* The Great Gatsby, 5.

17. Fitzgerald, *Gatsby*, ed. Bruccoli, 20.

18. Fitzgerald, *Gatsby*, ed. Bruccoli, 141

19. Fitzgerald, *Gatsby*, ed. Bruccoli, 141.

20. Fitzgerald, *Gatsby*, ed. Bruccoli, 142.

21. Fitzgerald, *Gatsby*, ed. Bruccoli, 134.

22. Greg Olear, "Ga(tsb)y," *Weeklings*, January 8, 2013, http://www.theweeklings.com/golear/2013/01/08/gatsby/ (accessed January 8, 2013).

23. Fitzgerald, *Gatsby*, ed. Bruccoli, 45.

24. Fitzgerald, *Gatsby*, ed. Bruccoli, 45.

25. Olear, "Ga(tsb)y."

26. Many scholars have written about these incidents, which have passed into general lore about both Fitzgerald and Hemingway. For more details, see Matthew J. Bruccoli, *Some Sort of Epic Grandeur: The Life of F. Scott Fitzgerald*, 2nd rev. ed. (Columbia: University of South Carolina Press, 2002), 275.

27. Bruccoli, *Epic Grandeur*, 275.

28. Scott Donaldson, *Fool for Love: F. Scott Fitzgerald* (New York: Congdon & Weed, 1983), 73.

29. Richard Brody, "Why *The Great Gatsby* Endures," *New Yorker*, April 30, 2013, http://www.newyorker.com/online/blogs/movies/2013/04/the-great-gatsby-the-raw-material.html (accessed May 1, 2013).

30. Ty Burr, "Baz Luhrmann's Eye-Popping Vision of *Gatsby*," *Boston Globe*, May 9, 2013 http://www.bostonglobe.com/arts/movies/2013/05/09/baz-luhrmann-eye-popping vision-gatsby/OZfgTicBuABNo7ZIRZI h3N/story.html (accessed May 17, 2013).

31. Donaldson, *Fool for Love*, x.

11. A HOPE FOR READING AND THE QUEST FOR THE GREAT AMERICAN NOVEL

1. Unless otherwise noted, all student quotes are from students in Denise Douglas's eleventh-grade English class at Greenfield School in Greenfield, Tennessee. Under Ms. Douglas's direction, the students studied *Gatsby* and watched the 1974 film and then saw the 2013 film. The author would like to thank Ms. Douglas and the students for participating in an online survey about the novel and film.

2. Paul Lauter, *Canons and Contexts* (New York: Oxford University Press, 1991), viii.

3. Joy Hakim, "Rescue the Wonder of the Printed Page," in *The Last Word: The Best Commentary and Controversy in American Education*, ed. Mary-Ellen Phelps Deily and Veronika Herman Bromberg (New York: Wiley, 2007), 94.

4. Marjorie Garber, *The Use and Abuse of Literature* (New York: Pantheon, 2011), 173–74.

5. John Updike, *More Matter: Essays and Criticism* (New York: Random House, 1999), 546.

6. All quotes from Quincey Upshaw are drawn from an e-mail exchange with her in which she reflected on her experiences teaching *Gatsby* and shared two student papers. Quincey Upshaw, e-mail to author, May 4, 2013.

7. Jackson R. Bryer and Nancy P. VanArsdale, eds., *Approaches to Teaching Fitzgerald's* The Great Gatsby (New York: Modern Language Association, 2009), xi–xii.

8. Morris Dickstein, *A Mirror in the Roadway: Literature and the Real World* (Princeton, N.J.: Princeton University Press, 2005), 81.

9. Mark William Roche, *Why Literature Matters in the 21st Century* (New Haven, Conn.: Yale University Press, 2004), 251.

10. Roche, *Why Literature Matters*, 256.

11. Colette Bancroft, "Author James Patterson Campaigns to Save Books," *Tampa Bay Times*, April 28, 2013, http://www.tampabay.com/features/books/author-james-patterson-campaigns-to-save-books/2117609 (accessed April 28, 2013).

12. James L. W. West III, "Fitzgerald's Posthumous Literary Career," *Journal of Scholarly Publishing* 28 (1997): 98.

13. Dan Sperling, "Classics Still Tops in Schools," *USA Today*, May 31, 1989, 1A.

14. "Promise of No Child Left Behind Falls Short after 10 Years," *USA Today*, January 7, 2012, http://www.usatoday.com/news/education/story/2012-01-07/no-child-left-behind-anniversary/52430722/1?csp=34news (accessed January 7, 2012).

15. Nel Noddings, "High Stakes Testing: Why?" *Theory and Research in Education* 2, no. 3 (2004): 263.

16. James G. Henderson and Richard D. Hawthorne, *Transformative Curriculum Leadership* (Englewood Cliffs, N.J.: Merrill, 1995), 5.

17. Philip W. Jackson, *What Is Education?* (Chicago: University of Chicago Press, 2012), 92–93.

18. Kathleen R. Kesson and James G. Henderson, "Reconceptualizing Professional Development for Curriculum Leadership: Inspired by John Dewey and Informed by Alain Badiou," *Educational Philosophy and Theory* 42, no. 2 (2010): 214.

19. Garber, *Use and Abuse*, 167.

20. R. Clifton Spargo, "Why Every American Should Read *The Great Gatsby*, Again," *Huffington Post*, April 9, 2013, http://www.huffingtonpost.com/r-clifton-spargo/great-gatsby-rereading_b_3046378.html (accessed April 10, 2013).

21. Anthony Larson, "*Gatsby* and Us," *Critical Horizons* 4, no. 2 (2003): 284.

22. Larson, "*Gatsby* and Us," 290.

23. Larson, "*Gatsby* and Us," 288.

24. Maxine Greene, *Variations on a Blue Guitar: The Lincoln Center Institute Lectures on Aesthetic Education* (New York: Teachers College Press, 2001), 20–21.

25. Julia Ingalls, "Is the Great American Novel Still Relevant?" *Salon.com*, November 8, 2012, http://www.salon.com/2012/11/08/is_the_great_american_novel_still_relevant/ (accessed May 4, 2013).

26. George Garrett, "Fire and Freshness: A Matter of Style in *The Great Gatsby*," in *New Essays on* The Great Gatsby, ed. Matthew J. Bruccoli (New York: Cambridge University Press, 1985), 101.

27. Bryer and VanArsdale, *Approaches to Teaching*, 27.

12. BOOM, BUST, REPEAT: POWER, GREED, AND RECKLESSNESS IN CONTEMPORARY AMERICA

1. F. Scott Fitzgerald, *The Great Gatsby*, ed. Matthew J. Bruccoli (New York: Cambridge University Press, 1991), 153.

2. Fitzgerald, *Gatsby*, ed. Bruccoli, 153.

3. Ronald Berman, The Great Gatsby *and Fitzgerald's World of Ideas* (Tuscaloosa: University of Alabama Press, 1997), 147.

4. Brian Way, *F. Scott Fitzgerald and the Art of Social Fiction* (New York: St. Martin's, 1980), 102.

5. July 16, 1936, *F. Scott Fitzgerald: A Life in Letters*, ed. Matthew J. Bruccoli with the assistance of Judith S. Baughman (New York: Touchtone, 1995), 302.

6. Arthur Mizener, "The Real Subject of *The Great Gatsby*," in *Readings on F. Scott Fitzgerald*, ed. Katie de Koster (San Diego: Greenhaven Press, 1998), 77.

7. Mizener, *"The Great Gatsby,"* 77.

8. Fitzgerald, *Gatsby*, ed. Bruccoli, 22.

9. November 18, 1924, *Life in Letters*, 86.

10. November 20, 1924, *Life in Letters*, 87.

11. Mizener, *"The Great Gatsby,"* 81.

12. Quoted in Jeannine Aversa, "Many Believe US Already in a Recession," Associated Press, February 10, 2008, http://ap.google.com/article/ALeqM5hJjzb-73g6-mEmgvyixbf7Vzw2lgD8UNNUBO2 (accessed February 11, 2008).

13. Aversa, "US Already in a Recession."

14. Aversa, "US Already in a Recession."

15. Matthew O'Brien, "Happy Birthday, Alan Greenspan," *Atlantic*, March 7, 2012, http://www.theatlantic.com/business/archive/2012/03/happy-birthday-alan-greenspan-the-housing-bubble-wasnt-your-fault/254089/ (accessed March 30, 2012).

16. Way, *F. Scott Fitzgerald*, 114.

17. Bethany McLean and Peter Elkind, "The Guiltiest Guys in the Room," *Fortune*, July 5, 2006, http://money.cnn.com/2006/05/29/news/enron_guiltyest/index.htm, (accessed September 15, 2006).

18. Penelope Patsuris, "The Corporate Scandal Sheet," *Forbes.com*, August 26, 2002, http://www.forbes.com/2002/07/25/accountingtracker.html (accessed November 15, 2007).

19. Quoted in "CEOs Defend Their Paychecks," *St. Petersburg Times*, March 8, 2008, 2D.

20. Gerald Russello, "The Smartest Guys on the Cell Block," *New York Sun*, April 22, 2005, http://www.nysun.com/arts/smartest-guys-on-the-cell-block/12708/ (accessed January 2, 2013).

21. Adam Cohen, "A Tale of Two Bills," *Time International* (South Pacific Edition) no. 4, January 25, 1999, 52, MasterFILE Premier, EBSCOhost (accessed February 1, 2013).

22. Cohen, "Tale of Two Bills," 52.

23. Cohen, "Tale of Two Bills," 52.

24. Cohen, "Tale of Two Bills," 52.

25. For a more detailed discussion of suicide and the Great Depression, please see José A. Tapia Granados and Ana V. Diez Roux, "Life and Death during the Great Depression," *Proceedings of the National Academy of Sciences* 106, no. 41 (2009): 17290–95; and Steven Stack, "The Effect of the Media on Suicide: The Great Depression," *Suicide and Life-Threatening Behavior* 22, no. 2 (1992): 255–67.

26. Aaron Reeves, David Stuckler, Martin McKee, David Gunnell, Shu-Sen Chang, and Sanjay Basu, "Increase in State Suicide Rates in the USA during Economic Recession," *Lancet* 380, no. 9856 (2012), 1813.

13. *THE GREAT GATSBY* (2013): THE FILM

1. Andrew Wilson, "Has the Moulin Rouge Director Created the Starriest, Glitziest, Greatest Gatsby of All?" *MailOnline* (U.K.), April 20, 2013, http://www.dailymail.co.uk/home/event/article-2311016/The-Great-Gatsby-Has-Moulin-Rouge-director-Baz-Luhrmann-created-starriest-glitziest-Greatest-Gatsby-all.html?ito=feeds-newsxml (accessed April 21, 2013).

2. Quoted in Wilson, "Greatest Gatsby of All?"

3. Quoted in Wilson, "Greatest Gatsby of All?"

4. "Libertine Presents Gatsby," Press Release, May 13, 2013, http://www.libertineclublondon.com/ (accessed May 18, 2013).

5. Misty Harris, "*The Great Gatsby* Is a Branding Phenomenon," *Canada.com/Postmedia News*, May 2, 2013, http://www.canada.com/entertainment/

movie-guide/Great+Gatsby+branding+phenomenon/8326042/story.html (accessed May 15, 2013).

6. Quentin Vieregge, "Whose Brand Is It Anyway? How Brands Become Cults by Becoming Inclusive," in *Cult Pop Culture: How the Fringe Became Mainstream*, ed. Bob Batchelor (Santa Barbara, Calif.: Praeger, 2012), 71.

7. Vieregge, "Whose Brand Is It Anyway?" 71.

8. David Edelstein, "Why I Sort of Liked *The Great Gatsby*," *Vulture/New York Magazine*, May 7, 2013, http://www.vulture.com/2013/05/movie-review-the-great-gatsby.html (accessed May 15, 2013).

9. Richard Lawson, "The Tragic Emptiness of *The Great Gatsby*," review of *The Great Gatsby* film, *Atlantic Wire*, May 8, 2013, http://www.theatlanticwire .com/entertainment/2013/05/great-gatsby-review/65020/ (accessed May 18, 2013).

10. Joanna Connors, "*Gatsby* in 3-D Is a Manic, Three-Ring Spectacle," *Cleveland Plain Dealer*, May 5, 2013, http://www.cleveland.com/books/index.ssf/2013/05/gatsby_in_3-d_is_a_manic_three.html (accessed May 6, 2013).

11. Edelstein, "*The Great Gatsby*."

12. Dana Stevens, "*The Great Gatsby*," review of *The Great Gatsby* film, *Slate*, May 9, 2013, http://www.slate.com/articles/arts/movies/2013/05/ the_great_gatsby_directed_by_baz_luhrmann_reviewed.html (accessed May 15, 2013).

13. Arthur Frank, *The Wounded Storyteller: Body, Illness, and Ethics* (Chicago: University of Chicago Press, 1995), 23.

CONCLUSION: *GATSBY* IS AMERICA

1. Ray B. Browne, "Folk Cultures and the Humanities," in *Rejuvenating the Humanities*, ed. Ray B. Browne and Marshall Fishwick (Bowling Green, Ohio: Bowling Green State University Popular Press, 1992), 24.

2. Ray B. Browne, "Redefining the Humanities," in *Eye on the Future: Popular Culture Scholarship into the Twenty-First Century*, ed. Marilyn F. Motz et al. (Bowling Green, Ohio: Bowling Green State University Popular Press, 1994), 249.

3. Richard M. Dorson, ed. *Folklore and Folklife: An Introduction* (Chicago: University of Chicago Press, 1982), 21.

4. Marjorie Garber, *The Use and Abuse of Literature* (New York: Pantheon, 2011), 174.

5. William Voegeli, "*Gatsby* and the Pursuit of Happiness," *Claremont Review of Books*, 2003, 71.

6. Thomas C. Foster, *Twenty-Five Books That Shaped America* (New York: Harper, 2011), 146.

7. Foster, *Twenty-Five Books*, 146.

8. Alfred Kazin and Ted Solotaroff, *Alfred Kazin's America: Critical and Personal Writings* (New York: Harper Perennial, 2004), 122.

9. Kazin and Solotaroff, *Alfred Kazin's America*, 122.

10. Arthur Mizener, *The Far Side of Paradise: A Biography of F. Scott Fitzgerald* (New York: Houghton Mifflin, 1965), 185.

11. Morris Dickstein, *A Mirror in the Roadway: Literature and the Real World* (Princeton, N.J.: Princeton University Press, 2005), 82.

12. Malcolm Cowley, "Dear Scottie, Zelda and Max," review of *The Letters of F. Scott Fitzgerald*, ed. Andrew Turnbull, *New York Times*, October 20, 1963, 272.

13. James L. W. West III, "Fitzgerald's Posthumous Literary Career," *Journal of Scholarly Publishing* 28 (1997): 95.

14. Mark William Roche, *Why Literature Matters in the 21st Century* (New Haven, Conn.: Yale University Press, 2004), 258.

15. Roche, *Why Literature Matters*, 258.

16. Frank B. Farrell, *Why Does Literature Matter?* (Ithaca, N.Y.: Cornell University Press, 2004), 19.

17. Clive James, *Cultural Amnesia: Necessary Memories from History and the Arts* (New York: Norton, 2007), 219.

18. John Updike, *More Matter: Essays and Criticism* (New York: Random House, 1999), 547.

19. Jonathan P. Fegley, "'If I Couldn't Be Perfect I Wouldn't Be Anything': Teaching Becoming and Being in *The Great Gatsby*," in *Approaches to Teaching Fitzgerald's* The Great Gatsby, ed. Jackson R. Bryer and Nancy P. VanArsdale (New York: Modern Language Association, 2009), 130.

20. Chris Hedges, *Empire of Illusion: The End of Literacy and the Triumph of Spectacle* (New York: Nation Books, 2009), 92.

21. David Minter, *A Cultural History of the American Novel: Henry James to William Faulkner* (New York: Cambridge University Press, 1994), 114.

22. Minter, *Cultural History*, 114.

23. Leonardo DiCaprio, "The Great American Dreamer," *MailOnline* (U.K.), April 20, 2013, http://www.dailymail.co.uk/home/event/article-2311016/The-Great-Gatsby-Has-Moulin-Rouge-director-Baz-Luhrmann-created-starriest-glitziest-Greatest-Gatsby-all.html?ito=feeds-newsxml (accessed April 21, 2013).

24. Quoted in Andrew Wilson, "Has the Moulin Rouge Director Created the Starriest, Glitziest, Greatest Gatsby of All?" *MailOnline* (U.K.), April 20, 2013, http://www.dailymail.co.uk/home/event/article-2311016/The-Great-Gatsby-Has-

Moulin-Rouge-director-Baz-Luhrmann-created-starriest-glitziest-Greatest-Gatsby-all.html?ito=feeds-newsxml (accessed April 21, 2013).

25. Voegeli, *"Gatsby,"* 70.

26. Kazin and Solotaroff, *Alfred Kazin's America*, 122.

27. Jim Cullen, *The American Dream: A Short History of an Idea That Shaped a Nation* (New York: Oxford University Press, 2003), 182.

28. Cullen, *The American Dream*, 182.

29. John Updike, *Odd Jobs: Essays and Criticism* (New York: Knopf, 1991), 37.

30. Roche, *Why Literature Matters*, 259.

BIBLIOGRAPHY

Abramowitz, Alan, and Ruy Teixeira. "The Decline of the White Working Class and the Rise of a Mass Upper-Middle Class." *Political Science Quarterly* 124, no. 3 (2009): 391–422.

Allan, John H. "Interest Rates Surge for Bonds." *New York Times*, August 7, 1966.

"All for Love." *Time* 86, no. 27 (December 31, 1965): 20. Academic Search Complete, EBSCOhost. Accessed December 23, 2012.

Anderson, Richard. "*Gatsby*'s Long Shadow: Influence and Endurance." In *New Essays on* The Great Gatsby, edited by Matthew J. Bruccoli, 15–40. New York: Cambridge University Press, 1985.

"Apple's Taxes Expose the Rotten U.S. Code." *Bloomberg*, May 21, 2013, http://www.bloomberg.com/news/2013-05-21/apple-s-taxes-expose-the-rotten-u-s-code.html. Accessed May 21, 2013.

Aversa, Jeannine. "Many Believe US Already in a Recession." Associated Press, February 10, 2008, http://ap.google.com/article/ALeqM5hJjzb 73gG-mEmgvyixbf/Vzw2lgD8UNNUB Q2. Accessed February 11, 2008.

Bahrenburg, Bruce. *Filming* The Great Gatsby. New York: Berkley, 1974.

Baker, Russell. "Too Far from West Egg." *New York Times*, August 23, 1989, A21.

Bancroft, Colette. "Author James Patterson Campaigns to Save Books." *Tampa Bay Times*, April 28, 2013, http://www.tampabay.com/features/books/author-james-patterson-campaigns-to-save-books/2117609. Accessed April 28, 2013.

Batchelor, Bob, and Scott Stoddard. *The 1980s*. Westport, Conn.: Greenwood, 2007.

Beale, Lewis. "Great *Gatsby* Expectation." *New York Daily News*, January 14, 2001.

Berger, Arthur Asa. *Ads, Fads, and Consumer Culture: Advertising's Impact on American Character and Society*. Lanham, Md.: Rowman & Littlefield, 2004.

Berman, Ronald. The Great Gatsby *and Fitzgerald's World of Ideas*. Tuscaloosa: University of Alabama Press, 1997.

Bewley, Marius. "Scott Fitzgerald's Criticism of America." In *F. Scott Fitzgerald: A Collection of Critical Essays*, edited by Arthur Mizener, 125–41. Englewood Cliffs, N.J.: Prentice Hall, 1963.

Bianco, Robert. "Duchovny Delights in *Californication*." *USA Today*, August 13, 2007, http://usatoday30.usatoday.com/life/television/reviews/2007-08-12-californication_N.htm?csp=34. Accessed August 13, 2007.

Bliven, Bruce. "The Revolution of the Joneses." *New York Times*, October 9, 1960.

Bloom, Harold, ed. *F. Scott Fitzgerald's* The Great Gatsby. New ed. New York: Chelsea House, 2010.

Boozer, Jack. "Wall Street: The Commodification of Perception." In *Cultural Power/Cultural Literacy: Selected Papers from the 14th Florida State University Conference on Literature and Film*, edited by Bonnie Braendlin, 76–95. Gainesville: University Press of Florida, 1991.

Bremner, Charles. "Is the American Party Over?" *Times* (London), September 30, 1989.

Brody, Richard. "Why *The Great Gatsby* Endures." *New Yorker*, April 30, 2013, http://www.newyorker.com/online/blogs/movies/2013/04/the-great-gatsby-the-raw-material.html. Accessed May 1, 2013.

Bronner, Simon J. *American Folklore Studies: An Intellectual History*. Lawrence: University Press of Kansas, 1986.

Browne, Ray B. "Folk Cultures and the Humanities." In *Rejuvenating the Humanities*, edited by Ray B. Browne and Marshall Fishwick, 24–34. Bowling Green, Ohio: Bowling Green State University Popular Press, 1992.

———. "Popular Culture as the New Humanities." In *Popular Culture Theory and Methodology: A Basic Introduction*, edited by Harold E. Hinds, Jr., Marilyn F. Motz, and Angela M. S. Nelson. Madison: University of Wisconsin Press, 2006.

———. "Redefining the Humanities." In *Eye on the Future: Popular Culture Scholarship into the Twenty-First Century*, edited by Marilyn F. Motz, John G. Nachbar, Michael T. Marsden, and Ronald J. Ambrosetti, 247–58. Bowling Green, Ohio: Bowling Green State University Popular Press, 1994.

Bruccoli, Matthew J., ed. *F. Scott Fitzgerald: A Life in Letters*. New York: Simon & Schuster, 1994.

———, ed. *F. Scott Fitzgerald's* The Great Gatsby: *A Documentary Volume*. Vol. 219 of *Dictionary of Literary Biography*. Detroit: Gale Group, 2000.

———, ed. The Great Gatsby: *The Revised and Rewritten Galleys*. New York: Garland, 1990.

———. *Some Sort of Epic Grandeur: The Life of F. Scott Fitzgerald*. 2nd revised ed. Columbia: University of South Carolina Press, 2002.

Bruccoli, Matthew J., and Judith S. Baughman, eds. *F. Scott Fitzgerald in the Marketplace: The Auction and Dealer Catalogues, 1935–2006*. Columbia: University of South Carolina Press, 2009.

Bruccoli, Matthew J., with Judith S. Baughman. *Reader's Companion to F. Scott Fitzgerald's* Tender Is the Night. Columbia: University of South Carolina Press, 1996.

Bruccoli, Matthew J., Arlyn Bruccoli, and Park Bucker. *The Matthew J. and Arlyn Bruccoli Collection of F. Scott Fitzgerald at the University of South Carolina: An Illustrated Catalogue*. Columbia: University of South Carolina Press, 2004.

Bruccoli, Matthew J., and Margaret M. Duggan, eds. *Correspondence of F. Scott Fitzgerald*. New York: Random House, 1980.

Bruccoli, Matthew J., Scottie Fitzgerald Smith, and Joan P. Kerr, eds., *The Romantic Egoists: A Pictorial Autobiography from the Scrapbooks and Albums of F. Scott and Zelda Fitzgerald*. Columbia: University of South Carolina Press, 2003.

Bryan, C. D. B. *The Great Dethriffe*. New York: Dutton, 1970.

Bryer, Jackson R. "The Critical Reputation of F. Scott Fitzgerald." In *The Cambridge Companion to F. Scott Fitzgerald*, edited by Ruth Prigozy, 209–34. Cambridge: Cambridge University Press, 2002.

———. "F. Scott Fitzgerald 1896–1940: A Brief Biography." In *A Historical Guide to F. Scott Fitzgerald*, edited by Kirk Curnutt, 21–46. New York: Oxford University Press, 2004.

Bryer, Jackson R., and Nancy P. VanArsdale, eds. *Approaches to Teaching Fitzgerald's* The Great Gatsby. New York: Modern Language Association, 2009.

Burr, Ty. "Baz Luhrmann's Eye-Popping Vision of *Gatsby*." *Boston Globe*, May 9, 2013, http://www.bostonglobe.com/arts/movies/2013/05/09/baz-luhrmann-eye-popping-vision-gatsby/OZfgTicBuABNo72IRZFh3N/story.html. Accessed May 17, 2013.

Callahan, John F. "F. Scott Fitzgerald's Evolving American Dream: The 'Pursuit of Happiness' in *Gatsby*, *Tender Is the Night*, and *The Last Tycoon*." *Twentieth Century Literature* 42 (Fall 1996): 374–95.

Canby, Vincent. "They've Turned *Gatsby* to Goo." *New York Times*, March 31, 1974, http://www.nytimes.com/books/00/12/24/specials/fitzgerald-gatsby74.html. Accessed December 19, 2012.

Carr, Nicholas. *The Shallows: What the Internet Is Doing to Our Brains.* New York: Norton, 2011.
Cartwright, Kent. "Nick Carraway as an Unreliable Narrator." *Papers on Language and Literature* 20, no. 2 (Spring 1984): 218–32. Reprinted in *Twentieth-Century Literary Criticism*, edited by Linda Pavlovski. Vol. 157. Detroit: Gale, 2005. Literature Resource Center.
Castle, Terry. "Home Alone." *Atlantic*, March 2006, http://www.theatlantic.com/doc/200603/house-porn. Accessed March 30, 2010.
Center for Media Research. "9.9 Billion Video Ad Views in February," *Research Brief Newsletter*, May 6, 2013, http://www.mediapost.com/publications/article/199678/99-billion-video-ad-views-in-february.html#axzz2UbwV6Xn8. Accessed May 6, 2013.
"CEOs Defend Their Paychecks." *St. Petersburg Times*, March 8, 2008.
Cohen, Adam. "A Tale of Two Bills." *Time International* (South Pacific Edition), no. 4, January 25, 1999, 52. MasterFILE Premier, EBSCOhost. Accessed February 1, 2013.
Coleman, Carter. "Riding a Ghost Train, *Gatsby*-Style." *Los Angeles Times Book Review*, June 9, 1996, 10. Reprinted in *Contemporary Literary Criticism Select*. Detroit: Gale, 2008. Literature Resource Center.
Connors, Joanna. "*Gatsby* in 3-D Is a Manic, Three-Ring Spectacle." *Cleveland Plain Dealer*, May 5, 2013, http://www.cleveland.com/books/index.ssf/2013/05/gatsby_in_3_d_is_a_manic_three.html. Accessed May 6, 2013.
Cowley, Malcolm. "Dear Scottie, Zelda and Max." Review of *The Letters of F. Scott Fitzgerald*, edited by Andrew Turnbull. *New York Times*, October 20, 1963.
Cross, Gary. *An All-Consuming Century: Why Commercialism Won in Modern America.* New York: Columbia University Press, 2000.
Crowther, Bosley. "*The Great Gatsby* (1949)," *New York Times*, July 14, 1949, http://movies.nytimes.com/movie/review?res=9502E6DC123CE53ABC4C52DFB1668382659EDE. Accessed February 14, 2013.
Cullen, Jim. *The American Dream: A Short History of an Idea That Shaped a Nation.* New York: Oxford University Press, 2003.
Curnutt, Kirk, ed. *A Historical Guide to F. Scott Fitzgerald.* New York: Oxford University Press, 2004.
Davis, Robert Gorham. "Is Our Past Becoming Irrelevant?" Review of *The Urgent West: The American Dream and Modern Man*, by Walter Allen. *New York Times*, March 16, 1969.
DiCaprio, Leonardo. "The Great American Dreamer," *MailOnline* (UK), April 20, 2013, http://www.dailymail.co.uk/home/event/article-2311016/The-Great-Gatsby-Has-Moulin-Rouge-director-Baz-Luhrmann-created-starriest-glitziest-Greatest-Gatsby-all.html?ito=feeds-newsxml. Accessed April 21, 2013.
Dickstein, Morris, ed. *Critical Insights:* The Great Gatsby. Pasadena, Calif.: Salem Press, 2010.
———. *A Mirror in the Roadway: Literature and the Real World.* Princeton, N.J.: Princeton University Press, 2005.
Dixon, Wheeler Winston. "The Three Film Versions of *The Great Gatsby*: A Vision Deferred." *Literature Film Quarterly* 31, no. 4 (2003): 287–94.
Dolan, Anthony R. "An Ascendant Conservative's Advice to Grim, Rejected Liberals." *New York Times*, August 25, 1987, A20.
———. "Don't Count the Gipper Out." *New York Times*, July 10, 1987, A35.
Donaldson, Scott. *Fool for Love: F. Scott Fitzgerald.* New York: Congdon & Weed, 1983.
Dorson, Richard M., ed. *Folklore and Folklife: An Introduction.* Chicago: University of Chicago Press, 1982.
DuMound, Joanne Berger. "*The Great Gatsby* Arrives at Berea High School." *Cleveland.com*, January 30, 2013, http://www.cleveland.com/berea/index.ssf/2013/01/post_14.html. Accessed January 30, 2013.
Ebert, Roger. "*The Great Gatsby.*" *Chicago Sun-Times*, January 1, 1974, http://rogerebert.suntimes.com/apps/pbcs.dll/article?AID=/19740101/REVIEWS/401010315. Accessed January 31, 2013.
Edelstein, David. "Why I Sort of Liked *The Great Gatsby.*" *Vulture/New York Magazine*, May 7, 2013, http://www.vulture.com/2013/05/movie-review-the-great-gatsby.html. Accessed May 15, 2013.

Edwards, Leigh H. *The Triumph of Reality TV: The Revolution in American Television*. Santa Barbara, Calif.: Praeger, 2013.

Eichenwald, Kurt. "Wall Street Cutting Muscle Now." *New York Times*, November 9, 1990.

Ewen, Stuart. *Captains of Consciousness: Advertising and the Social Roots of the Consumer Culture*. New York: Basic Books, 1976, 2001.

Farrell, Frank B. *Why Does Literature Matter?* Ithaca, N.Y.: Cornell University Press, 2004.

Fegley, Jonathan P. "'If I Couldn't Be Perfect I Wouldn't Be Anything': Teaching Becoming and Being in *The Great Gatsby*." In *Approaches to Teaching Fitzgerald's* The Great Gatsby, edited by Jackson R. Bryer and Nancy P. VanArsdale, 126–38. New York: Modern Language Association, 2009.

"Fire and Explosion Rock 42D Street." *New York Times*, April 3, 1920.

Fischler, Marcelle S. "Gatsby Would Feel at Home." *New York Times*, March 28, 2010.

Fishwick, Marshall. Introduction to *Icons of America*, edited by Ray B. Browne and Marshall Fishwick, 3–12. Bowling Green, Ohio: Bowling Green State University Popular Press, 1978.

Fitzgerald, F. Scott. *Afternoon of an Author: A Selection of Uncollected Stories and Essays*. Princeton, N.J.: Princeton University Press, 1957.

———. *F. Scott Fitzgerald: A Life in Letters*. Edited by Matthew J. Bruccoli with the assistance of Judith S. Baughman. New York: Touchstone, 1995.

———. *The Great Gatsby*. Edited by Matthew J. Bruccoli. New York: Cambridge University Press, 1991.

———. *Tender Is the Night*. New York: Scribner, 1934, 1962.

Foltz, Kim. "The Media Business: Advertising; A New Twist for Klein's Obsession." *New York Times*, August 15, 1990, http://www.nytimes.com/1990/08/15/business/the-media-business-advertising-a-new-twist-for-klein-s-obsession.html. Accessed November 15, 2010.

Foster, Thomas C. *Twenty-Five Books That Shaped America*. New York: Harper, 2011.

Frank, Arthur. *The Wounded Storyteller: Body, Illness, and Ethics*. Chicago: University of Chicago Press, 1995.

Frazier, George. "Scott Fitzgerald: The *Gatsby* Legend." *Saturday Evening Post*, May 1974, 60–63, 141.

Freeman, Joshua B. *American Empire: The Rise of a Global Power, the Democratic Revolution at Home, 1945–2000*. New York: Viking, 2012.

Garber, Marjorie. *The Use and Abuse of Literature*. New York: Pantheon, 2011.

Garrett, George. "Fire and Freshness: A Matter of Style in *The Great Gatsby*." In *New Essays on* The Great Gatsby, edited by Matthew J. Bruccoli, 101–16. New York: Cambridge University Press, 1985.

"*Gatsby*'s Influence Reaches Chinese Fashion." *Jing Daily*, May 22, 2013, http://www.jingdaily.com/gatsbys-influence-reaches-chinese-fashion/26871/. Accessed May 23, 2013.

Goodrum, Charles, and Helen Dalrymple. *Advertising in America: The First 200 Years*. New York: Abrams, 1990.

Granados, José A. Tapia, and Ana V. Diez Roux. "Life and Death during the Great Depression." *Proceedings of the National Academy of Sciences* 106, no. 41 (2009): 17290–95.

The Great Gatsby. Directed by Elliott Nugent. Los Angeles: Paramount, 1949. Video.

Greene, Maxine. *Variations on a Blue Guitar: The Lincoln Center Institute Lectures on Aesthetic Education*. New York: Teachers College Press, 2001.

Gross, Daniel. "Membership Has Its Penalties." *Newsweek*, January 2, 2009, http://www.thedailybeast.com/newsweek/2009/01/02/membership-has-its-penalties.html. Accessed March 30, 2013.

Gundle, Stephen. *Glamour: A History*. New York: Oxford University Press, 2008.

Gurko, Leo, and Miriam Gurko. "The Essence of F. Scott Fitzgerald." *College English* 5, no. 7 (1944): 372–76.

Hakim, Joy. "Rescue the Wonder of the Printed Page." In *The Last Word: The Best Commentary and Controversy in American Education*, edited by Mary-Ellen Phelps Deily and Veronika Herman Bromberg, 93–96. New York: Wiley, 2007.

Harlequin Enterprises. "Harlequin Romance Report—2012 Survey Results." Harlequin Media Center, February 9, 2012.

Harris, Misty. "*The Great Gatsby* Is a Branding Phenomenon." *Canada.com/Postmedia News*, May 2, 2013, http://www.canada.com/entertainment/movie-guide/ Great+Gatsby+branding+phenomenon/8326042/story.html. Accessed May 15, 2013.

Hedges, Chris. *Empire of Illusion: The End of Literacy and the Triumph of Spectacle*. New York: Nation Books, 2009.

Helm, Lynne. "Timeless Treasures." *Baltimore Sun*, October 14, 1990.

Hemingway, Ernest. *A Moveable Feast*. New York: Scribner, 1964, 2003.

Henderson, James G., and Richard D. Hawthorne. *Transformative Curriculum Leadership*. Englewood Cliffs, N.J.: Merrill, 1995.

Hensher, Philip. "*Great Gatsby*: A Story for the Modern Age." *Telegraph* (London), May 23, 2012, http://www.telegraph.co.uk/culture/film/film-news/9284394/Great-Gatsby-a-story-for-the-modern-age.html. Accessed March 30, 2013.

Hodges, Sam. "Frank Boykin: The Politician." *Mobile (Ala.) Press-Register*, December 17, 2001, http://www.al.com/specialreport/mobileregister/boykin_15.html. Accessed February 23, 2013.

———, "Teflon Tycoon." *Mobile (Ala.) Press-Register*, December 19, 2001, http://www.al.com/specialreport/mobileregister/boykin_08.html. Accessed February 23, 2013.

Huff, Richard. "Duchovny Says His Heel Has a Soul, Too." *New York Daily News*, September 25, 2009. LexisNexis Academic Solutions. Accessed December 24, 2011.

Ingalls, Julia. "Is the Great American Novel Still Relevant?" *Salon.com*, November 8, 2012, http://www.salon.com/2012/11/08/is_the_great_american_novel_still_relevant/. Accessed May 4, 2013.

Iwata, Edward. "Former CEO of National Century: Man of Mystery." *USA Today*, December 18, 2002, 1B.

Jackson, Philip W. *What Is Education?* Chicago: University of Chicago Press, 2012.

James, Clive. *Cultural Amnesia: Necessary Memories from History and the Arts*. New York: Norton, 2007.

Kazin, Alfred, and Ted Solotaroff. *Alfred Kazin's America: Critical and Personal Writings*. New York: Harper Perennial, 2004.

Kellogg, Carolyn. "Last Gasp of the Gatsby House." *Los Angeles Times*, April 20, 2011, http:// latimesblogs.latimes.com/jacketcopy/2011/04/last-gasp-of-the-gatsby-house.html. Accessed April 1, 2013.

Kemme, Steve. "King of the Bootleggers." *Cincinnati Enquirer*, August 1, 2011, http://cincinnati.com/blogs/ourhistory/2011/08/01/king-of-the-bootleggers/. Accessed May 4, 2013.

Kendall, Brian. "Golf with the Stars in a Celebrity Pro-Am." Canadian Golf Traveller, November 5, 2012, http://canadiangolftraveller.com/golf-with-the-stars-in-a-celebrity-pro-am/. Accessed January 8, 2013.

Kesson, Kathleen R., and James G. Henderson. "Reconceptualizing Professional Development for Curriculum Leadership: Inspired by John Dewey and Informed by Alain Badiou." *Educational Philosophy and Theory* 42, no. 2 (2010): 213–29.

Krugman, Paul. "For Richer: How the Permissive Capitalism of the Boom Destroyed American Equality." *New York Times Magazine*, October 20, 2002.

Larson, Anthony. "*Gatsby* and Us." *Critical Horizons* 4, no. 2 (2003): 281–303.

Lauter, Paul. *Canons and Contexts*. New York: Oxford University Press, 1991.

Lawson, Richard. "The Tragic Emptiness of *The Great Gatsby*." Review of *The Great Gatsby* film, *Atlantic Wire*, May 8, 2013, http://www.theatlanticwire.com/entertainment/2013/05/ great-gatsby-review/65020/. Accessed May 18, 2013.

Lears, Jackson. *Fables of Abundance: A Cultural History of Advertising in America.* New York: Basic Books, 1994.

Leboe, Jason P., and Tamara L. Ansons. "On Misattributing Good Remembering to a Happy Past: An Investigation into the Cognitive Roots of Nostalgia." *Emotion* 6, no. 4 (2006): 596–610.

Leslie, Larry Z. *Celebrity in the 21st Century: A Reference Handbook*. Santa Barbara, Calif.: ABC-CLIO, 2011.

Lewis, Anthony. "*The Great Gatsby.*" *New York Times*, August 6, 1987, A27.
Lewis, Paul. "*Ulysses* at Top as Panel Picks 100 Best Novels." *New York Times*, July 20, 1998, E1.
Lodge, David. *Language of Fiction: Essays in Criticism and Verbal Analysis of the English Novel.* New York: Columbia University Press, 1966.
Maimon, Elaine P. "F. Scott Fitzgerald's Book Sales: A Look at the Record." *Fitzgerald/ Hemingway Annual* 5 (1973): 165–73.
McConnell, Chloe. "How to Write about America." *New Yorker*, October 1, 2011, http://www.newyorker.com/online/blogs/festival/2011/10/how-to-write-about-america.html. Accessed January 2, 2013.
McDonald, Gail. *American Literature and Culture, 1900–1960.* Malden, Mass.: Blackwell, 2007.
McLean, Bethany, and Peter Elkind. "The Guiltiest Guys in the Room." *Fortune*, July 5, 2006, http://money.cnn.com/2006/05/29/news/enron_guiltyest/index.htm. Accessed September 15, 2006.
"Mia's Back and *Gatsby*'s Got Her." *People*, March 4, 1974, http://www.people.com/people/archive/article/0,,20197613,00.html. Accessed January 2, 2013.
Milford, Nancy. *Zelda: A Biography.* New York: Harper & Row, 1970.
Minter, David. *A Cultural History of the American Novel: Henry James to William Faulkner.* New York: Cambridge University Press, 1994.
Mizener, Arthur. *The Far Side of Paradise: A Biography of F. Scott Fitzgerald.* New York: Houghton Mifflin, 1965.
———. "*Gatsby*, 35 Years Later." *New Yorker*, April 24, 1960, http://www.nytimes.com/books/00/12/24/specials/fitzgerald-gatsby60.html. Accessed December 19, 2012.
———. "The Real Subject of *The Great Gatsby*." In *Readings on F. Scott Fitzgerald*, edited by Katie de Koster, 76–86. San Diego: Greenhaven Press, 1998.
Mount, Jane, and Thessaly La Force. *My Ideal Bookshelf.* New York: Little, Brown, 2012.
Nazaryan, Alexander. "Huge Incoherent Failures." *New York Daily News*, March 9, 2011, http://www.nydailynews.com/opinion/huge-incoherent-failures-doomed-mansion-great-gatsby-fitzgerald-america-article-1.120545. Accessed January 24, 2013.
Nichols, Lewis. "In and Out of Books." *New York Times*, January 8, 1961.
Noddings, Nel. "High Stakes Testing: Why?" *Theory And Research in Education* 2, no. 3 (2004): 263–69.
"No. 9." *Time* 79, no. 23 (June 8, 1962): 25. Academic Search Complete, EBSCOhost. Accessed December 23, 2012.
Norman, Philip. "The New Great Gatsbys." *MailOnline* (UK), June 15, 2012, http://www.dailymail.co.uk/news/article-2160115/The-new-Great-Gatsbys-Why-F-Scott-Fitzgeralds-book-relevant-Twenties.html. Accessed March 30, 2013.
O'Brien, Matthew. "Happy Birthday, Alan Greenspan." *Atlantic*, March 7, 2012, http://www.theatlantic.com/business/archive/2012/03/happy-birthday-alan-greenspan-the-housing-bubble-wasnt-your-fault/254089/. Accessed March 30, 2012.
Olear, Greg. "Ga(tsb)y," *Weeklings*, January 8, 2013, http://www.theweeklings.com/golear/2013/01/08/gatsby/. Accessed January 8, 2013.
Olsen, Eric. "The Great American Novel—What Is It, and Who Cares." *Portland Book Review*, February 4, 2012, http://portlandbookreview.com/2-4-12-the-great-american-novel-what-is-it-and-who-cares/. Accessed January 24, 2013.
"The $1.7 Trillion Dot-Com Lesson." *CNNMoney*, November 9, 2000, http://money.cnn.com/2000/11/09/technology/overview. Accessed November 15, 2000.
Osnos, Evan. "Reading *Gatsby* in Beijing." *New Yorker*, May 2, 2013, http://www.newyorker.com/online/blogs/comment/2013/05/reading-gatsby-in-beijing.html. Accessed May 20, 2013.
"Outsourcing Trends to Watch in 2007." *Fortune*, September 3, 2007, S2.
Oxman, Steven. "A&E Finds *Gatsby* Elusive." *Variety*, January 15, 2001.
Pastorek, Whitney. "David Duchovny." *Entertainment Weekly* 947 (2007): 21–22. Academic Search Complete. Accessed December 24, 2011.

Patsuris, Penelope. "The Corporate Scandal Sheet." *Forbes.com*, August 26, 2002, http://www.forbes.com/2002/07/25/accountingtracker.html. Accessed November 15, 2007.

"The People's Choice." *New York Times*, February 26, 1967.

"The People's Choice." *New York Times*, February 25, 1968.

"The People's Choice." *New York Times*, February 16, 1969.

Poore, Charles. "Two New Views of Fitzgerald and His Works." *New York Times*, July 20, 1963.

Prigozy, Ruth, ed. *The Cambridge Companion to F. Scott Fitzgerald*. Cambridge, U.K.: Cambridge University Press, 2002.

"Promise of No Child Left Behind Falls Short after 10 Years." *USA Today*, January 7, 2012, http://www.usatoday.com/news/education/story/2012-01-07/no-child-left-behind-anniversary/52430722/1?csp=34news. Accessed January 7, 2012.

"Reagan's 'Scrooge'?" *Newsweek*, December 19, 1983. LexisNexis Academic. Accessed December 23, 2012.

Reeves, Aaron, David Stuckler, Martin McKee, David Gunnell, Shu-Sen Chang, and Sanjay Basu. "Increase in State Suicide Rates in the USA during Economic Recession." *Lancet* 380, no. 9856 (2012): 1813–14.

Rich, Frank. "American Pseudo." *New York Times Magazine*, December 12, 1999, 80–87, 98.

Rielly, Edward J. *The 1960s*. Westport, Conn.: Greenwood, 2003.

Roche, Mark William. *Why Literature Matters in the 21st Century*. New Haven, Conn.: Yale University Press, 2004.

Rosenblatt, Louise M. *Literature as Exploration*. 5th ed. New York: Modern Language Association, 1995.

Russello, Gerald. "The Smartest Guys on the Cell Block." *New York Sun*, April 22, 2005, http://www.nysun.com/arts/smartest-guys-on-the-cell-block/12708/. Accessed January 2, 2013.

Samuel, Lawrence R. *The American Dream: A Cultural History*. Syracuse, N.Y.: Syracuse University Press, 2012.

Schudson, Michael. *Advertising, the Uneasy Persuasion: Its Dubious Impact on American Society*. New York: Basic Books, 1984.

Scribner, Charles, III. "Publishing—Past Imperfect." In *The Professions of Authorship: Essays in Honor of Matthew J. Bruccoli*, edited by Richard Layman and Joel Myerson, 68–77. Columbia: University of South Carolina Press, 1996.

Severo, Richard. "For Fitzgerald's Works, It's Roaring 70's." *New York Times*, March 3, 1974, http://www.nytimes.com/books/00/12/24/specials/fitzgerald-roaring.html. Accessed December 20, 2012.

Spargo, R. Clifton. "Why Every American Should Read *The Great Gatsby*, Again." *Huffington Post*, April 9, 2013, http://www.huffingtonpost.com/r-clifton-spargo/great-gatsby-rereading_b_3046378.html. Accessed April 10, 2013.

Specter, Michael. "The Age of the Sage (or Is It Money Talking?)." *New York Times*, January 4, 1998, WK5.

Sperling, Dan. "Classics Still Tops in Schools." *USA Today*, May 31, 1989, 1A.

Sriramesh, Krishnamurthy, and Dejan Veri. *Culture and Public Relations: Links and Implications*. New York: Routledge, 2012.

Stack, Steven. "The Effect of the Media on Suicide: The Great Depression." *Suicide and Life-Threatening Behavior* 22, no. 2 (1992): 255–67.

Stein, Ben. "*The Great Gatsby* in 3-D, the Third Dimension Is Money." *Forbes.com*, May 17, 2013, http://www.forbes.com/sites/schifrin/2013/05/17/ben-stein-great-gatsby-101/. Accessed May 19, 2013.

Stevens, Dana. "*The Great Gatsby*." Review of *The Great Gatsby* film. *Slate*, May 9, 2013, http://www.slate.com/articles/arts/movies/2013/05/the_great_gatsby_directed_by_baz_luhrmann_reviewed.html. Accessed May 15, 2013.

Strasser, Susan. *Satisfaction Guaranteed: The Making of the American Mass Market*. New York: Pantheon, 1989.

Sutton, Brian. "Fitzgerald's *The Great Gatsby*." *Explicator* 59, no. 1 (Fall 2000): 37–39.

Trask, David F. "A Note on Fitzgerald's *The Great Gatsby*." *University Review* 33, no. 3 (March 1967): 197–202. Reprinted in *Novels for Students*, edited by Diane Telgen. Vol. 2. Detroit: Gale, 1998. Literature Resource Center.

Troy, Gil. *Morning in America: How Ronald Reagan Invented the 1980s*. Princeton, N.J.: Princeton University Press, 2005.

Trumka, Richard L. "Why Working People Are Angry and Why Politicians Should Listen." *Vital Speeches of the Day*, June 2010: 268–71.

Turnbull, Andrew. "Speaking of Books: Perkins's Three Generals." *New York Times*, July 16, 1967.

Tuttle, Brad. "Southwest Airlines: We're Not Really about Cheap Flights Anymore." *Time*, March 26, 2013, http://business.time.com/2013/03/26/southwest-airlines-were-not-really-about-cheap-flights-anymore/. Accessed April 9, 2013.

"UN Report Cites Global Internet Growth Despite Economic Woes." *USA Today*, November 18, 2002, http://www.usatoday.com/tech/news/2002-11-18-global-net_x.htm. Accessed November 19, 2002.

Updike, John. *More Matter: Essays and Criticism*. New York: Random House, 1999.

———. *Odd Jobs: Essays and Criticism*. New York: Knopf, 1991.

Vieregge, Quentin. "Whose Brand Is It Anyway? How Brands Become Cults by Becoming Inclusive." In *Cult Pop Culture: How the Fringe Became Mainstream*, edited by Bob Batchelor, 71–85. Santa Barbara, Calif.: Praeger, 2012.

Voegeli, William. "*Gatsby* and the Pursuit of Happiness." *Claremont Review of Books*, 2003, 69–71.

Way, Brian. *F. Scott Fitzgerald and the Art of Social Fiction*. New York: St. Martin's, 1980.

Weinstein, Arnold. *Morning, Noon & Night: Finding the Meaning of Life's Stages through Books*. New York: Random House, 2011.

Welsh, James M., Gene D. Phillips, and Rodney F. Hill. *The Francis Ford Coppola Encyclopedia*. Lanham, Md.: Scarecrow Press, 2010.

West, James L. W., III. "Fitzgerald's Posthumous Literary Career." *Journal of Scholarly Publishing* 28 (1997): 92–101.

Will, George. "Fitzgerald Conjures Echoes from Jazz Age." *St. Louis Post-Dispatch*, December 20, 1990, 3C.

Wilson, Andrew. "Has the Moulin Rouge Director Created the Starriest, Glitziest, Greatest Gatsby of All?" *MailOnline* (UK), April 20, 2013, http://www.dailymail.co.uk/home/event/article-2311016/The-Great-Gatsby-Has-Moulin-Rouge-director-Baz-Luhrmann-created-starriest-glitziest-Greatest-Gatsby-all.html?ito=feeds-newsxml. Accessed April 21, 2013.

Wilson, Edmund, ed. *The Crack-Up*. New York: New Directions, 1965.

Yates, Donald A. "The Tragic Experience." Review of *F. Scott Fitzgerald: A Critical Portrait*, by Henry Dan Piper. *New York Times*, November 21, 1965.

Young, William H., and Nancy K. Young. *The 1950s*. Westport, Conn.: Greenwood, 2004.

INDEX

ABOUT THE AUTHOR

Bob Batchelor is James Pedas Professor of Communication and executive director of the James Pedas Communication Center at Thiel College. A noted cultural historian and biographer, Batchelor is the author or editor of twenty-four books, including *John Updike: A Critical Biography*. He is the founding editor of the *Popular Culture Studies Journal*, published by the Midwest Popular Culture / American Culture Association and a member of the editorial advisory boards of the *Journal of Popular Culture* and the *International Journal for the Scholarship of Teaching & Learning*. He serves as director of marketing and media for The John Updike Childhood Home Museum in Reading, Pennsylvania. Visit him on the web at www.bobbatchelor.com.